The Education of
Slow Learning Children

BY

A. E. TANSLEY, B.Sc., M.Ed.

Headmaster, St. Francis Residential School for Educationally Subnormal
Children, Birmingham

AND

R. GULLIFORD, B.A.

Tutor, Course for Teachers of Educationally Subnormal Children
University of Birmingham

LONDON
ROUTLEDGE & KEGAN PAUL

First published 1960
Second edition 1960
Reprinted twice

First published as a Routledge paperback 1965
with additions to references and book lists
by Routledge & Kegan Paul Ltd
Broadway House, 68–74 Carter Lane,
London, E.C.4

Reprinted 1967, 1969

Printed in Great Britain by
Western Printing Services Limited, Bristol

© *A. E. Tansley and R. Gulliford* 1960, 1965

SBN 7100 2170 4 (*c*)
SBN 7100 4650 2 (*p*)

CONTENTS

PREFACE

IN the last fifteen years there has been an increased interest in the education of very backward pupils in our schools. As we suggest in this book, we would hope for further developments in providing suitable education for them—for example, in the prevention or earlier discovery and treatment of backwardness; more special classes in ordinary schools; improved post-school guidance for backward leavers; a wider recognition of the fact that the aims of special educational treatment apply to all slow-learning children. We would like to stress that, while we have referred mainly to educationally sub-normal children and to the work of ESN schools, we believe that the type of education we have outlined is needed by many children who are not officially designated ESN and who remain in ordinary schools. There is no clear line of division between the better children in ESN schools and the most backward ones in ordinary schools. Hence, the use of the inclusive term 'slow-learning children' in our title.

Many teachers have found in this form of teaching not just a job to be done but a subject of absorbing interest as well as a source of personal satisfaction. We hope that teachers of backward children will find this book a guide in deciding the aims of the teaching and a help in planning the methods to be used. We have tried to present, in a simple form, some of the theoretical background to the teaching of backward children as well as an account of methods which have proved successful in teaching them. We have tried to strike a balance between practice and theory—to give not merely an account of methods and techniques but also a summary of the principles on which special methods should be based. These principles derive from the study of normal child development and from the knowledge of the characteristic limitations of backward children.

Although much has been achieved in this field of education, there are many opportunities for experiment and research. Throughout, we have been constantly aware of the need for further investigation of the learning, thinking and adjustment of slow-learning children so that teaching methods can be more precisely planned to suit their needs.

We would like to express our thanks to the many people who have helped us, and, in particular, to the staff of St. Francis Residential School, Birmingham, and the students and staff of the Education Department, University of Birmingham.

A. E. TANSLEY
R. GULLIFORD

Birmingham,
November 1959

I

SPECIAL EDUCATIONAL TREATMENT

DEREK is a thirteen-year-old in a secondary modern school. His reading is only as good as that of a seven-year-old; his mechanical arithmetic is a little better than his reading although he is not very good at dealing with numbers in practical situations such as shopping and measuring. In other ways he does not stand out as very different from his class-mates except that he is always slow on the uptake and is often teased by the other boys because of his slowness. He is quite well built physically but rather clumsy and uncoordinated in movement. He is no trouble in school. Although much of the work is too difficult for him, he is patient and co-operative. He is good-natured and takes his teasings in good part. His stability is no doubt partly the result of having a mother who is devoted to him and who gives him a great deal of affectionate support. When he was first noticed by an educational psychologist who was studying some of the backward children on entry to the school, he was recognized as a boy who probably needed special educational treatment in an ESN school. After some deliberation, it was decided that his needs might partly be met by arranging for some daily help in basic subjects from the remedial teacher who was working in the school. The fact that he had made a start on reading, that he was not troublesome in school, and that his mother would have been very upset if he had to go to a special school, all carried some weight in this decision. Eighteen months later, this decision was regretted because, although Derek had made some progress in reading, he was being increasingly teased by other boys and was clearly not able to benefit fully from the education given. He needed a school environment which was less complicated, work that was suited to his capacities in *all* aspects of the curriculum, and the more individual relationship with an understanding teacher that is possible in the special school and less likely to occur in a secondary school with its specialization and less thorough knowledge of backwardness.

There are many Dereks but not all of them are so fortunate in

1

having an affectionate mother to help and encourage them; some are much more limited in their capabilities and some have additional handicaps—physical, environmental, emotional—which impede their school progress and personal development. Some get the special help they need in an ESN school, others in a special class in an ordinary school; far too many struggle along in ordinary classes failing to have the special attention which they need.

The defects of children who are blind, deaf, or physically handicapped are readily apparent to the observer. The handicaps of educationally subnormal children are not always so obvious. Their handicap is broadly one of retarded all-round development, which is especially marked in relation to their powers of thinking and their ability to learn. They are therefore less able than most children to meet the normal demands of education and life in modern communities. It has often been pointed out that many of the children described as educationally subnormal might not have stood out as markedly different in former times or in other cultures. Even in present conditions, many of them will be absorbed into the life of the community as adults and will contribute usefully without drawing undue attention to themselves. (This is indeed one of the aims of special educational treatment.) The period at which their limitations are most obvious is that of the school years. Education values certain abilities such as verbal intelligence, the capacity for abstract, conceptual thinking and the intellectual skills made possible by them. In particular, education reflects the community's need for minimum attainments in reading, writing and simple calculation in its members —attainments in which comparisons are most obvious at school. A proportion of school children are so limited in their capacity to learn that they are seriously handicapped for meeting these demands of normal school learning. Others while not so seriously handicapped are, nevertheless, more likely than most children to have learning difficulties, especially if the teaching is not suitably geared to their slower rate of progress, and modified to achieve the most effective ways of learning.

Hence there is a need for special educational measures to ensure for these children the maximum progress of which they are capable in the traditional three Rs, and, no less important, in other developments—practical, personal, and social—which are valuable in adult life. This special attention could be justified on humanitarian grounds, for the unhappiness and personal inadequacy that are the concomitants of severe educational and social failure may be considerable. If added justification be needed, more utilitarian reasons can be advanced. First, the community needs the fullest development of its human resources, not only in those capable of development of higher skills but also in those capable of routine tasks which are equally essential for the maintenance of the social organization. Secondly, the cost to society of mental ill-health and delinquency which can result from educational failure may well be greater in the long-run than the cost of developing adequate means of special educational treatment in childhood.

The educational problem presented by these children became apparent after the beginning of universal education in the closing decades of the nineteenth century. An entry in the log book of one school reads:

> 27th Jan. 1879. I have thoroughly examined the newcomers. I find about half of the number can be decently prepared for Standard I. About 12 or 14 cannot say their letters and as to their writing they have no notion of writing from a copy, to say nothing of transcribing from a book or card.
> 4th Feb. I have taken Standard I again this week. What to do with about 20 of them I am at a loss to know. (4)

Such children had little chance of special attention in these early Board schools. There was no widespread understanding of the nature of the problem even if the teachers could have been freed from the problems of discipline, and the pressures of the payments-by-results system to deal with it.

By 1900, however, a number of special classes had been opened, first in Leicester and later in other large towns, for those pupils not capable of benefiting from instruction in the ordinary school.

The provision of classes and schools for mentally defective children was given sanction in the Education (Defective and Epileptic Children) Act, 1899. The Education Act of 1921 directed that children 'not being imbecile and not being merely dull and backward' should be provided for in special classes and schools. Pupils sent to such schools had first to be certified as feeble-minded by the School Medical Officer. It is not surprising that the special procedures and terminology, with their suggestion of something of an abnormal nature, aroused unfavourable emotions and attitudes. The stigma which was attached to schools for mentally-defective children has been partly but not completely shaken off by the later and more enlightened provision for educationally subnormal pupils.

Meanwhile, the application of psychology to education and to the study of child development began to have an increasing influence. Binet in 1905 devised a simple mental test, partly in response to the need for a reliable means of selecting the children most needing special schooling in Paris. The development of mental testing which followed played a big part in the study of individual differences

3

between school children and in the realization of the need for differential treatment. The expansion of research into child development, symbolized by such names as Gesell, Buhler, Susan Isaacs, and Piaget, influenced educational theory and methods. One of the most important influences has been the work of school psychologists, typified by the monumental work of Burt from the time of his appointment as psychologist to the London County Council in 1913. His work, and that of others (such as Schonell), provided a foundation of knowledge about the extent of backwardness, its causes and the broad lines of treatment. Forty years of research and experience paved the way for a new concept of the need for special educational treatment for a section of the school population. This concept reflected changes in attitudes towards handicapped children and has helped to bring about a broader approach to their education.

The category, educationally subnormal

The Education Act of 1944 required local education authorities to have regard 'to the need for securing that provision is made for pupils who suffer from any disability of mind or body by providing, either in special schools or otherwise, special educational treatment, that is to say, education by special methods appropriate for persons suffering from that disability'. Eleven categories of pupils needing special educational treatment were named and defined in the Handicapped Pupils' and School Health Service Regulations in 1945.[1] (6). Educationally subnormal pupils were defined as:

> Pupils who, by reason of limited ability or other conditions resulting in educational retardation, require some specialized form of education, wholly or partly in substitution for the education normally given in ordinary schools.

This definition was explained in a pamphlet 'Special Educational Treatment', 1946 (7) and by chapters in the reports of the Chief School Medical Officer at the Ministry of Education, 'The Health of the School Child', 1939–45 and 1946–47 (8).

The category is a broad one and draws attention to the educational problem of all seriously backward children, not only the small group who previously would have attended special schools. It thus avoids stigmatizing the most seriously backward as though they were a group apart. This is in line with current knowledge and thinking. The severely backward shade off into the low-average group, both in mental ability and other characteristics. It is not possible to draw a

[1] These were replaced by the School Health Service and Handicapped Pupil's Regulations 1953.

rigid line of demarcation. Furthermore, the criterion of the need for special educational treatment is to be essentially an educational one; the category is based on educational needs, not medical or psychological types. It is suggested that educationally subnormal children are those whose standard of school work falls below that of children who are 20 per cent younger. Thus, a child of 10 whose attainments are below those of average eight-year-olds, may be considered as educationally subnormal. It was estimated that this might apply to 10 per cent of the school population although a recent pamphlet (10) mentions the figures 5–10 per cent. The cause of the backwardness was not a vital issue in deciding the need for special educational treatment. It could be limited ability or 'other conditions' such as absences from school, ill-health, unfavourable home or school conditions, and emotional barriers to learning. The cause of the backwardness was relevant, however, to the question of the means by which special educational treatment was to be given. Thus, it was suggested that special schools would provide mainly for pupils whose backwardness was due to limited ability. Pupils who were not so limited intellectually would need suitable arrangements in ordinary school. At the borderline, weight would have to be given to the other conditions affecting a child's capacity to learn. Children from extremely unsatisfactory homes might need to be educated away from home in residential schools. The number of children needing special school provision was estimated as follows: 1 per cent needing to attend day special schools in urban areas; 0·2 per cent in urban areas might need in their own interests to be educated away from home in residential schools. It was estimated that in rural areas 0·4 per cent would need residential school provision, since the more scattered population of rural areas would not make it feasible to gather the most backward into day ESN schools. The number of children needing special educational treatment in ordinary schools was thought to be about 8 per cent. It is obvious that these estimates are rough indications and that the need for the special educational treatment in particular areas will depend on the local incidence of backwardness. The forms that special educational treatment should take will need to vary according to local circumstances.

These estimates were roughly in accordance with the results of surveys of the incidence of backwardness (mental and educational) reported in the previous thirty years. The figures in Table 1 show that the incidence of backwardness due mainly to low intelligence (i.e. IQs below 70) is likely to be between 1·5 per cent and 2 per cent in urban areas and in rural areas is more likely to be nearer to 3 per cent.

But the educationally subnormal group is defined in terms of

TABLE I

PERCENTAGES OF CHILDREN IN THE SUBNORMAL AND DULL GROUPS OF
INTELLIGENCE ACCORDING TO VARIOUS SURVEYS.

Source of survey	Subnormal Intelligence IQs below 70	Mental Dullness IQs 70–85
Burt (ages 7–14) (1)	1·5 (urban)	12·0
Lewis (ages 7–14) (5)	1·7 (urban) 3·3 (rural)	not obtained
Scottish Council for Research in Educa- cation. (13)	3·0 (urban and rural)	24 in IQ range 70–90

educational quotients not in terms of intelligence quotients. While it is reasonable to expect that children with poor intelligence will have greater difficulty with their school work, the relationship between attainment test and intelligence test results is by no means a perfect one. Moreover, to those children who would be educationally subnormal on account of intellectual limitations must be added those whose backwardness is due to other limiting conditions—physical, environmental, emotional. The estimates of general educational backwardness vary. Burt (1) has suggested the figure of 15 per cent; Schonell (12) 17 per cent. Estimates of the amount of backwardness in reading have been made by the Ministry of Education in 1948, 1952 and 1956 (11). In 1956, the percentage of children aged 11 in the backward category (roughly, reading ages between 7 and 9 years) was 20 per cent and in the semi-literate and illiterate category combined (roughly, reading ages below 7 years) was 1 per cent. The percentage of 15-year-olds in the backward category (roughly, reading ages between 9 and 12 years) was 21 per cent and in the semi-literate category (roughly, reading ages between 7 and 9 years) was 4 per cent.

Children who need special educational treatment

The experience of schools confirms that there are many children who are so backward in basic subjects that they need special help. The number of children involved varies from place to place, from one district of a town to another and from school to school. The type of provision also varies, partly for the reasons already stated, but also because of the nature of backwardness and its principal causes. Backward children may be considered in three broad categories:

1. Some are very backward because of retarded mental development which is often accompanied by additional handicaps, such as physical deficiencies, ill-health, limited verbal experiences at home, and emotional disturbances. Their educational problems are usually so acute that they need special treatment outside the ordinary school, i.e. in special schools, or, failing this, in special classes which have aims and methods similar to those of the special school.

2. There are others whose ability is not quite so limited but who nevertheless have more difficulty in learning than average children. Absences from school, unfortunate personal circumstances, or inadequate environmental conditions have often further limited their progress. Failure to recognize and provide for their problems must be counted among the contributory causes of their backwardness. These children are included in the 10 per cent of children who may be considered educationally subnormal but they can usually be provided for satisfactorily in ordinary schools, i.e. in special classes or other forms of organization. However, some children in this group may derive considerable benefit from education in a special school, particularly if their problems require close personal teaching which cannot be provided otherwise. As we shall see later, each child's needs must be considered in detail. It is not possible to draw a simple line of division between the children in groups 1 and 2.

3. A third group of children are manifestly not limited in intelligence, but, nevertheless, are not beyond the beginning stages of reading and writing. They reveal their higher ability sometimes by average attainment in arithmetic or in practical subjects, by the level of their oral expression, or by their interests. The causes of their failure range from specific perceptual difficulties to emotional maladjustments. Whether one includes these children in the broad category, educationally subnormal, or not, their special problem needs to be catered for in making special provision. Some form of special or remedial teaching is required.

Developments in the period 1945–55

The broad definition of the category, educationally subnormal, has already proved its worth in the developments since 1945. (9) These have mainly been in the field of special school expansion. In the ten-year period, 1945–55, 142 new schools for educationally subnormal pupils were opened and over 10,000 more pupils received special school education (9). One of the most gratifying developments has been the change in attitude of both parents and teachers towards the special school. The disappearance of the terms, Mentally Defective and Feebleminded, from the educational vocabulary has

7

assisted this change. Special schools are increasingly being appreciated not as places where children are sent as rejects from the ordinary school but as places where they receive the individual attention and specialist treatment needed to ensure their progress, not only towards literacy but, of equal importance, towards social and vocational adjustment. The fact that the category, educationally subnormal, defines a group of children in terms of their *educational* needs and not in terms of a medico-legal type has contributed towards this change of attitude. Other factors have played a part. The early special schools must have spent much of their energies on the physical welfare of pupils who were showing the effects of bad socio-economic conditions, but improved social conditions, resulting in better nutrition, clothing and general welfare, have enabled schools to concentrate more on strictly educational aspects. The surprisingly high standards achieved, not only in basic subjects but also in creative work and practical subjects, have helped to develop an awareness of the value of special educational treatment. New school buildings and good facilities have helped to promote public esteem. The increasing contact between ordinary schools and ESN schools has also been important, although much still remains to be done before it can be said that teachers in ordinary schools really appreciate the purpose of the special school.

One of the questions created by the wide definition of educationally subnormal is that of which kinds of backwardness should be treated in the ESN school. About one group of children there is little disagreement—the children in the middle range of the ESN school, usually children with intelligence quotients in the 60s whose personal and intellectual immaturity, often allied with other handicaps, establishes a clear case for special schooling. At the lower extreme of the ESN school range, the pamphlet, *Special Educational Treatment*, (7) was quite emphatic that a firm line should be taken about children who are severely mentally handicapped to the extent that they cannot benefit from education. However, a firm line is often not easy to take. Many teachers who have worked hard with such children, although with little success, often become attached to them and are unwilling to recommend their exclusion unless their presence is actually detrimental to other children. The problem would be easier if more occupation centres and other forms of care, e.g. home teaching, were available for these children in the community. There is no doubt that children who, for want of a better term, are described as *ineducable* should not be retained when a reasonable period of trial and any necessary specialist examination and treatment have given evidence of their very limited educability.

At the higher levels of ability, there is the question of what type of backward children to admit to special schools. The wide definition of the educationally subnormal category has encouraged a tendency to refer to the ESN school, some who, although very backward educationally, have intelligence quotients as high as the 90s. The greater willingness of parents and teachers to contemplate special schooling has contributed to this trend. There have even been one or two cases of schools which have a distinct remedial function, and aim at returning a large number of children to ordinary schools once their attainments have been improved. While the possibility of returning children to ordinary school should always be borne in mind, it would seem a sensible policy to try to select for special schooling those children whose all-round retardation seems to require, not just a temporary period of remedial help in order to boost their attainments, but the continuous experience which is going to influence their growth towards maturity. There are enough children of this type to fill the available ESN school places. This does not mean, however, that it is possible to adopt a rigid standard about the type of child who should go to ESN school, and certainly not in terms of a rigid interpretation of mental test scores. There will always be the unusual child whose problem calls for the specialist knowledge increasingly to be found in the ESN school. For example, John obtains a Terman-Merrill score in the 80s, his performance quotient is in the 60s, attainments are virtually nil. He is extremely immature in his personal-social development, and is very withdrawn and lacking in drive. A school for maladjusted children might meet his needs more suitably, but this would entail residential treatment which does not seem desirable in his case. Child guidance treatment is another solution but such treatment might not have quick results, and meanwhile he is quite out of place in his own class. The problem whether to admit such children to the ESN school would be considerably reduced if there were more adequate facilities in ordinary schools. For example, Kenneth, aged 11, has an IQ of 85. He has made no real start in reading. He is one of those children who seem to have profited little from any attempts to teach him. He seems to have extraordinarily poor powers of retention, difficulty in discriminating sounds, a very limited verbal background at home, and has developed a hopeless attitude towards reading. Various teachers have tried to help him but the teaching has been sporadic and there has been no careful diagnosis of his difficulties followed by systematic teaching. If he had had special class teaching during his junior school years, it is highly probable that his difficulties would have been resolved. He is now moving into a secondary modern school where, partly owing to staff shortages, there is little chance of his problem being tackled in a thorough way. There is in the town, however, an excellent ESN school which has been very successful with several similar children previously, and has returned them to ordinary school after a considerable improvement in their attainments. In present circumstances, it seems a reasonable expedient to place him in the ESN school, but it must be noted that (*a*) he may well be taking the place of a mentally more limited child still in ordinary school who, while making some progress in basic subjects, has nevertheless a greater need for the all-round preparation for life which the ESN school sets out to provide; (*b*) his problem is partly due to the lack of special educational treatment in ordinary schools. Special classes in the junior school would probably have prevented his backwardness becoming so serious; a special class would have been the best place for him at present.

While it would be convenient to have a neat specification of the types of children who should receive special education in the special school, it is scarcely possible to make it neat in practice. There are many factors that induce local variations. The most influential factor is the extent and variety of other special educational provisions. A more comprehensive system for discovering and educating backward children would enable ordinary schools to cope satisfactorily with some children who might otherwise be deemed in need of special schooling. The population of special schools in different areas will also vary according to the amount of other provision for handicapped children—in an area where there are few other facilities there are bound to be more children with secondary handicaps. But while recognizing the necessity for local variations, there is no justification for continuing to use the ESN school indefinitely as a convenient solution for a variety of types of problem which really need special arrangements in other ways. In brief, it is clear that the function of the ESN school can only be properly defined when there are adequate facilities for backward, maladjusted and other handicapped children.

Arrangements in Ordinary Schools

The pamphlet, *Special Educational Treatment* (7), suggested in 1946 that there was as yet no unanimity of view about how ordinary schools can best make arrangements for their backward children, and that how this can be done must be found by experiment. There has certainly been a growing interest in the problems presented by backward children in ordinary schools and an increased awareness of the size of the problem. But provision is hardly anywhere adequate to the need. More special classes with a manageable number of pupils have been started, but these are often the first victims of staff shortages. There is often, too, a shortage of teachers who are interested in backward children and knowledgeable about the methods of dealing with them. This often results in the young teacher fresh from college being assigned to the backward class, a practice which is to be strongly deprecated. There are experienced teachers who are enthusiastic about teaching backward children but who often feel handicapped by not having had instruction in college about methods of teaching basic subjects. There is a need for all teachers during training to have some instruction in methods of teaching the early stages of reading and number, and to be made aware of the methods of helping children who cannot keep up with their age group.

One useful trend has been the increasing interest taken by school psychological services in the problem of backwardness. One approach, often associated with this, has been the setting up of remedial teaching services. But remedial teachers can only tackle a section of the problem and one of their most effective functions has been as advisers and disseminators of ideas and information about methods and materials. Their work is needed as a supplement to that of special schools and special classes, not as an alternative.

A comprehensive attack on the problem is needed, extending *special educational treatment* into the ordinary schools. The aims and methods of the special school are needed not only for the 1 per cent who are selected as most in need of special schooling but also for the many backward children who remain in ordinary school. It would be a pity if the potentially fruitful concept of a broad category of educationally subnormal pupils did not gain acceptance. In the first place, it is illogical to make good arrangements for the most severely retarded and neglect, often through pressure of circumstances, those only slightly less retarded. Many delinquents and social misfits are drawn from this latter group whose experience of school has not had real meaning for them. It is not unusual for some of the backward children in ordinary schools to be achieving less than their contemporaries in the ESN school. In the second place, a more comprehensive attack on backwardness should result in earlier detection of children needing special schooling as well as a clearer recognition of which children are most in need of it. At the present time, while the majority of children admitted to special schools are educationally retarded owing to limited intelligence (often, of course, in combination with other conditions) there are varying proportions of children who are there chiefly because of 'other conditions', such as maladjustment, or who may be quite intelligent but have special learning difficulties. As Cleugh (2) has pointed out, the wide ESN umbrella is in danger of being misused to provide a haven for pupils who should have been provided for in other ways. We incline to the view that the ESN school *should* expect to provide for a proportion of such children, but it is equally probable that more of them could be provided for in ordinary schools were adequate facilities more widely available. We cannot be certain upon this point until there is a more comprehensive provision of special educational treatment in ordinary schools. Meanwhile, there is a danger that some children whose limited capacities really merit the support and the preparation for living given in the ESN school may be overlooked, while others whose immediate difficulties call attention to them are being admitted to ESN schools.

Our present arrangements for backward children often fail to observe the maxim 'a stitch in time saves nine'. A crucial time for getting to grips with backwardness is the last year of the infant school and the beginning of the junior school, i.e. from ages 7 to 9 years. Infant schools which are able to arrange a remedial or opportunity class in the last year know how valuable it can be in preventing backwardness in children who have fallen behind either because of earlier illness, absences or late maturing. ESN children would benefit from a greater realization that at this stage they are far from ready for formal work and that premature teaching only makes it more difficult to teach them later on. There is a need for a genuine special class in the first years of the junior school so that these children can be taught in ways very similar to those used for the young infant school child. In addition to the special class for slow-learning pupils, there is also a need for remedial help for children who, although quite intelligent, may be failing generally in school work or have difficulties in certain subjects. The intelligent school failure needs his problem investigated and dealt with thoroughly as soon as possible, i.e. before continuing failure sets up wrong habits of learning, or intensifies unfavourable attitudes which are such a marked feature of the older backward child. An early and thorough attack on the educational failure of these children would help to obviate the sad spectacle of the manifestly intelligent child whose low attainments necessitate his being placed in the C stream when he enters the secondary modern school at age eleven. There is a real need for special attention to these children who are capable of a higher level of functioning than the usual run of slow-learners. In addition, therefore, to special classes in the junior school, there is a need for the specialist remedial teacher operating as part of the school psychological service but working, for at least part of the time, in and with the co-operation of the schools.

The need for an adequate organization of special educational treatment is even more apparent when children move to the secondary modern school at age 11. The proportion of backward pupils is greater since children are usually drawn from several junior schools.

Moreover, the gap between the average pupil and the slow-learner is widening with age. The result is that most secondary modern schools need a teacher who is responsible for the education of backward children. He should be capable of taking on the teaching of the most difficult educational problems of two, possibly three, age groups, or of taking one of several special classes. But he needs also to be a person who has the knowledge and experience to be able to advise on the methods and curricula for all the work with the slower children. It follows that he must have qualities of personality as well as knowledge, and such people at present are in short supply. It should be possible to remedy this with the increase in the number of training courses for teachers of backward children. (10)

What is meant by a special class is not always understood. By special class, we mean a class that can keep its numbers as near to twenty as possible so that it is possible to give the individual attention that is needed. Secondly, the special class should not have merely a reduced curriculum but one that is, like the special school's, different in aims, methods and content. (See Chapter V.) In the secondary modern school, specialization should be very limited, especially in the first year or so, when slow pupils still need the security of a relationship with an understanding person as well as of a familiar classroom. However, a specialist teacher who is sufficiently interested to accept the challenge of presenting his subject in a way suitable for slower pupils has much to offer. He will also serve the useful purpose of freeing the teacher of backward children for some periods of a different form of teaching or for remedial work elsewhere in the school. One hears of 'special' classes which have to submit to a written examination 'to be like the rest of the school', yet such a demand runs counter to the principles on which the special class teacher will be working. Much of his work will be organized on individual lines and he will be anxious to avoid anything which will increase children's sense of failure. The special class, because of its smaller numbers and because of the psychological and educational needs of its members, must run on freer lines than its neighbours. For much of the day, it may not be adhering strictly to a timetable, except in relation to the use of the hall, gym, and practical rooms. Although its activities will be less academic, it will make similar demands to the A class on the requisition for books, and there may be extra, unusual requests for equipment and materials. In brief, if it is really special, in the sense of providing an education specially designed for slow-learning pupils rather than a pale imitation of the work of the ordinary streams, there must be differences in the atmosphere, the methods of discipline and the type of activity going on.

The exact nature of the organization of special educational treat-

13

ment can only be decided on the basis of the need in a particular school and the availability of staff. For example, if a school can only spare one teacher to run a special class it will be necessary to decide whether this should contain the most backward pupils from several age groups or concentrate on one age group. It is usually inadvisable to have too wide an age range—14-year-olds mixed with 12-year-olds or 11-year-olds with 8-year-olds. A compromise is to have a class covering two age groups, e.g. 8- and 9-year-olds in the primary school or 11- and 12-year-olds in the secondary school. It might be considered best to make a thorough job of the first-year entry, hoping thereby to reap the benefit in later years. Such action would, of course, need to be supported by some remedial teaching groups as the children moved up the school, since the progress in attainments might not have become sufficiently secure within a year. Another system is to have cross-classification or 'sets'. For example, if the English or Arithmetic periods throughout the backward classes can be arranged for the same time, pupils can be grouped according to attainment. The group with the lowest attainment can be reduced in number and one or two members of staff be available to give the maximum of individual attention. Another line of attack is for remedial groups to be organized, children being withdrawn daily from their own classes for remedial teaching. It is important in such a system that there is full co-operation with the class teacher or with the staff normally taking English and Arithmetic. While this system is suitable for the intelligent school failure, it is a method less satisfactory than the continuous special class for the slow learner. Usually, the method of organization must be a compromise, owing to shortage of staff and the numbers of backward pupils needing help. Where the need is greater than the facilities for coping with it, it is probably better to concentrate effort at one or two places early in the school rather than dissipate efforts at several.

There is sometimes a prejudice against special classes or other special provisions, on the grounds that they set pupils apart as different or inferior. If special educational treatment could be given without singling children out, we would be in sympathy with this view. But only too often children drag along year by year, unable to keep up with the rest of the class, worried and unhappy about their failure. In many cases, they are well on the way to becoming inadequate personalities. What, after all, singles children out more than their own failure? The real answer to those who doubt the wisdom of a measure of segregation under present conditions is to see the results of a good special class and the obvious happiness of its pupils. The good special class is often one to which children are happy to belong, and the improved attendance figures often demonstrate this.

In any case, whatever method of organization is adopted, it should not have the effect of isolating the children. The members of the special class should participate in the life of the school and it should be possible to maintain a flow of successful pupils back into the ordinary streams.

To summarize, it is desirable to think of the ESN category not just as the 1 per cent to 2 per cent of children whose educational and personal handicaps require special education in special schools, but as a wider group of backward children for whom special educational treatment should be available in ordinary schools. The form that provision takes must depend to some extent on local conditions. There is, in any case, room for a variety of approaches. What cannot be in question is the need for special teaching to be started earlier in the child's school career so that the backwardness of some children is prevented and in other cases is treated early enough to prevent the problem becoming severe. The greatest need now is for a more extensive provision of special classes (which are really special) both at the junior and the secondary stage. Remedial teachers can have a stimulating effect by increasing interest and knowledge about backward children, can meet the special need of more intelligent failing children and cope with the difficult cases who do not progress satisfactorily even with special class work. The ESN school fits into this scheme as the place where the most handicapped children can receive the specialist attention they need. The ESN school would benefit in this comprehensive scheme from the greater possibility of earlier ascertainment and a more careful selection of cases.

Ascertainment for the Special School

Local Education Authorities have to ascertain which children are in need of special educational treatment as educationally subnormal pupils. The word 'ascertainment' has come to be used to refer to the process whereby the child is examined to determine whether he is in need of special educational treatment. In practice, the procedure includes a report from the child's school, a medical examination, and an assessment of psychological, educational and social factors. On the basis of these examinations, the School Medical Officer makes his recommendation to the Local Education Authority.

The majority of day ESN schools admit children from seven years of age, although there are now more schools taking a small number of children before that age. It is a unanimous opinion in the special schools that the sooner children can be ascertained after the age of seven, the better for the child and for the working of the school. The average age of entry to special school varies according to the area but the peak age is probably about ten, with some children continuing to be admitted up to thirteen or fourteen. It is posing special schools with an unnecessarily difficult problem when they are expected to do in two or three years what could have been done so much more satisfactorily and thoroughly if they had had the child at seven or eight. It is unfair to the child to let him linger without special help in the ordinary school, for the experience of continued failure sets up unfavourable attitudes, creates emotional difficulties and intensifies the learning problem to a point at which it may be difficult to treat. Earlier ascertainment is one of the most urgent needs in special educational treatment.

Ascertainment from the Infant School (ages 5–7 years)

It is not possible to ascertain the majority of ESN children in the infant school period. There are indeed some children who stand out as being obviously extremely backward. Their mental retardation shows in their poor physical co-ordination, their clumsy manipulation, and their very retarded speech. Their drawing may be like that of a three- or four-year-old child. Their play and their whole behaviour may be strikingly immature; they are often not able to join with other children in free play. Infant schools can usually provide for these children up to a point, but where the ESN school has a class for children of infant age, it is as well for the most retarded to have the benefit of the smaller group and special attention. They should, in any case, be referred for special examination so that any reasons for their backwardness, such as hearing loss, visual defects, speech difficulties or other physical causes can be investigated and treated. Some of these children may indeed improve considerably; others will continue in the ESN school; some, after a period of trial in the ESN school, may be considered more suitably placed in an occupation centre.

One of the difficulties here is in distinguishing children whose backwardness is due to limited potentiality for development from those in whom emotional disturbance has retarded development. Some experts consider that children whose retardation is primarily due to their emotional condition should not be placed in the ESN school. Where a clear diagnosis can be made, this opinion has merit. But it is, in practice, not often easy to distinguish between the two, and in the absence of other provision the infant ESN class seems best suited to study and treat such children. However, the possibility of transfer back to ordinary school should always be kept in mind.

Many of the children who will later be rightly placed in ESN schools, could not be selected with any certainty before the age of seven. Apart from the greater unreliability of testing, especially with backward children, at these younger ages, there are many children who make a slow start in the infant school and it is not easy to distinguish between those who are likely to hold their own in the slower streams of ordinary schools and those who will need special schooling. It is sometimes difficult to judge how far their slow progress is due to mental retardation, emotional factors, to the limitations of the home background, the effect of poor health or of school absences. Many infant schools arrange for extra attention to be given to these children either by holding reading groups in the head teacher's room or by running a small remedial class (Highfield, *The Young School Failure* (3).) Such arrangements can be most valuable as a first step in the prevention of backwardness. They will also indicate a few children who can with fair certainty be judged as needing special schooling. It is advisable to put such children forward for ascertainment soon enough for them to go straight to ESN school rather than leave it to the junior school to do so. In the junior school, it may be another year before someone else refers the child for ascertainment. Sometimes such children drift on in ordinary school until ten or eleven, with the result that several years of useful foundation experiences in the special school have been lost.

Ascertainment from the junior school (age 7–11 years)

Children from this backward group at the top of the infant school may make progress in the junior school, especially if there is a continuing infant school approach, or if there is a special class. But fairly early in the junior school—say at age eight—there should be a systematic attempt to discover all children who need special educational treatment. It is a common observation that the referral of children for ascertainment is often not very systematic. Some schools readily put forward children for examination while others are slow to do so. Children whose backwardness is accompanied by difficult behaviour tend to be referred more quickly. It is sometimes suggested that the remedy would be a survey of backwardness at age eight, using group attainment tests for an initial screening, followed by individual testing. Group attainment tests can certainly reveal the pupils who are seriously backward educationally. The problem then is to discover which children in this probably quite large group need special schooling, and which can be dealt with in ordinary school. It must be pointed out that a group non-verbal test of intelligence will not provide a reliable pointer to the ones with low intelligence—there may be many backward children who score low on the tests because they lack the confidence, the persistence and the attention

17

to work pencil-and-paper tests. In any case, a non-verbal test is not necessarily predictive of *educational* development. The best step is probably an on-the-spot discussion between the psychologist and the staff, followed by individual examination of a short list of children who appear to have the greatest learning difficulty. (If time is limited, this testing could be done with the starred tests of Terman-Merrill Form M, (14) reserving Form L or the Wechsler Intelligence Scale for Children (15) for use if the child is put forward for ascertainment.)

Improving referral for ascertainment

The chances of early ascertainment can also be increased by propaganda about the importance of early referral and about the type of child who should be put forward. In many areas, especially where new schools have been started, this has been achieved by meetings of head teachers at which the head teacher of the ESN school explains the function, aims and work of his school. There is still surprising ignorance, many teachers and more parents confusing the special school with the occupation centre. Such a discussion needs to be followed by visits to the ESN school and by as much informal contact as possible. Where the ESN school is appreciated as the local source of specialist knowledge about methods and materials in teaching backward children, there is likely to be an attitude developing which is favourable to early ascertainment. One of the many reasons for late ascertainment is undoubtedly the feeling of reluctance on the part of head teachers to refer a child because they feel that they are condemning him, and that it is generally an unfortunate step to take. They may feel confirmed in their reluctance through knowing that there is still something of a stigma attaching to the special school and that the child may be teased by other children. No one would deny that there are disadvantages that have to be weighed but the advantages in terms of the child's preparation for life ultimately far outweigh any immediate disadvantages that may loom large. Happily there are more teachers who feel with real conviction that they can recommend the step as the right one.

Ascertainment procedure

Whatever steps are taken to discover the children who may need special schooling, the next step should be a thorough diagnostic examination. The examination must be sufficiently comprehensive to reveal the causes of educational subnormality. It will take into consideration the child's physical, mental and educational status, his life history, his family background and the other environmental influences to which he has been exposed. It therefore requires the co-ordinated efforts of doctors, teachers, psychologists and social workers. The diagnosis of a child's difficulties does not, of course, end with the special examination but is a continuous process which should be carried on once the child has arrived at the ESN school. It is rarely possible, even with a most thorough examination, to unravel all the factors in a child's problem; there are some aspects of backwardness in which our knowledge is so uncertain. Moreover, the results of treatment may provide indications upon which a better diagnosis can be made. For example, the medical treatment of a sensory or organic deficiency may lead to such marked improvements as to indicate that an earlier finding of severe intellectual deficiency was inaccurate; remedial educational treatment may result in marked improvements in personality in children previously diagnosed as severely disturbed for reasons other than educational failure; psychiatric treatment may be so successful that an original pessimistic prognosis has to be abandoned. While changes in the child's condition may not merit a different form of schooling, they may at least require a re-thinking of the child's educational needs. The relationship between diagnosis and treatment must be a close one.

The special examination should be concerned not only with assessing the child's need for special schooling but also with providing information upon which special educational treatment can be based. Information about the child's earlier development, his previous school history and his home background may be vitally important in tackling his problem when he comes to the special school. The results of the psychological and educational examinations should give the teacher a clearer insight into the nature of the child's difficulties in learning and adjustment. It is apparently not unknown for the information from the special examination not to be made available to the staff of the special school. Yet if the teachers are to do their job well, they should surely be made as fully aware as possible of the nature of the child's difficulties.

Close co-operation and consultation between doctors, psychologists, teachers and any others who know the child seem essential, if only because physical, social and psychological problems are so often associated with educational backwardness. Each profession should, therefore, know enough of the other's work to be able to make team-work fully effective.

A thorough diagnostic examination would include:

(a) *A medical examination which is more than the usual school medical examination.* Many school medical officers take a particular interest in the work with special school children and their careful medical scrutiny is a most valuable aspect of special educational treatment. A careful examination of eyes, ears, throat, speech organs and the central nervous system is certainly called for. Today consultants are more accessible and the services of paediatricians, ophthalmologists, audiologists, neurologists, and speech therapists should be used freely. In special schools, there are many children with visual defects other than loss of acuity, hearing defects which may only be revealed by audiometric examination, and brain damage which cannot be confirmed without a neurological examination or electroencephalography. It is of interest to note here that a recent examination of twenty-four children, selected because they were very restless and distractible, showed that ten had definite neurological signs of organic damage. These ten are responding to psychiatric and educational treatment. There are also children whose physical development and muscular co-ordination are so retarded that remedial measures are necessary, e.g. remedial physical education, physiotherapy. Others are malnourished because either feeding has been poor or the metabolic processes are faulty. Such children may need special diets and treatment by nutrition experts.

(b) *A psychological examination.* This will include an assessment of the child's present intellectual level and an objective assessment of educational attainment. It is advisable that a verbal intelligence test, such as the Terman-Merrill Scale, should be supplemented by a performance test. Many psychologists are now using the Wechsler Intelligence Scale for Children which provides Verbal, Performance and Full Scale Quotients. Whatever the tests used, the examination should result in more than the production of test scores. Testing is, in effect, a standardized interview. The quality of the child's thinking, his intellectual strengths and weaknesses, his attitudes to success and failure, along with many other personal characteristics, can all be noted. Such observations may be important not only in assessing the child's need for special schooling but also in understanding his needs once he has arrived at the ESN school. The examination is preferably undertaken by a trained educational psychologist since the emphasis is on the child's educable capacity and requires not only knowledge about the interpretation of test scores but also about schools and the educational process. Above all, it should be done by someone who has a real interest in very backward children and who is able to ensure their full co-operation.

(c) *An educational assessment.* This should provide a detailed description of the child in the school setting, giving information about:

(i) The child's level of attainment in the basic subjects in terms of what he can do, what his special difficulties appear to be, and what steps have already been tried, e.g. whether remedial measures have been attempted, and if so, by what method and with what result.

(ii) The child's level of language development and speech.

(iii) Standards of achievement in other areas of the curriculum, e.g. in art, practical subjects, physical education.

(iv) Emotional and social behaviour as displayed both in and out of the classroom.

(v) Interest in and attitude towards school.

(vi) Previous school history with particular reference to attitudes towards school, changes of school and regularity of attendance.

(vii) The child's interests and background knowledge.

(viii) Degree of parental co-operation.

(d) *A social history of the child in his family and cultural setting.* Most discussions about backward children lead to the point when the importance of the home as a powerful factor in the child's response to school is agreed upon. The information obtained at the special examination is a useful starting point but in many cases the school feels a continuing need for work with the home. The school nurse and the welfare officers can provide useful information, but there is no doubt that a trained social worker able to devote part of her time to helping the special school with this problem would be a great asset. At the initial examination there is a need to acquire basic information about:

(i) The child's developmental history. Efforts should be made to find out about birth conditions, age of passing the 'milestones', stages in speech development, illnesses and accidents and any marked irregularities in development. It is often difficult to get reliable information. Other sources such as previous schools, welfare departments, and family doctors might be referred to.

(ii) Details about the family history, particularly with reference to mental or physical illnesses that may have a bearing on the child's condition. Facts about the cultural and economic factors in the home.

(iii) Family attitudes and relationships. This is a most important aspect to assess, for the emotional climate of the home, the attitudes towards the child, and the way difficulties in development have been met can be powerful determinants of the child's capacity to learn. It is here that a social worker's special training and experience have most to offer in assessing and changing attitudes and relationships within the family.

When the examination and investigations have been completed, some form of conference is desirable to collate the information that has been obtained. A conference between the various workers concerned is to be recommended. In some places this purpose is served by an admissions' committee at which the school medical officer, psychologist and the headmaster of the ESN school together with other people concerned meet to discuss which children are most in need and suitable for admission. The practice whereby the school is informed of new entrants merely as an administrative action seems inadequate. The headmaster is likely to know what children on the waiting list can most suitably be catered for, taking into account the distribution of ages, educational and behaviour problems as well as the staffing resources to deal with them.

A person who should be taken into consultation and co-operation right through the ascertainment procedure is the parent. It is a good thing if this consultation starts well before the child is referred for ascertainment. Head teachers of ordinary schools should, wherever possible, discuss the child's difficulties with the parent while he is in ordinary school. If the parent appreciates that the ordinary school has taken some trouble to help the child, he is more likely to accept the head teacher's reasons for referral and to see the probability of special school as a positive step. A visit to the ESN school often dispels some of the anxieties and opposition when the parent sees the wide range of educational work undertaken and the good results obtained. It must be remembered that many parents conceive of the ESN school as a place for mental defectives and may need more than verbal descriptions and persuasions to understand that it is special *education* that is being advised. It is easy to be impatient with parents' misconceptions, and their mixture of motives for unwillingness, especially when the child's need is so patently obvious to the objective observer.

We have stressed earlier that the diagnosis should be continuous. The first case conference should not be the only one. The ideal should be for each case to be reviewed annually, and particularly so for those in residential schools. We suggest elsewhere that case conferences among the staff should be arranged to consider the broad lines of educational treatment. We hesitate to suggest further calls on the time of educational psychologists, school medical officers and social workers but at least some cases should be discussed at frequent intervals—for example, children with serious behaviour disturbances or inexplicable learning difficulties.

REFERENCES

1. BURT, C. *The Subnormal Mind.* O.U.P., 1935.
2. CLEUGH, M. F. *The Slow Learner.* Methuen, 1957.
3. HIGHFIELD, M. *The Young School Failure.* Oliver and Boyd, 1949.
4. INGRAM, A. J. *Elementary Education in England during the period of payment by results.* Dissertation for Dip. Ed. Univ. Birmingham, 1958.
5. LEWIS, E. O. *Report of the Mental Deficiency Committee.* Part IV, H.M.S.O., 1929.

SPECIAL EDUCATIONAL TREATMENT

Nos. 6–11 are Ministry of Education Publications.

6. *Handicapped Pupils and School Health Service Regulations, 1945. School Health Service and Handicapped Pupils Regulations, 1953.*
7. Pamphlet No. 5, *Special Educational Treatment*, 1946.
8. Reports of the Chief School Medical Officer, Ministry of Education, *The Health of the School Child*, 1939–45, 1946–7, 1956–7. H.M.S.O.
9. Pamphlet No. 30, *Education of the Handicapped Pupil*, 1945–55. H.M.S.O.
10. Training and Supply of Teachers of Handicapped Pupils, 1945. H.M.S.O.
11. Pamphlet No. 32, *Standards of Reading, 1948–56.* H.M.S.O.
12. SCHONELL, F. J. *Backwardness in Basic Subjects*, 1942. Oliver and Boyd.
13. SCOTTISH COUNCIL FOR RESEARCH IN EDUCATION. *The Intelligence of Scottish Children.* U.L.P., 1933.
14. TERMAN, L. M. and MERRILL, M. *Measuring Intelligence.* Harrap, 1937.
15. WECHSLER, D. *Intelligence Scale for Children.* Psychological Corporation, 1949.
16. W.H.O. *The Mentally Subnormal Child.* W.H.O. Technical Report, No. 75.
17. SCHONELL, F. J., RICHARDSON, J. A. and MCCONNEL, T. S. *The Subnormal Child at Home.* Macmillan, 1958.

FURTHER READING

DUNN, LLOYD. *Exceptional Children in the Schools.* Holt, Rinehart & Winston, 1963.

JOHNSON, O. *Education for the Slow Learners.* Prentice-Hall, 1963.

KERSHAW, J. D. *Handicapped Children.* Heinemann, 1961.

KIRK, S. A. *Educating Exceptional Children.* Houghton-Mifflin, 1962.

MINISTRY OF EDUCATION. *Half our Future.* A report of the Central Advisory Council for Education. Her Majesty's Stationery Office, 1963.

PRITCHARD, D. *Education and the Handicapped, 1760–1960.* Routledge & Kegan Paul, 1963.

ROTHSTEIN, J. *Mental Retardation: Readings and Resources.* Holt, Rinehart & Winston, 1961.

SCHONELL, F. J., MCLEOD, J. and COCHRANE, R. G. *The Slow Learner—Segregation and Integration.* Univ. of Queensland Press, 1962.

SEGAL, S. S. *Dull and Backward Children: Post-war Theory and Practice.* Educational Research, Vol. III, No. 3.

II

INTELLECTUAL DEVELOPMENT
OF ESN CHILDREN

THE limited intellectual development of ESN children is an essential fact to be taken into account in considering what methods of learning and teaching should be employed and what standards may be achieved. Many other things must of course be considered. In fact, once children have been placed in an ESN school, the level of intelligence, as indicated by a test result, is less useful and important than the teacher's observation of the child's ways of thinking and learning, and the way his personality and previous experiences affect his response to school. But since low intelligence is so marked a characteristic of ESN children we have to examine what is meant by intelligence and the significance of test results.

It is our impression that many teachers are uncertain about the meaning of intelligence and especially the interpretation of test results. In regard to the former, they are in good company since the experts have been arguing about intelligence for the last fifty years. Recently there has been a change of emphasis in views about intelligence and this is of interest to teachers of backward children.

A definition of intelligence given by Schonell (26) in *Backwardness in the Basic Subjects*, is a good starting point.

> *General intelligence may be defined as an inborn, all-round mental power which is but slightly altered in degree by environmental influences although its realization and direction are determined by experience.*

Most teachers would agree with the first part of the definition—*an inborn, all-round mental power*—but would probably be rather uncertain about how to interpret the last part of the definition—*although its realization and direction are determined by experience.* In the last thirty years the emphasis has been placed on intelligence as an innate ability, determined by heredity and but little influenced by experience. The benefits of a superior environment and the handicaps of an inferior one have usually been thought of as affecting the child's progress in school work rather than the *realization and direction* of his mental growth. There has in fact been a good deal of controversy about the relative effects of inheritance and environment on intelligence with rather fruitless attempts to estimate the exact contribution of each. In recent years a concept of intelligence has been developing which rather by-passes this controversy about the effects of nature and nurture. The innate basis of intelligence is admitted, but intelligence is viewed not merely as an unfolding or maturing of this innate potentiality but also as something that grows and develops in the course of the child's active experience of his environment. The infant's simple ways of perceiving and behaving are modified and added to as new needs arise and new environmental demands are encountered; verbal and other concepts are built up; more mature ways of thinking are acquired in the course of his experience. In current views, more emphasis is being placed on the last part of Schonell's definition of intelligence—*its realization and direction are determined by experience.*

Hebb (10) has suggested that there are two meanings of the word intelligence. He refers to these two meanings as Intelligence A and Intelligence B. Intelligence A is the innate potentiality for development, 'which probably amounts to the possession of a good brain and a good neural metabolism'. Intelligence B is the quality and level of functioning that has developed; it has been acquired in the course of experience. We have no means of knowing or measuring Intelligence A although it is reasonable to assume that individuals vary in their inherited potentiality for development, and we know also that damage to the brain and nervous system, as in the case of some handicapped children, can impose another limitation on that potentiality. Intelligence B is what we are referring to when we describe a child as being of high or low intelligence or as having more intelligence than he uses. Vernon (34) has suggested a third meaning—Intelligence C for the mental ages, Quotients or other scores resulting from attempts to measure Intelligence B. The concept of Intelligence C is a reminder that our measurements may or may not be good estimates of Intelligence B.

In children who come from similar environments, differences in Intelligence B are mainly due to the differences in their inherited potentiality, Intelligence A. This is probably true of the majority of children in our culture. They are exposed at school and home to a very similar kind of stimulation to intellectual growth. Where environments are much more varied, it is likely that the influence of

25

environment on mental growth is greater. To quote Vernon (33), 'When environments vary more widely, as between white and negro sub-cultures in America, between secondary modern D streams and Grammar school A streams or between institutionalized and vocationally adjusted imbeciles, the relative influence of environment is more clearly apparent.'

The question of the effect of environment and experience on the growth of intelligence is a matter of obvious interest to teachers of handicapped children. Many ESN children grow up in circumstances which limit rather than foster the development of Intelligence B and this must be remembered as well as the probability that they have a poor Intelligence A. Very poor homes rarely provide as good opportunities for the incidental learning as average or good homes do. There may be few means for play with toys and other materials through which so many productive ways of thought and activity are developed. In one problem family recently, a boy was observed on his return from school. It was a back-to-back house in a small area behind other houses on a main road. At first, he sat down in a chair, listening to Mom and the visitor talking. After a minute or two he began to play with the baby, which he did for a short while before picking up a comic. Then he wandered round the room, eventually sitting down in another chair. In a few minutes, he went to the larder to get something to eat. Having finished this, he was on the move again. There was nothing, in fact, capable of holding his attention for very long.

In such a home, there may be no books; no picture books in early childhood to extend knowledge and vocabulary; no story-telling from which children gain in language and in understanding of the ways of the world. There may be little conversation worthy of the name. There may be few trips away from the immediate surroundings, no holidays in the country or at the seaside. Such deficiencies may be severe enough to limit, to some extent, the development of concepts and the ability to think which we measure in intelligence testing.

It is interesting to speculate how far special education may improve not only attainments and social adjustment but also the level of mental functioning in children who have not experienced the best conditions for mental growth. We are unfortunately a long way from any precise and practically useful knowledge about the effects of experience on mental growth but some investigations which have a bearing on this problem are worth mentioning.

Studies of children in unusual environments

One of the earliest studies demonstrating the effect of unusual cultural and social background was Gordon's report (9) on mental test scores of children who had had little or no schooling—physically handicapped children, canal-boat and gypsy children. He found that the youngest canal-boat children had an average IQ of 90 whereas the oldest (average age, 11 years 11 months) had an average IQ of 60 on the Stanford Binet test. These figures illustrate, as Binet noted in his original work, that the Binet test measures intelligence as developed by environment and that it is not really appropriate to children whose experience has been very different from that of the type of children on whom the test was standardized. These older children had no doubt developed skills well suited to their particular canal-boat environment but their lack of schooling and other cultural experiences had limited the development of abstract and verbal concepts which are sampled by the Binet type of test. There is a similarity here with *some* children in ESN schools who have been brought up in unusually inadequate environments or with children who have been deprived of normal experiences owing to long periods of hospitalization.

It is interesting that studies of children in very isolated mountain areas of the U.S.A. showed the same tendency for intelligence quotients to decrease with age. In one community, the investigation (39) was repeated ten years later. Intelligence quotients showed the same decline with age but in each age group the quotients were slightly higher than before, suggesting that increased school attendance and improved contacts with the outside world had had a stimulating effect. Similar trends have been observed in Britain. The Scottish Intelligence Survey (32) compared the mental test results of eleven-year-olds in 1947 with those in 1932; Cattell (4) compared the scores of Leicester children in 1950 with those he obtained thirteen years before. In both cases, slight but significant gains were recorded instead of the decreases which had been predicted on the grounds of a differential birth rate. There are various explanations, such as test sophistication, for these results but improved social and educational conditions may well be having some influence.

Studies of foster children

Several investigators have tried to show that children who have been placed in good foster homes have benefited in their mental growth from the better environment. Over a period of fifteen years, Skodak (28) followed the progress of sixteen children of defective mothers.

27

These children had been placed in foster homes before the age of six months. The average IQ of the foster children was close to 100 throughout the period of investigation suggesting that these children had developed mentally more at the level of the foster parents. Freeman, Holzinger and Mitchell (8) produced evidence to suggest that children who lived with their own defective parents for a longer period before being placed with foster parents were lower in intelligence than children who had lived with defective parents for a shorter period. Skeels (27) found that young children who were removed from an unstimulating orphanage to an institution where they received very much more attention and affection showed quite considerable gains in the level of mental functioning as measured by scores on tests for young children. These results depend on considerable differences between the two environments. Removing children from an extremely unfavourable environment to one which is very much more favourable would seem to result in quicker mental development, especially with young children in the formative pre-school period.

The effect of early adverse experiences

It is not only the intellectual stimulation provided by the environment in these early years which is significant for children's mental development. Emotional relationships may be important in determining the child's attitude to himself and the vitality of his response to his environment. The work of Bowlby (2), Spitz, Goldfarb and others has highlighted the effects on personality and mental growth of severe maternal deprivation in the early years. We can do little more than speculate at the moment about the effect on mental growth of other variations in family relationships—the inadequate and inconsistent mothering which has been the lot of some ESN children, the effect of different types of discipline and attitudes towards children. Hebb (10) has shown that animals brought up as pets with the freedom of a varied environment are more capable at maturity of solving problems than are animals which have been brought up in the restricted environment of a cage. In the case of children it may well be that mental growth can be limited by restricted living conditions, by parents' attitudes or by emotional upsets which prevent children being fully active in relation to their environment. We have little evidence on such points at the moment nor do we know whether or how we could help children to recover from such effects.

Some recent work in this country however shows that the process of recovery from adverse experiences in childhood can continue in adult life. Clarke and Clarke (6), psychologists at a mental deficiency hospital, have reported improved mental functioning in high-grade patients. In particular, they found that twenty-five patients who had come from extremely adverse home environments (gross poverty, neglect, families with no fixed abode, N.S.P.C.C. cases, etc.) made the largest gains on intelligence tests over a period of about two years. The average gain was 9·7 points of IQ and this was at an age when it has commonly been assumed that mental growth has ceased. The Clarkes attributed these changes to the effect of removal from unsatisfactory environments.

The effects of educational experiences

Does a specially stimulating school environment accelerate mental growth? Wellman (38) and other workers at the University of Iowa thought so and claimed definite gains in intelligence as a result of nursery school experience. This stimulated other investigations to check the validity of this claim but it must be admitted that there are few researches which give conclusive evidence (or which have escaped serious criticisms) about the effect of special educational experiences on mental growth. (For recent work see Kirk, 40.)

Several investigations with subnormal children have shown that there was a relatively marked tendency for IQs to decline while the child was in unfavourable school and home conditions and that this trend was reversed, at least for a while, after the child was admitted to the special school (Kephart (12), Phillips (18)). Oliver (17), working with subnormal children in a residential school, reported that mental tests scores had improved slightly during the three-month period of a special physical education programme.

One well-known but doubtful claim is that of Schmidt (25) who worked with 12- to 14-year-old boys and girls in special centres in Chicago. They had been classified as feeble-minded on the basis of test results. The experimental groups were provided with a programme very like that of the good special school, aiming at developing academic and practical skills, and personal and social adjustment through experiences designed to prepare them for work and life. They were tested at the beginning of the experiment, at the end of the course, and at the end of a five-year follow-up period. From the various test measurements, we may take the results of the Stanford-Binet intelligence tests. From an average IQ at the beginning of the experiment of 52·1 the experimental groups moved to an IQ of 71·6 at the end of the three-year course, and after five years the average IQ had moved to 89·3. Similar progress was reported on social and personal adjustment. While one can accept that these children improved in many respects as a result of the special centre work, the changes reported in terms of test results are very considerable and much greater than anything else that has been published. Attempts by Kirk (13) to verify the data raised serious doubts regarding the accuracy and validity of the claims. These were not adequately dispelled by Schmidt in her reply. She claimed that similar investigations were being undertaken but so far these have not been reported upon.

More recently, several investigations, not related to the special school field, have given indications that the length and type of schooling may have an appreciable effect on the level of intelligence reached and the kind of mental abilities developed. Husen (11) has shown that a man who has full secondary and university education has on average a 12-point advantage on tests over the man who was equally intelligent at 15 but did not continue his formal education. Vernon (35) found that after the age of 17, boys not attending school declined in tests related to scholastic abilities but continued to gain in mechanical and spatial abilities. It is possible too that the slight average increases reported by the Scottish Intelligence survey (1947) and Cattell at Leicester may be partly due to educational influences.

Our personal impression is that the effect of unsatisfactory (and to the child, unsatisfying) educational experience can often be observed in the mental testing of older ESN children, who have remained in the ordinary school. Their response to the tests and the pattern of successes and failures often show, not just a poor response to the test situation but also some retardation in aspects of mental growth that seem to depend, at least to some extent, on a full participation in school experience. Although they may obtain scores well into the subnormal range, one feels that these are not a true picture of their possibilities and that more adequate realization of their potential would have been possible if they had received special educational treatment.

It is unfortunate that in spite of the amount of mental testing of ESN children that takes place, there has been little attempt to report on the amount of variability in the mental status of ESN children receiving special educational treatment. Lloyd (15) mentions cases at her own school of children 'who may appear to have a low intelligence level for a very long time and may gradually climb upwards or may suddenly "find themselves" after years of misunderstanding.' She quotes three cases who moved during a period of two and a half to four years from IQ 72 to 83; from IQ 73 to 88; and from IQ 45 to 89. In each case five or six tests were given over the period and the final quotient shows a fairly dramatic change from the previous level. Lloyd argues that these were maladjusted children whose problem should have been diagnosed before entry to the school and dealt with in some other way. It is, however, not always easy to make a certain diagnosis about such children at ages five to eight years. Moreover, there are few places which have adequate facilities for treating such children in a thorough manner over a period of time.

In this connection, an investigation by Mundy (16) at the Fountain Hospital is worth mentioning. She gave psychological treatment to fifteen children whose average IQ was 45. They were compared with a matched group who did not receive treatment. The experimental group gained 9 points of IQ on average compared with 2 points for the control group. One measure of the success of the treatment was that eight children in the treatment group appeared to be ready for education in an ESN school although before treatment there had been no suggestion of this possibility. Teachers have long felt the need for some psychological or child guidance treatment for a proportion of the children in ESN schools. There are many justifications for such treatment but one is that a *few* children whose mental retardation is partly due to failures in personality development would be helped. The earlier these children can be treated the greater the chance of improved mental growth.

The constancy of intelligence

The doctrine of the constancy of the intelligence quotient has at times been so literally accepted in the schools that surprise has been expressed at small changes in quotients. It is true that, on the whole, children remain roughly in the same group of intelligence over the school period, but variability is greater than is often realized. The amount of variation in quotients in a *normal* population of children has usually been expressed as 50 per cent of the cases remaining within 5 points up or down from the previous IQ. Vernon (36) has suggested that the average change in IQ would be about 6 points when the tests are of a similar kind and about 10 points when they are very different, or when re-testing is done after a lapse of several years. Longitudinal studies of children's development show that, while the majority stay roughly in the same group of intelligence, there are a few cases where considerable upward or downward changes occur. Variability is great enough to suggest that the IQ should never become a label which is permanently fixed to the child.

We have, however, inadequate evidence about the amount of variability with ESN children. Childs (5) quotes figures supplied by Lloyd for all the children in a Junior ESN school. The children were tested mostly by the same person, roughly at nine-month intervals, and it was found that the successive IQs for each child could be classified into four groups. 24 per cent showed a steady rise; 19 per cent showed a steady fall; 50 per cent showed an irregular series of ups and downs; only 7 per cent showed anything like a consistent IQ. Those who showed an upward tendency obtained an average increase of 19 points in an average of three and a half years' schooling. A number of things would need to be known about these figures before drawing firm conclusions but at least they bring home the fact that the intelligence quotient can be more variable than we have often supposed. What we really need is more evidence on this point. At least one investigation is in progress by Port-wood (22) in Sheffield ESN schools in which annual testing of ESN children on the Wechsler scale should give reliable information.

This is not a matter of mere academic interest. If there are children who are capable of higher levels of mental functioning, we should know more about them in case there is anything we can do in addition to providing good special schooling to facilitate the process. How far special schooling can improve mental abilities is an open question at present although an expression of opinion by Professor Vernon (33) is worth quoting: 'It is quite probable that first-rate schooling, which encourages intellectual exploration and keenness, does do more to stimulate and develop the mind all-round than does the mechanical instruction of bored pupils; though we have little direct evidence and should not forget the negative findings of so many experiments on transfer.'

The meaning of low intelligence

What does it mean when we say that a child is of low intelligence? It is useful in answering that question to look at a sample of an ESN child's thinking and see in what respects it is limited. Here are some responses of Pat, an 11-year-old ESN girl, to some questions which belong to the 7-year-old group of tests on the Terman-Merrill Scale (30)—the intelligence test which most ESN children meet in the examination before they come to the ESN school.

Question	Answer
In what way are:—	
(a) apple and orange alike?	round and juicy.
(or like each other or the same)	
(b) coal and wood alike?	coal has got wood in it.
(c) a ship and a motor car alike?	ship sails and car doesn't.
(d) iron and silver alike?	silver shines, iron doesn't.

The answer to the second question is unusual for ESN children. She had heard her father talk about coal but characteristically could not explain her answer further. The usual answer is that coal and wood both burn but many ESN children of nine or ten would say that they are both black. In these replies Pat showed a characteristic weakness of the thinking of ESN children—the difficulty of thinking of relationships. She was able to say something about each of the items but she found it hard to think of a point of similarity, and when the objects were less familiar to her she could only think of differences. Many ESN children about this age would persist in giving differences for all the questions as though they did not grasp the idea of a likeness (however the question was worded). The average child of seven or eight finds no great difficulty with this type of problem; the more intelligent ones would probably give answers of good quality such as 'fruit' for (a) or 'metal' for (d).

We have here an example of one of the chief weaknesses of the ESN children's thinking—a difficulty with the complex mental operation of reasoning. They are slower to notice the features of things and to perceive relationships between things in their experience. They are therefore poorer in the process of developing concepts or general ideas which underlie a great deal of school work, especially in language and number. For example, developing a vocabulary is not just a matter of learning to attach the right word to the right thing. There are many words which do not refer directly to particular *things*—the words 'metal', 'tools', 'transport' each refer to a *class* of different things; other words are even further removed from the concrete and actual—honest, truthful, more, less, equal. Our talk, and the stories and reading books we use, are full of words which stand for concepts which are built up as the result of processes of abstracting, classifying and generalizing. The less intelligent child finds this kind of thinking difficult, and all the more so if it is not based on actual experiences.

Piaget (19) has described the stages through which children pass as their thinking develops. It is interesting to see how far ESN children get in these stages. The first stage, which need not concern us, is the *sensori-motor stage* from birth to about eighteen months when the child is learning to pattern his sense impressions of the world around him and to act in a variety of ways in relation to it. In the next stage of *pre-concepts*, he makes his first attempts at conceptual thinking. Words begin to be used for partially formed concepts. The inaccuracies of his concepts can often be detected in his errors in using words, for example, when he says 'dog' for any four-footed animal, or calls 'Dadda' after any man, or says 'two' when he means any amount more than one. It will be apparent that many ESN children between the ages of five and seven are still in this stage of thinking. Many ESN children below the ages of 10 or 11 years are still in the next stage of *intuitive thought*. Here the child has a basic store of concepts and a more considerable vocabulary and he can think about many more things that interest him. But his thinking is still not rational. He can be led astray by particular, irrelevant features in what he perceives. For example, in Piaget's well-known experiment, a child is shown two glasses of water which he agrees are equal. When the water from one glass is poured into another glass which is thinner and taller, the child at the intuitive stage will say that there is now more water, his judgment being led astray by the greater height of the glass. Something similar to this seems to have been happening in Pat's answers about the iron and silver—she can think of the shininess of silver but not of the similarity with iron. Also at this stage, children tend to explain physical phenomena animistically. Thus the movements of the wind, the clouds, the sun and moon are interpreted as though they were living beings. In the understanding of the causes of events, these children are still in the intuitive stage. Similarly, their judgments about behaviour are likely to be based on personal feeling and attitudes rather than on any real idea of rules and moral principles.

At the next stage, of *concrete operations*, roughly from seven to eleven, the normal child becomes able to think more rationally. He begins to make simple classifications—to put things together that are alike, or to put things in order, e.g. he can make a series from shortest to longest or lightest to heaviest, and can begin to think about the relationships between number groups. At first, these operations are concrete operations, i.e. children need to reason in relation to things; the thinking must be based on experiences.

The final stage of thinking is the stage of *formal operations* from about eleven or twelve onwards when the child can think and reason in the abstract. This is the stage that permits the academic studies of the able secondary school child. ESN children do not, of course, reach this stage of logical abstract reasoning. What we can hope to do is to provide the best conditions for their development from the intuitive stage into the stage of concrete operations where simple reasoning is possible about things and events which they can perceive or imagine.

Piaget (20) and his collaborators are not very precise about whether children's progress through the stages of thinking can be hastened by the right sort of experiences. But their work does suggest that the development of intelligence is not just a matter of the maturing of some innate potentiality; it is also partly the result of the child's activity in relation to his experience. At the very least, therefore, it is reasonable to suppose that providing children with rich opportunities for experience, and encouraging their mental activity in relation to it, is a step in the right direction. For example, in the development of number thinking they need plenty of experience of amounts and quantities before we try to develop the number concepts. In developing the ability to reason about the world around them and how that world works, they need not only to observe but to do things themselves, to experiment, notice and compare. Then they need to talk and think about what they have observed in order to progress from the immature ways of thinking characteristic of the intuitive stage to the more objective thinking of the stage of concrete operations. Similarly in the development of moral concepts, we cannot just impose our mature concepts of good, fair, truthful, etc. upon them. These concepts must develop and are likely to be more firmly based if they have been built up in the course of their own thinking about many situations in class or school, or about events happening in the community around them. The fact that ESN children are so much less able to think about experience in this way does not remove the obligation to attempt this type of approach, at least with the more able children in ESN schools, and with the backward children in ordinary school.

Returning to Pat's answers to some of the test questions, we can see some other weaknesses in her thinking. The following were her replies to the vocabulary test of the Terman-Merrill Scale in which she is asked to give the meanings of a list of words.

orange.	round one; got pips in it.
envelope.	put the letter in it.
straw.	drink through it.
puddle.	paddle in it. On further questioning she said, "Lake".
tap.	water comes out of it.
gown.	what you wear at night.
eyelash.	close it down to go to sleep.
roar.	lions roar.
scorch.	scratch the bottom of your shoes.
muzzle.	put it on the dog's nose to save him from getting away.
lecture.	sit on it.
Mars.	bar chocolate.

Her replies illustrate the poor verbal ability of ESN children both in terms of the words she knew and in the brief and simple explanations given. (This is discussed further in Chapter VI.) Pat knew the examiner well; they were on very friendly terms and the brevity of replies was not due to shyness. It was interesting to note how the words were described by referring to simple actions or uses, showing again the tendency to think of the particular and the actual. Another feature was the confusion between similar words, a confusion which was not due to hearing loss—eyelid for eyelash, scratch for scorch. The answer to 'muzzle' showed that she knew what was referred to but her knowledge, as so often with ESN children, was incomplete.

In another test she was asked to say what was silly about some statements—the Verbal Absurdities tests from Terman-Merrill Scale, Year VIII.

> They found a young man locked in his room with his hands tied behind him and his feet bound together. They think he locked himself in.
> Answer: The policeman locked him in.
> A wheel came off Mr. Smith's motor car. As he could not get the wheel back on by himself, he drove the car to the garage for repairs.
> Answer: The garage man mended his car; the wheel came off.

She was obviously completely lost with these questions although she passed several other tests at this age level (questions about a story that was read to her and some simple comprehension questions). It is as though there are too many details and relationships to be thought about at once. She can reason about one or two ideas but not several ideas simultaneously. It suggests that, in teaching her, the material to be learned should be presented wherever possible step by step, so that she can think about one thing at a time rather than have to cope with several things at once.

These examples of an ESN girl's thinking in certain items of the Terman-Merrill test illustrate the difficulty ESN children have in thinking about words, relationships and other abstractions. Their limited abilities are usually obvious in other mental tasks even where verbal concepts are not needed, such as in drawing or matching shapes, completing jigsaws, completing or remembering patterns. They are, however, often rather better in these tests than in those which are mainly verbal. Indeed there is a fair amount of evidence to show that *on the average* ESN children obtain higher scores on performance tests than on verbal tests. The results obtained by Duncan (7) at Lankhills will be familiar to many teachers. They are compared in Table I with those obtained by Tansley (29) at Leeds.

TABLE I
VERBAL AND PERFORMANCE QUOTIENTS OF ESN CHILDREN

	Binet		Alexander Scale	
	Range of IQ	*Mean*	*Range of PQ*	*Mean PQ*
Duncan	54–76	66	67–119	96
Tansley	53–87	67	50–122	77·7

It is possible, as Kirk suggests, that the ESN children Duncan refers to are not quite typical (verbal quotient 66; performance quotient 96). Coming largely from a rural area there is probably a more pronounced cultural factor in the discrepancy. It will be noted that Tansley's results for an urban area are much less pronounced. Moreover, a preliminary report by Portwood (22) on the testing of 150 Sheffield ESN children, using the Wechsler Intelligence Scale for Children, states that twice as many children had higher verbal than performance quotients. The difference between Portwood's results and those of Duncan and Tansley needs elucidation but it is probably partly due to the difference between the tests used, the Wechsler Performance Scale containing less strictly *performance* material than the Alexander.

The important thing is not so much the general tendency as the existence of discrepancies between verbal and performance quotients in individual children. That these can be quite large is shown by the analysis of Wechsler results of 100 children in a residential school. (Table II).

TABLE II

PERFORMANCE QUOTIENT 5 OR MORE POINTS HIGHER THAN VERBAL QUOTIENT

No. of points higher	Girls	Boys
5–9	4	10
10–14	6	10
15–19	4	5
20–24	1	4
Over 25	0	4

VERBAL QUOTIENT 5 OR MORE POINTS HIGHER THAN PERFORMANCE QUOTIENT

5–9	6	7
10–14	3	4
15–19	2	2

Where there are big differences between verbal and performance quotients in individual cases, it is worth considering to what they are due and whether there are any implications about methods of dealing with the child. One explanation of lower verbal quotients immediately suggests itself—that they reflect the subnormal child's retardation in language and his greater difficulty in thinking with verbal concepts and symbols. Faced with tests set in a concrete form, he can solve them by doing rather than by abstract thinking and is therefore able to function at a relatively higher level. Many teachers will be familiar with the educational approach of Duncan who believed that higher performance quotients showed that subnormal children should be taught by methods based on thinking and problem-solving in practical activities. 'That their attainments have been low is due to an educational approach through the medium of words, their weakest factor.' No one will doubt the value of practical activities and concrete experiences but the problem is perhaps not as simple as Duncan states it. An equally valid conclusion would be that a special attack on the language backwardness of subnormal children is required, both indirectly through the concrete and practical and directly through the medium of language and verbal experiences.

Duncan's explanation does not take account of social and emotional factors. In the case of the 100 children whose Wechsler results given in Table II, the tendency towards a performance bias may be related to the fact that many of the children come from broken or unstable homes which do not provide the best conditions for language development. Pringle and Bossio (23) using the Wechsler scales have shown that, on the average, groups of deprived children obtain lower verbal quotients. Sarason (24) has suggested that lower verbal quotients may be due to the subnormal child's emotional response to a face-to-face interview in which oral replies are required. In such an interview, emotional factors resulting from the child's previous experiences of failure in school and in inter-personal situations might be expected to inhibit verbalization. It is indeed noticeable how some children turn with relief from verbal to practical tests. In support of his suggestion Sarason points out that of twelve items on the Terman-Merrill Scale which Thompson and Magaret (31) showed to be easier for subnormals than for normals of the same mental age, eight require a response to a visual stimulus (e.g. a picture) and that six of the eight do not require any oral response; of the items on which normals surpass subnormals, all but two require an oral response.

Bijou (1) attempted to relate the comparison of verbal and performance quotients to educational and social achievement. He found that boys having a performance bias had high arithmetic attainments relative to reading, were rated higher in practical subjects and were judged to be better in adjustment than boys of comparable mental age who had low PQs. In contrast, boys with low PQs split into two groups, half succeeding in arithmetic, half failing in the subject. They were poorer at practical work and were considered to be poorer in personal adjustment. A number of other workers have found that a performance bias is a favourable sign for future adjustment and social competence and that a low performance quotient relative to verbal quotient suggests a poor prognosis.

But it would be unwise to generalize in the present state of our knowledge; any child whose test results showed a big discrepancy should be studied as an individual problem. But as Kirk (14) points out, 'Discrepancies in these results indicate that mentally handicapped children not only differ among themselves but also show different abilities within the individual.' It would seem desirable that wherever possible the psychological examination of ESN children should include a performance test.

It is to be hoped that further work will provide the means for a more detailed assessment and interpretation of these individual differences so that special educational treatment can be more precisely planned to suit individual needs. The Terman-Merrill test is an extremely useful all-round measure of scholastic potential but we cannot assume that it is the last word in examining children for special schooling. It often reveals strengths and weaknesses in the abilities of children, but since the different types of item are not consistently or equally distributed throughout the scale, it is often unwise to make statements about the child on the basis of his Terman record. The Wechsler Intelligence Scales, providing verbal and performance quotients and sub-tests which are statistically comparable should have something to offer if the significance of different test patterns can be established. In educating ESN children, a more detailed diagnosis would often be of value. We are sometimes operating rather in the dark, hoping that the recipe that has worked in the past with most children will work again.

Memory

One of the most frequent complaints about backward children is the weakness of their memory. As Burt (3) remarks, 'Of all the special mental disabilities that hamper educational progress, the most frequent is a weakness in what may be termed long-distance memory.' Dull children seem to need to go over material more times before it is fixed in their minds, and more frequent revision is required to prevent forgetting. Teachers often raise particularly the problem of the child who appears to have markedly poor powers of memory, forgetting from one page to the next words that he has supposedly learned, or being unable to remember the simplest number facts in spite of having plenty of practice with interesting apparatus. At the same time such children are often able to remember other things reasonably well, sometimes to the point of being specially knowledgeable about footballers, makes of cars or aeroplanes, names of birds, etc.

What we refer to as memory is, of course, not one power of the mind but involves several different processes. The efficiency of the initial learning is important as well as actual retention and recall; these are all influenced by attitudes, interests and emotional states.

There is no doubt that ESN children have poorer powers of retention than average children, but it would be a mistake to assume, as there is sometimes a tendency to do, that the remedy lies only in increasing the amount of repetition. What is at fault is often the quality of the initial learning rather than the amount of time spent going over the same material.

One of the causes of poor memory in dull children is weakness in attention. What is to be learned must be attended to and its main features observed. Failure in this may be due to factors in the child such as restlessness and distractibility. Motivation may be poor. For example, there may be an attitude of avoidance resulting from previous experience of failure and dislike of a subject. This is often evident in backward readers of all levels of intelligence. They often glance at words rather than scrutinize them carefully, with the result that their errors in recall are the result of guessing from slight clues such as initial letters or superficial similarities. Attention may be poor because the material to be learned is unsuitable—too difficult or outside the child's experience. It may be that it is presented in a way that does not facilitate accurate perceptions of it. This sometimes happens when a game or activity, which is used to clothe the learning with interest, distracts from the essentials to be learned; or when a correct response is obtained with reading and number apparatus on the basis of colour or shape without real mental activity by the pupil.

One way in which remembering can be improved is by ensuring that as many useful associations are made as possible. One reason for the poorer memories of dull children is, however, that they are slower to perceive and use possible associations—indeed this is another way of saying that they are less intelligent. The teacher must therefore pay special attention to getting children to see links which brighter children would probably see for themselves, and encourage various modes of learning the material so that several associations are available. Learning the word 'night' is not just a matter of associating the word with naming the sequence of letters, n-i-g-h-t. In fact such rote mmeorization is not likely to be very successful. The associations which can be used are between the word and its visual pattern; the word and its auditory pattern as it is spoken or sounded; the word and the kinaesthetic memory of writing it. All these should be mutually linked and with the meaning of the word. A network of associations such as this can be added to by linking the word to other groups. For example, teaching *night, light, sight, fight* together in spelling or phonics enables the association of similarity to play some part in the learning and recall. Meaningful relationships as between *light* and *night* might also be used. Wherever possible several links should be used to improve the chances of recall; associations should not, however, be so elaborate that the child is confused—it is often more a matter of presenting the material in a way that facilitates the making of generalizations.

Meaningful associations are of great importance. We recognize this fact in teaching reading when we try to use only words which the child understands, or try to enrich his understanding of words by using pictures and actions, and by talking about experiences in connection with the word. It is significant that nouns and verbs which hold interest and meaning for the child are often remembered better than small words which are colourless and abstract. It is often an aid to remembering if words like 'here', 'there', 'down', 'up', 'over', and, 'under' can be related to appropriate actions or pictures. Similarly, in arithmetic, memory for numbers has to be based on real concepts of number derived from active experiences. It is a fallacy to think that because ESN children are limited in intelligence, they can only learn by rote memorization. They must understand as much as they can of what they are learning; and *then* they need more repetition, revision and practice to ensure retention.

The meaning of tests results

Individual intelligence tests are extremely useful in examining children for the special school and in other aspects of school psychological work. They provide a reliable and quick method of assessing the child's present level of mental functioning as well as his strengths and weaknesses in the variety of types of test-item of which the tests are composed. A test such as the Terman-Merrill consisting of a variety of items (although with a predominantly verbal bias) has been shown to be a good measure of school aptitude and, as such, is a valuable part of the ascertainment examination. A further value of the individual test is that it is a more or less standard situation which gives the examiner many opportunities for observing the way the child behaves—his response to the examiner, his attitude to success and failure, his persistence and many other personality characteristics.

But the usefulness of the IQ in the ascertainment procedure, its undoubted value in drawing attention to certain individual differences and its apparent simplicity and objectivity, have tended sometimes to give the IQ by itself more importance than it merits. The majority of special school teachers will claim to view the IQ as 'only a guide', yet it is deceptively easy to quote the IQ as though the figure were pregnant with meaning and significance. In fact, the IQ by itself does not provide much information beyond indicating the child's standing relative to other children of his age. It does not tell us how that child is different from other children with the same score, how he is likely to react in different situations, nor how successful his future adjustment will be. It is, in fact, no substitute for the knowledge that can be gained from observation of the child's learning and thinking in the classroom. It is only the *beginning* of our study of his intellectual capacities and must always be considered in relation to all the other information which can be acquired—about his health and physical development, his emotional and social maturity, his keenness to learn and his attitudes to school.

The Intelligence Quotient

The intelligence quotient is one way of expressing the child's score on the test. We need to consider first of all whether it is a reliable measure. At the time of the original test the child may have been insecure or unhappy owing to his failure in school or because of his parent's attitude to the special examination. The younger the child was at the time of the examination, the less likely he would have been to co-operate with the examiner. There is also the possibility with a child of any age that the examiner was not able to get the best out of the child. The individual intelligence test is a form of personal interview and children who are aware of their verbal and social limitations may not be completely at ease in such an interview, particularly in one conducted by an unfamiliar person. Children who are emotionally unsettled may have difficulty in applying themselves to the test although under other conditions in the familiar classroom with a familiar teacher they may be capable of somewhat better mental functioning. The psychologist who gives the test normally indicates when there is reason to suppose that the result is an underestimate.

In using the test result, the possibility must also be borne in mind of some change in mental status since the last test was given. The longer the time interval, the more cautious we need to be in interpreting the result. The child may have become more happy and settled during his period in the ESN school; difficulties in his environment may have cleared up; defective speech, sensory deficiencies and other handicaps may have been corrected. As we have said earlier, there is at present little evidence about the variability of IQs in ESN children.

These comments have not been made to detract from the value of intelligence tests but merely to point out some of the considerations in using the results. Measuring intelligence cannot be as simple and accurate as measuring height.

The mental age

The mental age is a way of expressing the child's score on the test. It would be better to think of it as the test age in order to avoid the misleading inference that a mental age of six implies a six-year-old's mentality. The child may indeed have passed tests which the average six-year-old passes but he may well have passed tests in several different age groups in the tests. In some children the scatter of passes through the age groups is wide; in other cases, children pass only a few tests beyond the basic year group of tests. Two children may obtain the same score by virtue of very different mental achievements on the tests. For example, Sheila and Brian both obtained mental ages of six on the Terman-Merrill Scale of intelligence. Sheila failed on tests such as copying a square, diamond and a bead chain and did not do well on tests involving the matching and explanation of pictures. She was relatively better in vocabulary, repeating sentences, remembering the details of a story and other items using words. Brian, however, failed on tests of vocabulary, remembering sentences and following verbal instructions, although he did well in many of the practical tests in which Sheila was poor. Sheila had a history of poor physical development and ill-health but she came from a good home which had promoted verbal development. Brian came from a poor home which had not helped him to develop verbally. Sheila had made a start on a reading Book 1; Brian had not done so and seemed unlikely to do so for some time.

We need, therefore, to look beyond the actual test score and notice the abilities and levels of functioning of which it is an average. We need to think not only of *altitude* of intelligence, i.e. high or low, but also of its *breadth*, i.e. the different abilities in which it is manifested.

A further objection to too literal an interpretation of the mental age is that an older ESN child with a low mental age is different in many respects from a young normal child with the same mental age. A ten-year-old with a mental age of six will differ from a normal six-year-old in physical development and skills; his interests and experience may be more like those of his age group although their range and his understanding of them will be poorer. He will perhaps be less curious, spontaneous and active; the quality of his learning and remembering will be poorer. Moreover, the wrong habits of learning and thinking established during his period of failure, make him a different problem from the normal infant whose behaviour has been less modified by such experience.

The relationship between intelligence and attainment

In teaching backward children, the mental age is often taken as a guide to the levels of attainment to be expected of pupils. Thus, if a child's mental age is 10 years we assume that his attainment ages should also be at the 10-year level. If his reading age is two years below his mental age he is considered retarded and special efforts must be made to get him 'working to capacity' or 'up to expectation'. It has usually been assumed, on this view, that it would not be expected that children should get attainment ages in advance of their mental ages. One would not expect them to be working *above* their capacity, if capacity for learning is defined in terms of scores on a verbal test of intelligence. Yet it is not unusual to find a child whose reading age exceeds his estimated mental age. In such a case, it has been the practice to suspect the intelligence test as inaccurate, or that the child's reading is mechanical without good comprehension—the result of over-emphasis on word-recognition skills. Both these explanations may apply in some cases but it is equally possible that the results are valid and reliable. First, there is no reason why determination, good motivation and a high degree of interest should not result in surprisingly good attainments in some cases. Learning in school does not only depend on intellectual ability. Second, a child might have special abilities which enable him to do well in certain subjects. Third, the nature of test construction and statistical errors in test measurements lead to attainment ages scattering above and below mental ages.

Although over-achievement has been noted in school and referred to by psychologists, e.g. Burt (3), it has tended to be an issue to explain away and has largely been neglected. The question has recently been discussed at length following the publication by Pidgeon and Yates (21) of evidence that in a normal sample of children, the proportion who are over-achieving is almost as great as the proportion of those who are under-achieving. This evidence, together with the shift in emphasis in views of intelligence (referred to earlier) is resulting in some rethinking about the relationship between educational attainment and intelligence. Further investigation is needed.

Some practical implications do emerge immediately. One is that, while we would expect attainment and intelligence test results to approximate, anything like an exact numerical equivalence should not be expected. There is no reason why some children should not have attainment ages above their mental ages. This is not a signal for applying academic pressure but rather for intensifying the attention to all the other factors which promote educational progress—the quality of learning, social and emotional factors in the child. Statements such as 'not working to capacity' should not be made solely in terms of apparent differences between intelligence and attainment test ages. A broader view of 'learning capacity' should be taken.

REFERENCES

1. BIJOU, S. W. *An experimental analysis of Arthur Performance Quotients.* J. Consult. Psych. No. 6, 1942.
2. BOWLBY, J. *Maternal Care and Mental Health.* W.H.O., H.M.S.O., 1951.
3. BURT, C. *The Backward Child.* U.L.P., 2nd edition, 1946.
4. CATTELL, R. B. *The fate of the national intelligence.* Eugenics Review, No. 42, 1950.
5. CHILD, H. A. T. Studies in Education, No. 7. London Institute of Education. Evans, 1955.
6. CLARKE, A. D. B. and CLARKE, A. M. *Cognitive Changes in the Feeble-minded.* Br. J. of Gen. Psych. 45, 1954.
7. DUNCAN, J. *The Education of the Ordinary Child.* Nelson, 1942.
8. FREEMAN, F. N., HOLZINGER, K. J. and MITCHELL, B.C. *The influence of environment on the intelligence, school achievement and conduct of foster children.* Year book. Nat. Soc. Stud. Educ. 27, 1928.
9. GORDON, H. *Mental and Scholastic Tests among Retarded Children.* Educ. Pamphlets. Bd. of Educ. No. 44, 1923.
10. HEBB, D. O. *The Organisation of Behaviour.* Wiley, 1949.
11. HUSEN, T. *The influence of schooling upon IQ.* Theoria, 17, 1951.
12. KEPHART, N.C. in *Intelligence: its nature and nurture.* Yearbook of the Nat. Soc. Stud. Educ. 39, 1940
13. KIRK, S. A. *An evaluation of the study by B. G. Schmidt.* Psychol. Bull. 45, 1948.
14. KIRK, S. A. *Educating the retarded child.* Harrap, 1954.
15. LLOYD, F. *Educating the subnormal child.* Methuen, 1953.
16. MUNDY, L. *Therapy with physically and mentally handicapped children in a mental deficiency hospital.* J. Clin. Psychol., 13, 1955.
17. OLIVER, J. N. *The effect of physical conditioning exercises on the mental characteristics of ESN boys.* Br. J. of Ed. Psych. Vol. XXVIII, 1957.
18. PHILLIPS, G. E. *The constancy of the IQ in subnormal children.* Melbourne University Press, 1940.
19. PIAGET, J. *The Psychology of Intelligence.* Routledge and Kegan Paul, 1950.
20. PIAGET, J. *The Child's Conception of the World.* Kegan Paul, 1929.
21. PIDGEON, D. A. and YATES, A. et al. *The relationship between ability and attainment.* Bulletin N.F.E.R. No. 8, 1956.
22. PORTWOOD, P. F. *Progress Report on the Sheffield ESN study.* B.P.S. Bulletin, No. 34, 1958.
23. PRINGLE, M. L. K. and BOSSIO, V. *A study of deprived children. Part 2.* Vita Humana. Vol. 1, 1958.
24. SARASON, S. *Psychological Problems in Mental Deficiency.* Harper, 1949.
25. SCHMIDT, B. G. *Changes in personal and social behaviour of children originally classified as feeble-minded.* Psych. Monog. 60, No. 5, 1946.
26. SCHONELL, F. J. *Backwardness in the Basic Subjects.* Oliver and Boyd, 1942.
27. SKEELS, H. M. and DYE, H. B. *A study of the effects of differential stimulation*

in mentally retarded children. Proceedings of the American Association on Mental Deficiency. 44, No. 1, 1939.

28. SKODAK, M. and SKEELS, M. M. *A final follow-up study of one hundred adopted children.* J. Genet. Psych. 75, 1949.

29. TANSLEY, A. E. *The use of mental and scholastic test data and case history information as indications for the treatment of ESN children.* M.Ed. Thesis. Univ. of Leeds, 1951.

30. TERMAN, L. M. and MERRILL, M. *Measuring Intelligence.* Harrap, 1937.

31. THOMPSON, C. W. and MARGARET, A. *Differential test responses of normals and defectives.* J. Abn. and Soc. Psych. 42, 1947.

32. THOMSON, G. H. *et al. The Trend of Scottish Intelligence.* U.L.P., 1947.

33. VERNON, P. E. *The relation of intelligence to educational backwardness.* Educational Review, XI, 1958.

34. VERNON, P. E. Studies in Education. No. 7. Evans, 1955.

35. VERNON, P. E. *Changes in ability from 14–20 years.* Adv. Sc. 5.

36. VERNON, P. E. *A New Look at Intelligence Testing.* Educational Research, Vol. 1, No. 1, 1958.

37. WECHSLER, D. A. *Intelligence Scale for Children.* Psychol. Corp., 1949.

38. WELLMAN, B. L. in 39th Yearbook, Nat. Soc. Stud. Educ., 1940.

39. WHEELER, R. L. *A comparative study of the intelligence of East Tennessee mountain children.* J. Educ. Psychol. Vol. 33. 1942.

40. KIRK, S. A. *Early Education of the Mentally Retarded.* Univ. of Illinois Press, 1959.

41. CLARKE, A. M. and CLARKE, A. D. B. *Mental Deficiency—the changing outlook.* Methuen, 1958.

FURTHER READING

CASHDAN, A. *The intellectual powers of subnormal children.* Educational Research, Vol. IV, No. 2.

KIRK, S. A. and MCCARTHY, J. J. *The Illinois Test of Psycholinguistic Abilities— An approach to differential diagnosis.* American Journal of Mental Deficiency, Vol. 60, No. 3.

KIRK, S. A. *Educating Exceptional Children.* Houghton-Mifflin, 1962.

MORAN, R. E. *Levels of attainment of educable subnormal adolescents.* Br. J. of Ed. Psych., Vol. XXX, Pt. 3.

STOTT, D. H. *Observations on retest discrepancy in mentally subnormal children.* Br. J. of Ed. Psych., Vol. XXX, Pt. 3.

III

EMOTIONAL DEVELOPMENT

IT would be wrong to assume that, because ESN children are limited in intelligence, their emotional life is similarly limited. They may be less capable of a varied and subtle expression of emotions but they have the same basic needs as normal children. It is obvious even with severely subnormal children that the experience of love, approval, security and personal attention can have a considerable effect on their personal growth. They are quick to sense those who are genuinely fond of them. The basic emotional needs of children have been variously stated but the following summary includes the essential ones and considers them briefly in relation to ESN children.

(i) *The need for security*. Children need the security of a stable family; the security of a familiar place in which to live and work; the security of familiar people whose attitude and behaviour are consistent and predictable; and the security of a known routine. With handicapped children, we must note too the insecurity that can come from a sense of personal inadequacy, either because of physical weaknesses, or the awareness of mental limitations or the inability to control feelings in temper outbursts or aggressiveness.

(ii) *The need for giving and receiving affection*. Much experience and research has shown how vitally important it is for children to have someone who loves them, and who watches and encourages each step they take in growing up. The inadequate satisfaction of this need is often apparent in those ESN children who are continually seeking the close attention and approval of the teacher. Even senior children will go into a childish sulk or do work well below their best, because they are harbouring a grievance that the teacher has been giving more attention to another child. Children who have been deprived throughout childhood of the full attention and affection of parents will often use the teacher as a parent substitute.

(iii) *Need for acceptance by other children*. Even normally adjusted children may become distressed by the temporary rejection of their playmates. How much more serious is the case of the child who has never learned the elementary techniques of making friendships and getting on with the group. Some ESN children remain isolated because they have had little experience of mixing with others or because they have additional handicaps which set them apart. Rejection by other children is often due to the child's personal appearance, his lack of cleanliness or his spitefulness. The isolated child may withdraw still further or, alternatively, try to get approval and acceptance from the group by boasting, showing-off, and daredevil behaviour.

(iv) *Recognition and self-esteem.* Every child wants to feel successful and get recognition for what he can do. Since ESN children have fewer talents with which to satisfy this need, it is most important that the school should provide many means for successful achievement. If the need is not satisfied in worthwhile ways in school, it may be satisfied out of school, possibly in delinquent ways.

(v) *The need for independence and responsibility.* The urge to become increasingly independent, self-reliant and responsible is a marked feature of normal development. It is easy to overlook this with ESN children because they are more dependent on other people and have more limited capacities for taking responsibility. Yet their satisfaction and pride in themselves when they do accomplish a step forward in independence is most marked. Opportunities for learning to become more independent and responsible are, of course, vitally important for their future.

(vi) *The need for new experience and activity.* The normal child has a strong urge to explore and find out; he welcomes the challenge of new situations and new learning. Although ESN children are less spontaneously curious, and tend to prefer the security of the known and familiar, they do show a similar pleasure in new experiences and in activity. Since their mental and social handicaps tend to limit the satisfaction of this need, a variety of activities and interests in school are all the more necessary.

The growth of personality and the achievement of mental health depend upon the satisfaction of these needs at each stage from infancy to adolescence. Security and affection are the essential needs of infancy and if these have not been fully met, as in the case of many ESN children, there is a poor foundation for the later building-up of personality. Even so, the security and affection offered in the school can go a long way to make up for the lack of them in the child's own home life. The needs for acceptance by the group, for recognition and for independence become increasingly important as the child gets older, and are especially relevant to developing the qualities children should have if they are to be successful when they leave school.

Emotional factors in learning

These needs are also important in relation to the child's motivation for learning .The success of learning and teaching in school does not only depend on the quality of the teaching materials and the methods used. The learner must want to learn. The process of learning must provide one way of satisfying his emotional needs. While there are many ways in which we try to motivate children's learning, the basis of good motivation is in the satisfaction of the needs we have mentioned. For example, children learn something in order to:

(i) gain adults' approval and retain their affection;
(ii) be like other children and be able to join in activities with them;
(iii) achieve success and get recognition for it;
(iv) satisfy the need for play and activity.

In other words, good motivation depends on a good teacher-pupil relationship, the enjoyment of group participation, on feelings of success and mastery and on employing the child's natural interests and activity. We shall hope, of course, that as children progress through the school, they will respond to higher forms of motivation; that they may feel some of the satisfaction of puzzling through a problem or task and feel the satisfaction of mastering it; and that eventually they will develop sufficiently in personality and character to set standards for themselves and become self-involved in doing as well as they can.

Children whose basic emotional needs have been inadequately satisfied may be difficult to motivate. It is difficult to interest children in arithmetic if they are continually pre-occupied with their relationship to parents. They cannot organize their emotional energies for learning in school if they are continually being upset by feelings of hostility and jealousy, or riddled with anxieties about their own failures. Research into the causes of educational failure, whether in bright or dull pupils, has made us realize that anything which interferes with the fulfilment of these basic needs can result in a lowered capacity for learning. Teaching means not only providing them with the right books and using the best methods but also meeting emotional needs, as the following case illustrates.

Jimmy was the last child of a large family. He was not unintelligent but was very backward educationally. He came from a stable working-class family. Closer inquiry showed that although Jimmy was the 'baby' of the family he was not treated as such. He was left very much to his own devices and given the minimum of attention. Father, because of ill-health, had little to do with the boy and mother was pre-occupied with her own worries and interests. Yet Jimmy was a very active, lively boy who loved to be in the limelight. He was good at dramatic work in school; he was thrilled to be chosen to do any special job. When he could not get approval in school in legitimate ways, he obtained it by naughty behaviour, and was often in trouble. When his teacher gave him extra help with his school work, a close relationship was established. On many occasions he showed what this meant to him when he called his teacher 'Dad'. The teacher felt that this relationship partly satisfied Jimmy's longing for approval and affection and largely accounted for the improvements in attainments which were made.

Inadequate satisfaction of any of these needs has different effects on different children. Children vary in the way they react to circumstances and in their ability to withstand strain and stress. Some children develop reasonably well in situations which would upset others to the point of maladjustment or delinquency. Some withdraw, are silent and unforthcoming in school, and are distrustful of adults' attempts to help them. Others in similar circumstances may react in the opposite way with hostile behaviour, although this may conceal an underlying desire for acceptance. No doubt innate, constitutional factors play a part in this. But certain patterns can be detected in the way children behave when basic needs are not satisfied. These are:

(i) *Immaturity*. Children may remain fixed at an immature stage of emotional development, being unable to risk making the next step in growing up. Some ESN children continue to seek affection very much in the way that pre-school children do. They may only be able to work when the teacher is standing over them, encouraging, helping and approving. They may react to frustration or the denial of their immediate wishes very much as young children do—by temper-tantrums, childish sulks, throwing materials away in annoyance. Because of a pupil's age and size, we may fail to recognize that his behaviour is an indication of an immature level of development.

(ii) *Regression*. A period of difficulty in school work or renewed unsettlement at home may result in a return to babyish behaviour, such as wetting, soiling, over-dependence, temper-tantrums. There may be a regression to infantile play.

(iii) *Compensatory activity*. If a need is not met, substitute satisfactions may be found. Lack of affection at home can be compensated for to some extent by the relationship with the teacher. Lack of success in basic subjects may be compensated for by success in practical subjects or in physical activities. Less happily, compensation may be found in undesirable ways such as disturbing behaviour in class or delinquent behaviour outside school.

(iv) *Withdrawal*. Some children react to difficulty and failure by withdrawing. They make little contact with other children or with teachers, and therefore do not benefit fully from school experience. Withdrawn behaviour can be serious from a mental health point of view, and the fact that it does not present a disciplinary problem should not result in its being overlooked. Much can be done to help the withdrawn child by forming a close relationship between teacher and child, by helping him to join in group activities such as drama, by ensuring success in school work and by the gradual development of responsibility and resourcefulness.

(v) *Fantasy*. Needs not satisfied in real life may be satisfied in daydreams. An imaginary good parent may take the place of a non-existent or neglectful one. Failure in school work may result in withdrawing from the difficulties and imagining successful achievements. The child who is not accepted by the group may satisfy his needs by solitary imaginary play, as did the child who did not know how to join in the class games but spent the time going round the playground being a train.

Factors influencing the emotional development of ESN children. The effect of low intelligence

Naturally there are differences between bright and dull pupils especially in those aspects of emotional life which are modified by or dependent on intelligence. For example, ESN children, like young children, tend to live more for the present moment without foreseeing the consequences of impulses. They tend to act upon the first idea or suggestion without waiting to judge between alternatives. Their behaviour is more likely to be modified by the influence of previous training and example than by abstract notions of right and wrong. They have a poorer understanding of situations and this, combined with their greater suggestibility and greater dependence on other people, can result in their being more easily led astray. As adolescents and adults, they will be less able to think out solutions to their emotional and social problems. Much, therefore, depends on the development of positive attitudes and the appropriate channelling if the emotions during school life.

Because they have limited mental abilities, fewer skills and fewer opportunities in their environment, their means of finding emotional satisfaction and expression are less varied than with average children. This is one reason why the curriculum should offer many opportunities for developing practical interests and give scope for emotional expression in various forms of creative work.

The effects of educational and social failures

Many of the emotional problems of ESN children are not related directly to low intelligence so much as to the educational and social consequences of low intelligence. Having less to contribute in class or in the play groups in the street, they easily get left on the fringe and are denied the full participation with others through which so many social and emotional developments are possible. Their early experiences of school are often unsatisfying and this often results in feelings of inferiority and lack of confidence. Even in the favourable conditions of the ESN school it requires a great deal of planning and effort on the school's part to ensure that success and confidence are maintained. When this cannot be done, because of circumstances outside the control of the school, such as tensions in the home, it is not surprising that the child's feelings of frustration sometimes result in outbursts which may appear incomprehensible as well as reprehensible to a teacher.

Emotional development is slower

Whereas the average child beginning school soon acquires sufficient emotional control to be ready to settle to the tasks of formal learning, the young ESN child needs a much longer period of informal activity and the support of a sympathetic teacher to reach that stage. With ESN children below the age of eleven, it is a case of 'more haste less speed'. Premature attempts to teach basic subjects formally before the child has enough self-control to focus his emotional energies upon the task of learning may defeat their object. While many children will be sufficiently mature by the age of eight or nine, there will be many others whose urgent emotional problems require a continued informal approach to learning, as well as special efforts to help them grow up emotionally.

Uneven development

It is almost inevitable that ESN children should show uneven development in the different aspects of growth—physical, intellectual, emotional. Where the discrepancies are considerable, it is important

52

that they should be recognized and taken into account. Physically, a fourteen-year-old ESN boy can be as well developed as the majority of boys of his age. He may have reached puberty. Intellectually, he may have the reasoning ability of an eight- or nine-year-old. Emotionally, his reactions to frustration and his need for attention may be like those of a pre-school child. Socially, he might not have that ability to co-operate with other children and with adults which we would expect in the average six-year-old. Disparities of this kind present a problem to the boy himself as well as to his teachers. For the child, it may mean that he has impulses with which he is intellectually and emotionally incapable of controlling. For the teacher, it means that expectations for responsibility, co-operation and behaviour will be very different from those appropriate to most boys of his age and size. Another child may be physically under-developed but fairly mature emotionally and socially. Similar irregularities occur at all ages in the ESN school and are highly significant in relation to learning as well as to behaviour and disciplinary problems. All teachers should be aware of them.

In trying to promote social and emotional development, we need to recognize the stage the child has reached so that we can start from that point. Stages in development cannot be missed for the maturer attitudes are built on less mature ones—just as in learning to read, quick reading for comprehension depends on first achieving good recognition skills. We cannot therefore expect the immature child suddenly to be able to conform to our expectations. We need to lead him through some of the experiences which will help him to grow up—for example, by giving him gradually more responsible routine jobs to do in school; by arranging the work of the class so that he has many experiences of learning to get on with others; by giving him opportunities for emotional expression in art and drama. Similarly, the child has to learn how to control socially unacceptable expressions of temper, jealousy and ego-centricity. He is helped in this task by having adults at home and school who do not expect him emotionally 'to run before he can walk'. The urgency of the problems arising from uneven development is particularly apparent when one considers the immaturity of some of our school-leavers.

The importance of home influence

A vital matter is the nature of the child's home and upbringing both as they affect him now and as they have nurtured his growth as a person from infancy. It is impossible to realize fully the countless ways in which he has been influenced in the years before he came to school—by the ways in which he has been loved or rejected, rewarded or punished, accepted as he is or urged to be something he cannot be We cannot undo the past but knowing something of the child's previous history may at least make us a little more tolerant of him. It nearly always helps us to understand why he behaves as he does and, therefore, how best to help him. Although the early period of life is undoubtedly most important in determining the way personality develops, this does not mean that later influences are unimportant.

The family is of first importance in creating a sense of security. Some family causes of insecurity are obvious enough, such as parental separations and disharmony, permanent or temporary break-ups in the family, long illness or unemployment. But a child in a family which is outwardly stable may feel insecure if he feels that he gets an insufficient share of affection or that he is a disappointment to his parents by not being able to live up to their expectations in behaviour or achievement. There may be brighter and more successful brothers and sisters to be compared with. It is essential for the child's adjustment that he should be able to accept his limitations, balancing the knowledge of his difficulties and failures with a knowledge of success in other directions. School experience usually provides him with some ways of achieving success but the attitude of the family can be crucial, especially in the case of the child from the better home or from a family where the other children are more able. If he is aware that he is loved for his own sake and accepted in spite of his limitations, and that his small successes are received with approval and pleasure, he is better able to face his inevitable frustrations whether they be due to his personal difficulties or the taunts of quicker children in the neighbourhood. This was illustrated by the story of Brenda.

She was the middle child of a working-class family with one older and one younger child of average ability. Her IQ was 68. Her physical development was normal but she was personally immature. Her parents encouraged her development in every way possible, giving her if anything a larger share of their attention than the other children. At the same time they were not unduly protective. As soon as they sensed that she was ready for the next step forward in independence they helped her to achieve it. Each new gain in educational development and social competence was received with mutual pleasure and congratulation. This child was in the backward class of an ordinary junior school and although backward was not the worst in her class. The fact that there was not an ESN school in the vicinity was not at this time a matter of concern because school and home had co-operated to ensure that she did not feel a failure.

One important feature of this case was that both parents were united in their affection for the child and in the desire to do everything they could to help her.

There are innumerable variations in family attitudes. It sometimes happens that one parent is not prepared to accept the child's backwardness and attempts to force the child's development by undesirable methods. Such inconsistency of standards and the resulting tensions in the family can be very unsettling for the child. The importance of the father's role is often not sufficiently realized. Where the father is uninterested or actually rejectful, it is not only the child but the mother who suffers from his lack of interest. For many mothers, a child who needs extra attention and effort is an added burden which can become almost intolerable if it is not shared. The child suffers both from the lack of father's interest and also from mother's increased anxieties and the divided standards within the family.

In trying to appreciate these family situations, one has also to take into account the possibility that some parents have to contend with feelings of guilt or shame about having a backward child. Such feelings are not always revealed as obvious rejection of the child but may be concealed by excessive concern. This is sometimes so in the case of parents who persist in being over-protective or who have difficulty in accepting reasonable suggestions about the child's education and welfare. Even when parents accept the child as he is, they may have difficulty in adjusting to the attitude of relations or neighbours, especially when backwardness is accompanied by undesirable habits or minor delinquency.

A large proportion of ESN children come from poor homes, and in some cases the living conditions may be very inadequate. It is easy to label such homes as bad but we really need to consider in what ways they are bad. Although they may be squalid and hygienically unsatisfactory, they are not always completely inadequate from a mental health point of view. They may provide a measure of security and affection. 'Mom' retains many of the essential and desirable qualities of Mother even though she be feckless and a bad manager; even Dad shows a rough affection, coming home with treats for the kids. One has to be wary of making easy generalizations. In homes where both parents are working, the provision made for the child when he comes home from school and the kind of attention shown by mother when she is at home are what matter. Though Father may drink, the important question is his attitude to the children, how he treats them and what they think of him.

Other homes, better placed socially and economically, can have more disturbing effects on the ESN child's emotional development.

The better-off home is more likely to have expectations of maturity in play and general behaviour which are in advance of the stage the child has reached. Although he may have many play materials, play opportunities suited to his level may be restricted. He is expected to play according to his age; standards of tidiness and cleanliness are expected prematurely. The children in the neighbourhood may be very much brighter and quicker so that he is left out of their play groups. The parents may be over-anxious about him when he is out of their sight. He may have less chance of fending for himself and so of developing independence.

Keeping a check on personality growth

Stott (9) has remarked that 'the emotional growth of every child should be watched just as carefully and in just as routine a manner as we watch his physical growth'. This is true not only for the sake of the child but also for the greater efficiency of our teaching methods. It must be admitted that it is not easy to assess emotional growth. Whereas intelligence tests help to assess differences in ability, we have rather inadequate measures of personality. Our estimations of children's ability can be based on many impressions of their actual performance in drawing, talking, acting on instructions, in practical work and other classroom situations, but it is rather more difficult to be sure that we are making sense of the many impressions of children's behaviour and emotional response. For one thing we are less certain of what we are looking for, and of its significance. Extreme variations from the average are quickly noticed, particularly if the behaviour has nuisance value—such as sullenness, temper tantrums, or over-active behaviour—or if the behaviour makes it difficult to make contact with the child—as in the case of the child who is very withdrawn or refuses to talk. But noting a few prominent characteristics does not constitute 'watching the child's growth'. The child's personality needs to be seen as a whole. His behaviour in many situations both in and out of school, his relationships with other children and with different members of staff should be observed. Full understanding can only be achieved if we know about his relationships at home and the previous experiences which have helped to form his present attitudes and ways of behaving.

What can be done to watch emotional growth? In the first place, a congenial teacher-pupil relationship and a relaxed class atmosphere which permits a normal, spontaneous expression of the child's personality is necessary. Secondly, the observer needs to have insight which is a result partly of sympathy and intuition, partly of experience. Some background knowledge of normal child development and of the processes of adjustment is also needed if the teacher is to have an adequate standard by which to judge how normal or how deviant the behaviour is. Thirdly, a method inducing systematic observation is of value. Record cards usually incorporate rating scales for personality traits such as co-operativeness, emotional stability, attitude to school, persistence, etc. These are not without value but they are often not sufficiently comprehensive, and in any case are descriptive of surface traits and do not necessarily reveal the underlying causes of behaviour.

Many teachers, especially of younger children, keep a weekly diary in which observations of children's behaviour are recorded. This can be well worth the time spent, even if only undertaken for a short period, since it compels the teacher to observe and think more carefully about individual children. It is often interesting how isolated observations made at different times can be seen to be related. Making a thorough case study of all the children in the class is normally too time-consuming but is to be recommended in the case of at least one or two children whose difficulties are rather baffling. In essence, the case study aims at gathering together all the available evidence about the child's physical and psychological growth, and his social setting of school, home and neighbourhood. An attempt is then made to see these, not as a mere collection of facts, but in terms of the forces that make the child act as he does, and so provide an adequate basis for formulating ways to help him.

Some schools use a case conference for which a regular time is set aside to discuss one or two children. Medical and psychological reports are considered, the class teacher reports on the child's progress and on any special problems, other teachers who take the child add their observations, and general discussion follows. The case discussion has several benefits. The comments and questions of colleagues may help the class teacher to see the child in a new light and may suggest alternative methods of teaching or discipline. All the staff will learn something about the child under consideration and there is therefore a greater unity of approach, which is highly desirable in the case of difficult children. It also makes for continuity of treatment when the child moves up to another teacher. The discussion method is perhaps most valuable since everyone learns from other teachers' observations and educational beliefs. There is nothing revolutionary about the notion of staff discussions of this kind for most staffs engage informally in discussion of children at playtime or dinnertime. Making it more formal ensures that all the available evidence is brought forward for consideration and also that discussion is spread over as many children as possible, not merely those awkward ones whose misdemeanours are likely to bring them up for informal discussion in the staffroom.

One aspect which should be watched at all ages is growth in social maturity. Children should be gradually developing the ability to look after themselves and to participate in those activities which lead towards ultimate independence as adults. *The Vineland Social Maturity Scale* (2) provides a method of assessing the development of personal and social competence. It consists of 117 items of behaviour, grouped according to age-levels. The items cover: Self-help (general, eating, dressing); Locomotion; Occupation; Communication; Self-direction; Socialization. It is not, however, a Scale that would be easy to apply in school conditions and the following check list is therefore suggested to serve as a basis for making observations of children. The questions as set down are general ones and the observations made would have to be related to the child's age and ability and to the teacher's knowledge of the normal sequence of development in personal and social competence. More specific lists could be made, appropriate to particular age-groups in schools, the items being checked as children become able to perform them.

Personal competence

1. Can he look after his personal needs?
   e.g. in eating, toileting, washing, dressing, physical safety.
2. Can he go about by himself?
   e.g. to school; in the neighbourhood; into town.
3. Is he independent in undertaking jobs and in work habits?
   e.g. at school: Can he work by himself? Does he need continuous help and supervision?
   Can he be relied upon to do a job? Can he think out how to do things for himself in the classroom or in practical subjects?
   at home: Does he help in simple household tasks? Does he have any routine jobs at home, e.g. cleaning shoes, chopping wood, fetching coal? Does he go on errands for his mother?
4. Has he any interests or hobbies appropriate to his stage of development? Does he show any particular skill?
5. What is his attitude to himself?
   e.g. is he reasonably self-confident? What is his reaction to difficulties?

Communication

6. Does he talk easily to teachers? To other children?

7. Can he carry messages? Can he comprehend simple oral instructions?

Social

8. Does he mix with other children?
9. Does he make friends with other children?
10. Does he co-operate with other children at play? In the classroom?
11. Has he an awareness of right and wrong behaviour?
12. Does he try to co-operate and conform to routines?
13. What is his attitude to authority? To rules? To correction?

A consideration of these items should help to focus attention on those children, who, because of personal limitations, lack of experience or maternal over-protectiveness, are lagging behind in the development of independence and social competence. Such children may do quite well in school work and because of this their personal and social immaturity can be overlooked.

There are other means of looking systematically at the behaviour and relationships in the classroom. Two which are practicable and useful in school will be referred to. Stott's *Bristol Social Adjustment Guides* (10) are designed to provide a means of assessing which children in a group are showing behaviour serious enough to be characterized as Unsettled or Maladjusted. The assessment has the advantage that it is based entirely on the teacher's everyday observation of the child in various situations. For the first stage of the assessment, four-page forms are available listing descriptions of children's behaviour under the main headings of Attitude to Teacher, Attitude to Schoolwork, Games and Play, Attitude to other Children, Personal Ways, Physique. The teacher underlines, in each section, phrases which are applicable to the child in question. The completed form is then scored by means of a Key and items indicative of unsettlement or maladjustment are noted on a diagnostic form. The number of items so noted gives some indication of the seriousness of the problem. In addition, the symptoms are grouped according to their type—for example, depression; hostility towards adults or towards other children; anxiety about adult interest and affection, etc. This classifying of symptoms helps to show in what directions the behaviour is disturbed and how serious is the disturbance. Many teachers have commented that while the Guides do not provide new information, they do help to give insight into the nature of children's difficulties since a variety of impressions are systematized.

Another technique that helps to supplement casual observations is sociometry (5), which is quite simple to apply in the classroom. The technique aims at discovering the friendships and social preferences within a class. One value of the sociometric study is that knowledge of the relationships in the classroom enables the teacher to arrange groups for work and informal activities in a way which promotes social development. This can be especially important in the case of the child who is always on the fringe. It is sometimes argued that without resorting to this technique the teacher knows the friendships within the group, the children who are popular and those who are isolated. This is usually so in special schools but it is worth noting that the teacher's judgement may be unduly influenced by what happens in the classroom, rather than the playground or the street.

We would emphasize most strongly that we are not in favour of using such techniques casually because they sound interesting or look impressive. They should only be used as part of a genuine attempt to understand the children in a class with a view to planning more effectively for them. Their use should be supported by the teacher's study of child development from the many books and sources now available. Any methods of assessment (whether of intelligence or personality) can so easily end in fixing a label to a child instead of being seen as a first step to greater understanding and appropriate action.

Some frequent patterns of behaviour and their causes

The aim of all this observation and recording should be to penetrate the surface impressions and to understand the causes of the attitudes and behaviour shown by children. Common characteristics of ESN children such as laziness, inattention, showing-off, aggressiveness, may occur for different reasons in different children. We cannot handle the individual child's problem in the wisest fashion unless we have some idea of these underlying causes.

Laziness. In some children, laziness seems to have a constitutional basis, for some are slower and less energetic than others by nature. A slow tempo characterizes all their activity. In some, laziness may be the result of physical factors—glandular dysfunction, poor health, fatigue resulting from inadequate sleep and nutrition. In others, what is condemned as laziness is the result of emotional conditions such as anxiety, conflict, or day-dreaming which absorb the child's energies and attention. In yet others, laziness may be a sign of a deep-rooted sense of failure—they are not buoyed up by the pleasurable and stimulating anticipation of success in any work that they undertake. Only too often, laziness is another way of saying that a satisfactory way of motivating the child in particular activities has not been found. All of us have experienced the somewhat annoying sight of the child who is lazy in the classroom scampering off enthusiastically to woodwork or P.E.

Inattention. It is not enough to accept that a short span of attention is just one of the characteristics of children of low intelligence. On average, slow-learning children do have a shorter span of attention than normal children but many are able to concentrate on enjoyable and successful work for a considerable time. The degree to which the work is suited to the child's capacity, and engages interest and activity is important. The child's physical condition and his expectations of success or failure are also influential. Children who are emotionally unsettled are understandably often restless and distractible. Concentration on 3R work may be largely irrelevant to their fundamental needs for security and affection. In addition, the ability to concentrate seems to be, to some extent, a product of experience and training. Children who have had adequate opportunities for absorbing personal and social play are more likely to have developed the capacity to persist, and be able to accept the more formal requirements of class routines. Creative and practical activities seem to promote the development of good attention and of work habits.

Aggressiveness. Bullying, spiteful, hostile behaviour may be due to feelings of inadequacy and frustration or to the child's inability to form relationships with other children and be accepted by the group. As the child begins to feel more successful in school and is accepted by his group, such reactions often abate. But the behaviour may be due to a generalized hostility towards the world, resulting from the inadequate satisfaction of the basic needs of childhood, from experience of aggressiveness in the environment or severe physical punishments at home. The attitude of the school towards physical punishment can also have an influence here.

In dealing with aggressive children, it is often hard to adopt that sympathetic attitude which can be so valuable in overcoming other personality difficulties, yet the teacher should try to distinguish between the child and his bad behaviour. He should try to like the child and to develop a relationship with him, even though he disapproves of his behaviour.

It is hard to accept that the child who is continually causing trouble to the point of inviting punishment may in certain circumstances be asking, in a roundabout way, for personal attention, or for someone to control him because he cannot control himself. His behaviour may indeed be merely an expression of extreme mischievousness or lack of developed standards of co-operativeness but it could be a way of testing out the relationship with the adult. If he could find words for his unconscious feelings he might say: 'Does teacher really like me? How much can he stand from me before he gives me up?' It demands a strong conviction and faith to go to the limits of toleration with a child like this in order to convince him that he is liked in spite of his behaviour. If such a trial can be won or even partially won, the child's chances of eventual adjustment are so much the greater.

Deprived children. Many ESN schools have a number of children on roll who are in care of the Children's Committee and probably live in Children's Homes. These are children who for varying periods, sometimes from babyhood, have not lived in their own home owing to the death or separation of parents or have been removed because of neglect. The importance of a continuous and happy relationship with parents, especially mother, is one that commonsense will recognize, but it is only recently that psychological interest in children who have been deprived of normal home life has focused attention on the problem and led to increased efforts to minimize its effects. Thus there has been greater recognition of psychological factors in caring for them. One trend has been to accommodate children in smaller groups, providing family homes in houses on new estates. But with the best will in the world it is hard to make up for the lack of the intimate relationships of the ordinary home, and even harder to heal some of the psychological scars of earlier deprivations and changes in circumstances. It is not surprising therefore that some of these children have greater difficulties in their emotional growth and adjustment and that these sometimes interfere with their capacity to learn and to make relationships. Frequently they are more retarded educationally owing to their restlessness and general unsettledness. They are often retarded verbally. The growth of language is intimately associated with emotional relationships and social opportunities and many studies have confirmed that deprived children are more retarded in this respect. Their unsatisfied need for personal attention is often shown in attempts to seek attention or affection— e.g. by boasting or showing off, by an excessive desire to please, by greediness or by over-affectionate and clinging behaviour. Emotional immaturity is often revealed in behaviour such as thumb-sucking, tantrums, sullenness, petulance, jealousy. Such characteristics may persist even though the child has been happily placed in a foster-home, for children do not grow up overnight or even over a period of months. Some are preoccupied with anxieties and fantasies about their parents, and, surprising though it may be, even children who have been ill-treated, neglected or deserted may build up an idealized picture of their parents and long for the moment of return to them. Such preoccupation with one of the basic needs of living is bound to distract from the other tasks of growing up which they should be tackling.

Perhaps the most difficult problem which deprived children present to those looking after them is that many have failed to learn satisfactorily 'the art of living with other people, i.e. to enjoy them, to identify with them, and to appreciate their friendship and affection'. Occasionally one finds a child who shows this to a marked degree as in the case of Kevin who was found abandoned as a baby. He spent periods in various institutions and now attends a residential special school. Many sympathetic people, knowing his history, have shown him affection, have sent him presents and have maintained contact with him, only to be baffled by the lack of emotional response from him. In its most severe form, we have what has been described as an affectionless personality, sometimes superficially responsive but incapable of deeper and consistent feelings towards others; and at other times aggressive, suspicious and lacking in moral control.

It must be stressed, however, that many deprived children may grow and adjust normally. In a study of 142 children living in cottages of a large institution, Pringle and Bossio reported that more than a third of their sample showed no symptoms of maladjustment or deprivation, reacting emotionally in ways very similar to those of ordinary children of their own age. There are, of course, many variables in this situation—the child's own make-up, the age at which he was separated, the quality of his foster-mothering and schooling.

Maladjustment

It is obvious from what has been said already that successful growth in personality is much more difficult for ESN than normal children. Their slower development and low intelligence increase the chances of serious failure in school work and in relationships with other children. Their home life may not provide the best conditions for total growth; parents may be uncertain how to help them. It is not surprising, therefore, that a high proportion of ESN children are unsettled and at odds with life when they come to an ESN school. However, the majority of them settle down reasonably well and fairly quickly. Smaller classes, suitable work, sympathetic and individual attention are sufficient in the majority of cases to bring about a satisfactory adjustment.

However, there is a minority of severely disturbed children whose difficulties are due to more deep-rooted causes than educational failure. In this minority, their fundamental needs for security and affection have been so imperfectly met that there has been no firm foundation for personality growth. In the home, insecurities and tensions continue to upset them and thwart the efforts of the school to help them. In school, their inability to apply themselves means that they are unable to satisfy their need for recognition and success. Their longing for affection and personal attention are difficult to satisfy. They do not respond to ordinary methods of teaching and their problem becomes cumulatively more serious. Some of these children may, after a short while in school, appear to be quite well-adjusted in the classroom, but they nevertheless remain disturbed in other situations—in the playground, at home or in the street. The problem of these children is often aggravated by the fact that they arrive at the ESN school at a fairly late age when their attitudes and reactions have become more fixed and difficult to modify.

The concept of maladjustment

The report of the Underwood Committee on Maladjusted Children (4) describes maladjustment in the following terms: *A child may be regarded as maladjusted who is developing in ways that have a bad effect on himself or his fellows and cannot without help be remedied by his parents or his teachers and other adults in ordinary contact with him. It is characteristic of maladjusted children that they are insecure and unhappy, and that they fail in their personal relationships. Receiving is difficult for them as well as giving, and they appear unable to respond to simple measures of love, comfort and reassurance. At the same time, they are not readily capable of improvement by ordinary discipline.*

Maladjustment is not, of course, synonymous with difficult behaviour. The child who is perpetually in trouble, a nuisance in class, annoying to other children and generally unable to adjust to school life usually merits the description of maladjusted. But the quiet, unobtrusive behaviour of the child who has begun to withdraw from human contacts presents just as serious a problem as that of the hostile, aggressive child. Such a child may lack the drive to tackle difficulties in school learning. His failure to make relationships and to make contact with the life around him can be just as serious from a mental health point of view as the unsatisfactory relationships of the awkward, aggressive child.

Janet[1] is an example of this kind of maladjusted child. She was described by the psychologist in the following way: 'Small, undeveloped and strikingly pale in colour. Shows many nervous habits—sucks thumb, scratches head. She is somewhat better in her potential intelligence level than her appearance and manner suggest but there is a serious lack of drive and vitality. She needs a great deal of stimulation. Left to herself she slips into a state of dreamy inactivity. She often

---

[1] We are grateful to Mr. D. Evans for his permission to quote this and the following case from his study of a group of maladjusted children.

wears a vacant or faraway look. She is in very poor contact with her environment. Educability is doubtful owing to lack of interest and drive.' Her IQ was 65; attainments were virtually nil. Janet's mother was subnormal in intelligence and provided a most inadequate home life with the result that Janet was recommended for residential schooling at the age of nine years. Her low intelligence, her school failure, the insecurity and anxiety resulting from the absence of normal family relationships had resulted in the extreme withdrawal. Her behaviour in a special class set up to help a group of maladjusted children at first showed the same pattern of inactivity. She would sit for long periods day-dreaming or watching the other children. The only moments of animation were during periods of hostility or irritation. At other times attempts to stimulate activity by giving her a job to do or trying to draw her into activities were never successful for long. Later, however, she was caught up in house-play with several other children. In make-believe domestic play—'cooking', 'cleaning', 'looking after the baby'—she found a means of expression that was denied to her in art and craft (her work was messy and crude) or in speech. She began to make some relationships with other children and especially with the teacher. Unfortunately, as so often happens in these cases, progress was impeded by the continued effects of her unsatisfactory home. She wept when she had no visitors on visiting days. She was unsettled by the letters from home suggesting that she should 'hurry up and come home'. She was upset by the death of a grandmother who had given her some of the affection she did not get at home.

The severity of maladjustment cannot therefore be judged by the nuisance value of the symptoms. Indeed, it is possible to have a maladjusted child who has tried to adjust by excessive conformity or by an unusual application to school work. Shirley, for example, never participated with other children in their games and activities but escaped into reading which she could do reasonably well. She concentrated all her efforts to get recognition and teacher's approval on the one thing in which she was confident of success. The rest of her behaviour gave serious doubts about her ability to adjust to life after school. The symptoms must also be evaluated in relation to the child's age, level of ability and social background. For example, such behaviour as temper-tantrums, romancing and over-dependence on adults must be expected to continue with ESN children to a later age than with normal children. If, however, such behaviour continues beyond the age of about nine years it may indicate more serious disturbance, although the child's level of intelligence would also have to be taken into account. Petty pilfering in a child from an inadequate home might be due to lack of moral training in the home;

in a child from a good home, it might be a sign either of pressure by the parents for standards of behaviour and attainment which are beyond the child's capacity, or a sign of failure to meet some of the child's basic emotional needs. Similarly, incontinence can be the result either of lack of training or the child's reaction to tension and insecurity.

One of the characteristics of maladjustment is that it spreads into many areas of the child's activity. A lack of adequate home relationships may result in attention-seeking or other behaviour which is disliked by other children. The child feels rejected and isolated and this may lead to annoying behaviour which still further isolates him. At the same time, his insecurity leads to distractibility in school. He fails to make progress; he becomes anxious about his failure and this anxiety and frustration make it more difficult for him to learn. He is in a vicious circle. The cumulative effect of all these failures can be seen in the case of Edna:

Edna's mother was of low average intelligence; her control of the child was weak and ineffectual. The step-father, however, was stern and repressive. At an early age, Edna reacted to this by pilfering, lying, wandering and truanting. School progress was nil. Praise and encouragement seemed to make no difference to her. By the time she was admitted to a residential school, she was suffering long periods of depression during which she would sit with a vacant, miserable look on her face. She sulked a lot especially when she thought other children were getting more attention than she, and often caused trouble by saying spiteful and malicious things about other children. She was therefore very unpopular. There were complaints about her stealing things from other children. She was restless, unable to concentrate and tired very quickly. The impression of several adults who knew her was that her IQ of 61 was depressed by her emotional condition. There were many indications of better ability but she never seemed to realize her potential because of the continual drain on her emotional energies.

There is no doubt that a proportion of ESN children are so maladjusted that they need child guidance treatment or something akin to it. There are several reasons why few children receive such treatment. (1) The shortage of trained personnel and the many other calls on the time of school psychological services. (2) Many parents might be uncooperative or not sufficiently intelligent to benefit from the intensive work of a psychiatric social worker. (There is, however, a great need to develop the work of parent guidance and, as we note later, a social worker could make a great contribution in the education of ESN children.) (3) An IQ in the subnormal range has usually been taken as a sign that psychotherapy would be ineffective.

There is a growing body of research evidence, particularly in the U.S.A., which shows that psychotherapy is possible and profitable with many subnormal children. There are several surveys of this research (Sarason (7), Cruikshank (1), Stacey and DeMartino(8)) and it is sufficient here to express the hope that more experiments in individual and group therapy with subnormal children will be attempted in this country.

It is sometimes possible to make some special provision for maladjusted children within the school. Thus in one junior ESN school, a well-equipped playroom is used for periods of group play with children who need something more than can be provided in the normal classroom situation. In some schools, it has been possible to organize a special class with smaller numbers and a more definite therapeutic approach. Evans (3) describes the work of a senior class of severely disturbed children in which the relationship with the teacher, the interaction of the group and the freedom and activity of the class programme produced improvements in personal and social adjustment.

What can be done in the classroom to help maladjusted children?

There are no clear-cut remedies for maladjustment which can be described step by step. Any summary is therefore bound to appear rather vague and somewhat remote from the difficult reality of the classroom where one so often has to compromise between what one knows is right for a particular child and what is needed for the rest of the class. However, the following general principles should be applied as far as possible.

A case study is needed. A case study should be made to discover some of the reasons for the maladjustment. In many cases, knowing the causes indicates the approach that is needed, and in others, enables us to afford the child some relief by encouraging him to talk about his anxieties, instead of bottling them up. At least, knowing some of the reasons why the child behaves as he does makes us more sympathetic and tolerant. For example, Dennis was so aggressive to other children and so difficult in class that his teacher was in despair and had given up trying to be tolerant and positive. When Dennis moved to another class, the new teacher visited the boy's home as part of her attempts to deal with Dennis's problem. She discovered that Dennis's mother and father, although living in the same house, were almost completely estranged and the boy was torn by conflicting loyalties as well as upset by the continual tension in the home. It was a family situation about which a teacher could do little, but at least the school knew more about the reasons for Dennis's behaviour. It was easier, therefore, to be tolerant. Sympathy with the boy's predicament gave an impetus to the school's efforts to help him. We could quote other cases of children who baffled us until eventually some new piece of information helped to explain their disturbed behaviour.

A good teacher-child relationship. The teacher's understanding of the child should lead to the child realizing that he is understood. While it is rarely possible to give maladjusted children as much attention as they need, there are many subtle ways in which a child can sense that an adult is anxious to help him—the extra word of encouragement, the extra help with work, the teacher's willingness to discuss his problems, to trust him and give him some simple responsibility. As the definition of the Underwood Committee notes, a difficulty with relationships is one of the characteristics of maladjusted children, and a relationship built up with the teacher can be a most effective therapeutic measure. This is not always easy. The withdrawn child takes a long time to respond. The over-active boy so often causes trouble that it is difficult to avoid nagging at him. As far as possible, misdemeanours should be played down and minimized; issues should be avoided. A sense of humour in the teacher can be most valuable here. Children can be jollied out of moods; laughter in the class, as long as it is not derisive, can dispel feelings of tension and grievance.

It is important to recognize that these efforts may not be rewarded by startling improvements. At one moment, when the teacher has the child alone, there seems to be a wonderful relationship; then a little later in class the child is as difficult as ever. This may be due to jealousy at having to share the teacher with others or it may be his way of testing out the strength of the relationship. In such situations it is important to appear as confident and imperturbable as possible in order to increase the child's confidence and security.

Discipline must be positive. As the Underwood report states, 'Maladjusted children are not readily capable of improvement by ordinary discipline'. A rigid, strict class discipline may induce apparent improvement in class but is likely to provoke maladjusted children to other forms of difficult behaviour elsewhere, e.g. bullying in the playground, temper tantrums at home, delinquency in the neighbourhood. They need a more permissive discipline so that they do not find themselves up against authority at every turn, or breaking rules which they do not understand and are therefore unable to conform to. The withdrawn child needs a permissive atmosphere to encourage him to 'come out of his shell'. Indeed, a degree of naughtiness in a withdrawn child is a favourable sign. However, a permissive discipline does not mean that children can do as they like. It is essential for their sense of security that they know that there are limits beyond which adults will not let them go. These limits should be drawn a little wider for maladjusted children until gradually they learn to control themselves and conform. This is likely to cause difficulties: 'Jimmy can do that. Why can't I?' This problem can to some extent be met, if the atmosphere in the class is a positive one. Children can be hard on each other but they can also be encouraged to be helpful towards others. A child can sometimes be moved into a class which will have a beneficial effect on him—for example, placement in an older, more stable group may quieten a child who was a disruptive influence in a younger class.

A broad curriculum is needed. A more permissive atmosphere is easier to maintain if the curriculum includes many outlets for activity and emotional expression. The freedom and variety of play with younger children; art and craft, physical activity, movement and drama for older ones provide the means for achieving success and outlets for strong emotional energies. Emotional release is an essential feature of any form of therapy.

The value of the educational approach

We have referred to the maladjusted child as being in a vicious circle. It is often not easy to assess at what point to try to break that vicious circle. Irrespective of what other treatment can be given, it is often profitable to tackle the child's problems through his educational failure. It can be easier to give the child the extra attention that he needs through some special help in basic subjects, and if progress can be made in these, there is often an all-round improvement.

There are, however, other children with whom an approach in this way would be premature, either because their attitude to basic subjects is so extremely negative or because there is little chance of their being able to apply themselves. For them, a period when the educational side is not emphasized may be needed. This period should be used to build up a better relationship with the child, to help him make more contact with other children, and to establish confidence by success in other aspects of school work.

REFERENCES

1. CRUIKSHANK, W. (ed.). *Psychology of Exceptional Children and Youth.* Staples, 1956.
2. DOLL, E. A. *The Vineland Social Maturity Scale.* Vineland Training School, 1935.

3. EVANS, D. *An experimental study of a group of seriously maladjusted ESN children.* M.A. thesis, 1956, Univ. of Birmingham.
4. Ministry of Education. *Report of the Committee on Maladjusted Children.* (The Underwood Report.) H.M.S.O., 1955.
5. NORTHWAY, M. L. *Primer of Sociometry.* Univ. of Toronto Press, 1952.
6. PRINGLE, M. L. K. and BOSSIO, V. *A study of deprived children.* Vita Humana, Vol. 1, No. 2, 1958.
7. SARASON, S. *Psychological Problems of Mental Deficiency.* Harper, 1949.
8. STACEY and DE MARTINO. *Counselling and Psycho-therapy with the Mentally Retarded.* Free Press, Illinois, 1958.
9. STOTT, D. H. *Unsettled Children and their Families.* U.L.P., 1956.
10. STOTT, D. H. *The Social Adjustment of Children; Manual to the Bristol Social Adjustment Guides.* U.L.P, 1958.

FURTHER READING

BOWLBY, J. *Maternal Care and Mental Health.* W.H.O., H.M.S.O., 1951.
BOWLBY, J. *Child Care and the Growth of Love,* Pelican, 1954.
BOWLEY, A. *Psychology of the Unwanted Child.* Livingstone, 1947.
BURBURY, W. M., BALINT, E. and YAPP, B. S. *Child Guidance.* Macmillan, 1945.
FORD, D. *The Deprived Child and the Community.* Constable, 1955.
ISAACS, S. *Social Development in Young Children.* Routledge, 1933.
ISAACS, S. *Psychological Aspects of Children's Development.* Evans, 1935.
SYMONDS, P. M. *Dynamics of Parent-Child Relationships.* Columbia University, 1949.
WALL, W. D. *Education and Mental Health.* (UNESCO.) Harrap, 1955.
WALL, W. D. *The Adolescent Child.* Methuen, 1948.
WILLS, D. *The Barns Experiment.* Allen and Unwin, 1947.

Bibliography
AXFORD, W. *Handicapped Children: their problems and education. Publications in G.B., 1944–58.* Library Association.

IV

PHYSICAL CONDITIONS

The physical development of ESN children

ONE cannot generalize about the physical development of ESN children on the assumption that low intelligence and retarded physical growth invariably go together. Certainly the lower the level of intelligence the greater is the likelihood of associated physical defects and retarded growth. But although there is a greater incidence of physical retardation and minor defects in the ESN group than among normal children there are those whose growth approximates to or even exceeds normal. Oliver (4) compared the growth of 100 ESN boys with 100 normal boys by graphing their growth on the Wetzel (10) grid. The results showed that there were more smaller boys among the ESN group: 57 ESN boys and 36 normals being below the standard growth line. There were more deviations from normal growth among the ESN boys—37 compared with 26 in the normal group. Above-average growth was noted, however, in 13 ESN boys and 15 normal boys. Oliver concludes from an examination of the literature on the subject that the all-round fitness of the ESN child tends to be below par compared with that of normal children and that this is likely to lead to fatigue, general muscular debility and postural defects. This general conclusion has implications for the physical demands made on children in school. It also emphasizes the importance of the physical education programme which will be considered in Chapter XI.

In physical development, ESN children can be considered in three groups (which are not distinct but overlap).

(1) There is the group of children who are slow to develop both mentally and physically, and in whom there appears to be a slow growth potential resulting in all-round immaturity. These are children who need extra practice for developing physical skills. At the early stages of the ESN school they will need attention to the development of finer manipulation as in dressing, using drawing and writing

71

materials and tools such as scissors. At all stages, they need plenty of opportunity for practising larger movements—climbing, jumping, skipping, dancing—and the acquisition of socially useful games techniques such as catching and kicking balls. These skills are important in themselves, but also because they promote feelings of success and self-confidence which can affect the child's attitude to himself and to school in general. Moreover, they assist social development. There are many occasions when playing with others or joining in class activities are impeded by the lack of simple physical skills.

(2) There is a group of children whose physical development, being average or above average for their age, is in advance of their mental development. Many schools achieve with these children high standards in P.E. and provide a wide range of activities directing their vitality and energy into acceptable channels. The problems posed by this unevenness of development were referred to earlier (Chapter III).

(3) A third group of children are those whose capacity to learn is reduced by the effects of illness, minor ailments and defects, some of which result from poor standards of living and hygiene at home. In Burt's (1) surveys of backwardness in the 1930s, he reported that 60 per cent of the children examined showed some physical handicaps, and that among those who would then have been considered certifiably defective the figure rose to 80 per cent. Improved health and welfare services have effected a considerable improvement in child health since then, and ESN children have shared in the improvement, but the effects of unsatisfactory home conditions, inadequate diets, and insufficient sleep have still to be reckoned with. The effect of good hygienic conditions is often very evident with children in residential schools who increase in alertness and general vitality throughout their stay. Attention still needs to be paid to the effects of malnutrition, throat and ear conditions, poor health resulting from a series of infectious illnesses and other ailments.

Poor health is important from the educational point of view not only because of lowered efficiency in learning but also because it results in absences from school. Regular absences of a day or so at a time are likely to result in educational failure becoming cumulative, especially if the child is in a large class in an ordinary school where the work that has been missed may not be made up. Longer absences on account of illness may restrict the child's experience of play and his contact with other children, thus retarding social development. This is particularly likely in the case of children who have had long periods in hospital. Moreover, the child who has been ill a great deal has often been over-protected and indulged within the family so that

72

he has not learned to do things for himself nor acquired those traits of self-activity and persistence which count for so much in school learning.

There are also those children whose ailments are of a psycho-somatic nature. Headaches, pains in the stomach, vomiting may be reactions to social and educational difficulties, as is often demonstrated by the way these symptoms clear up when the child is feeling more happy and successful at school. If one suspects that a child's ailments have a partly psychological origin, the remedy is to try to remove their main causes. Since such children are often sensitive to reprimand and correction, firm measures are rarely called for. What is needed is to tackle the social and educational difficulties by suitable school work.

Sensory Defects

The teacher is well placed to notice minor physical conditions which are interfering with the child's progress and since some parents are unobservant and unconcerned about these, the teacher should consider it as a part of his function to arrange for something to be done. This applies particularly to sensory defects. It is always worth arranging a sight test for a child who shows any sign of visual defect; for example, signs of apparent eye-strain, or visual difficulties in reading. However, omitting letters, words, or lines in reading is more likely to be a sign of faulty attitudes to reading, or of faulty reading habits, than of eye-defects.

Similarly, reversals and mirror writing tendencies are symptoms of immature visual perception rather than defective vision.

Severe hearing loss is usually apparent in the pre-school period; slighter defects go undetected, even in school. The latter may involve deficiencies in hearing sounds on certain frequencies, particularly high ones. In a case of high-tone deafness, there is a reduced ability to hear many of the consonants; the most frequently affected sounds are: *s, z, sh, f, ch, th*. The existence of partial losses of hearing cannot be reliably discovered by crude methods of examination, e.g. a whisper test. The child with high-tone deafness will 'get by' in school because he has learned to rely to some extent on lip-reading, the interpretation of gestures and expressions, and noticing what other children are doing. A test by a pure-tone audiometer is required to ascertain the nature of the loss. An aural examination is always worth asking for if there is any doubt about hearing.

The possibility of hearing loss should be considered in cases of defective speech articulation that cannot be adequately explained in other ways. If the child attends a speech clinic hearing will usually have been tested. Obvious physical symptoms of ear trouble may also be indications of impairment—running ears, earache, chronic catarrhal conditions. There may be behaviour characteristics which suggest the possibility of deafness—the child does not respond when spoken to; asks for remarks to be repeated; turns his head when listening; appears quite bright in some ways yet very slow to comprehend or react in others; is 'detached' and restless, e.g. in listening to a story.

When hearing loss has been established by the clinic, the teacher can do much to help the child in class. It is usually recommended that the child should sit on one side of the class near a window so that light falls on the faces of the teacher and the rest of the class, making it easier for the child to get help from the lip-movements and expressions of those speaking. If a hearing aid is supplied it often takes some time for the child to get used to it. Some children feel self-conscious about the contraption. Demonstrating it to other children makes it less something to be ashamed of and hidden away in the desk. One of the things that children find difficult in the early stages of using a hearing aid is getting accustomed to the amplification of extraneous noises. In normal hearing, we learn not to notice all the background noises—pages of a book being turned over, tables and chairs scraping on the floor, and all the other noises incidental to a classroom. A hearing aid amplifies these as well as speech, and it may be many weeks before a child can ignore them. If the hearing aid is persisted with, the child usually learns to adapt to this situation. Sometimes it will need attention and the local clinic which supplied it will be helpful in adjusting it and in giving advice on its use. The handling of a child with some hearing loss is certainly worth a little thought by the staff.

Epilepsy

Another secondary handicap sometimes found in ESN children is epilepsy. The nature and causes of epilepsy are still not completely understood but a good deal of progress has been made in recent years with the use of new techniques and treatment. One such technique is that of electro-encephalography (the E.E.G.) by means of which the electrical activity of the brain can be studied. Electrodes are placed on different areas of the head and the electrical activity of the brain is recorded and studied. One well-established pattern of activity is found in epilepsy. The most frequent forms of the condition are *grand mal* in which there are major convulsions with loss of consciousness, and *petit mal*, in which there are brief losses of consciousness lasting only a few seconds. In *petit mal*, the patient usually does not fall; there is merely a momentary lapse of attention or interruption of activity. There are other epileptic conditions which are not completely agreed on or understood, e.g. temporal lobe epilepsy.

From the point of view of the school, the problem of the epileptic child has been eased by the anti-convulsant drugs which effectively control the seizures. Medical treatment, however, needs to be supported by adequate environmental treatment which ensures that, as far as possible, the child is happy and well-adjusted. The medical officer will advise on any restrictions of activity which may be deemed necessary in particular cases. In general, it is better to run slight risks rather than over-restrict the child for this results in psychological upsets and frustrations. Attacks are usually more infrequent when the child is busily engaged than when idle and bored. The aim should be to enable the child to lead as normal a life as possible. The teacher may be in a position to help parents adopt a sensible, balanced attitude to the problem, avoiding undue risk on the one hand and over-protection on the other.

It is doubtful whether there is an epileptic personality pattern. Many of the behaviour problems popularly believed to be associated with epilepsy are due to stresses in the child's environment, aggravated by family and social attitudes to the condition. There is, however, a proportion of epileptic children who do show behaviour problems. Fifty per cent of children with 'temporal lobe' epilepsy are said to show behaviour problems, but these can be alleviated by wise handling. (11).

Speech defects in subnormal children

Defective speech is often and justifiably a matter of particular concern to special school teachers, especially in areas where the advice and help of a speech therapist is not available or not easily obtained. This is understandable in view of the consistent finding of surveys that speech defects are far more common among educationally subnormal than among normal pupils. Wallin (9) found nine times as many speech defects among subnormal children in St. Louis schools and Burt (1) found severe defects of speech in 1 per cent of his normal group, in 5 per cent of the backward and in 11 per cent of the mentally defective. Mary Sheridan (6), examining 100 subnormal children aged 11 to 13, found that 55 had speech defects, grouped as follows:

	Single defect	2 or more defects
Girls (19 out of 45)	24·5%	17·7%
Boys (36 out of 55)	41·8%	23·6%

Tansley (8) in a survey of 155 boys and 92 girls aged 7 to 16 found that 37·4 per cent of the boys and 20·7 per cent of the girls had speech defects ranging from single mispronunciations to complete unintelligibility. It is gratifying that more ESN schools are now having regular visits, sometimes several sessions a week, from speech therapists to meet this problem. But even where such help is provided, teachers are often keen to know how they can co-operate with the therapist. Most teachers recognize that well-intentioned but uninformed attempts to correct speech defects may do more harm than good, and possibly make the child more self-conscious and anxious about the difficulty. Wherever possible, the class teacher should discuss a child's speech defect with the speech therapist who will indicate the line on which she is working and how it can be followed up and supplemented. The class teacher can probably help most by providing the type of language programme we outline in Chapter VI, ensuring that there is plenty of stimulation for oral expression and language growth as well as a favourable emotional atmosphere. In addition, many of the slighter defects of articulation benefit from speech training done in an interesting and enjoyable fashion (see list of suitable sources at the end of the chapter). It is also well to remember that many minor defects of articulation clear up as the child matures.

In preparing to tackle speech problems, it should be realized that they do not result only from physical defects in the speech organs, or from defects in the brain and nervous system which affect the establishment of associations or the fineness of motor co-ordination. In some cases, the defect may have its origin partly in emotional and other psychological difficulties, and it is often not easy to say whether psychological factors are present as causes or as results of the defect. Speech depends not only on the efficiency of the speech organs but also on the personal maturity of the child, his attitude to himself, his relationships with others, and the degree to which the home has stimulated and encouraged speech.

Defective speech can be a handicap in many ways. Teaching reading may be difficult because what the child reads may not be intelligible, and it may be desirable to minimize the amount of oral reading. Enunciation difficulties interfere with word recognition and spelling; the poor articulator is often poor in auditory discrimination with resulting handicaps in phonic work and spelling. The difficulty in communicating with others may impede participation in play and group activities, especially if the child is self-conscious about his speech. There may be behaviour difficulties as a result of social isolation or because of frustration in not being able to make wants and desires known. It should also be realized that the effect of serious defects, and especially of language retardation, can be deeper and more far-reaching than an interference with the process of teaching. According to the severity of the defect the child can be more or less cut off from the chief means of mental growth. To appreciate this one has only to consider how the development of knowledge and thinking is stimulated and guided in young children by verbal interchange between parent and child. One of the problems in examining young children with retarded speech is that of trying to decide whether the speech is retarded because of mental retardation or whether the mental retardation is due to the retarded speech. This difficulty can lead to wrong diagnosis and placement.

In noting speech defects in class, it is useful to classify them in the following groups:
1. Defects of articulation—in the pronunciation of sounds and words.
2. Language retardation—delayed speech, aphasia.
3. Defects of rhythm—stammering.
4. Defects of voice production.

Defects of articulation are by far the most common defects of speech among subnormal children, ranging from defects in one or two sounds to a jumbled utterance which is difficult to follow. Some of these defects have a physical basis in malformations of the mouth or teeth, or they may be manifestations of poor motor co-ordination. In other cases, they are just another indication of the subnormal child's slow rate of maturation, poorer discrimination of sounds, and poorer learning. Baby talk (fwee for three, fumb for thumb, anoder for another) may partly be due to personal immaturities, as in the case of the child who is babied and over-dependent in the family, or to mispronunciations which are copies of the speech at home or in the locality.

It is with this group of defects that the class teacher can make a more direct contribution by giving the child practice in using the correct sound after it has been elicited by the speech therapist. Speech training activities aimed at particular children may be given to groups and will not be superfluous if taken as a class activity, for most ESN children can do with practice in clear and precise enunciation. Many activities, such as rhymes, jingles and speech games are suggested in speech training texts. (See list at the end of this chapter.)

Language retardation or delayed speech is not rare in the younger classes. Speech and language are retarded well below the level that would be expected for the child's age and apparent mental ability; a particularly late start in talking is usually the case. Articulation is often defective or unintelligible, but the distinguishing feature is in language itself—in the acquisition and the use of words. The vocabulary mainly consists of nouns and verbs referring to the most common objects and actions; sentences may consist of two or three words, prepositions, auxiliary verbs, conjunctions and pronouns being omitted. Gestures and signs may be used a great deal, and very effectively, to get what is wanted. The type of problem is illustrated by the following case:

> Peter at five seems quite intelligent in some directions although it is difficult to test his intelligence because of the lack of speech and his poor co-operation in a formal test setting. Physical skills had been acquired at the normal time—e.g. walking, running, pedalling a tricycle. He has always been interested in shapes and can complete a difficult jigsaw of twenty to thirty small pieces quite quickly. He is also quite quick to size up a situation if he needs to do so for his own ends; he displays some of the curiosity of the five-year-old about how things work. He certainly attempts the names of a number of common objects and his articulation of them is just recognizable. His continuous vocalization is an unrecognizable chatter. He seems to comprehend much that is said to him. His behaviour at home has usually been uncontrolled and even as a three-year-old he wandered off a long way from home. He has not made warm and affectionate responses to his parents, appearing detached and emotionally distant. At one time he was impulsively aggressive and awkward towards other children, often with little apparent reason.

In cases like this it is difficult to unravel the problem and its causes. A failure in the development of the basic relationship with mother in early childhood seems strongly indicated by his detachment, his wandering off and his uncontrollability. There is almost certainly some mental retardation although some of his achievements contra-indicate this. Deafness has been ruled out by several audiometric examinations.

A further possibility in this case is that he is an example of *an aphasic child*. This is the name given to a defect in the child's ability to form the necessary associations between words and the concepts and objects to which they refer—an inability to think in terms of symbols. True aphasia has an organic basis, resulting from injury or improper development of certain association areas of the brain, commonly caused by diseases of the brain such as encephalitis or meningitis, brain injuries at birth or accidents involving the cortex. It is not easy to diagnose aphasia except in the presence of clear neurological evidence, and any special techniques for aiding learning are not usually within the scope of the teacher. For practical school purposes, it may be thought of as a case of language retardation.

In providing for cases of language retardation, the efforts of the speech therapist can be supplemented most valuably by the teacher. As we note in Chapter VI, the desire to communicate occurs in relation to experiences and activities. Contact with other children and a close relationship with the teacher are most important. The activities and the relationships of a class run on nursery school lines can be very effective in stimulating speech development.

The *main defect of rhythm* is stammering. Stammering includes the abnormal repetition of certain sounds and words and also the speech blockage which occurs when the child cannot utter a sound although he is trying desperately to do so. The causes of stammering are still the subject of some controversy. There is a variety of factors in the child and in his environment which can start off the habit. There is fairly general agreement that tensions, frustrations, anxieties and feelings of insecurity increase the chances of stammering occurring in children who are pre-disposed to it. The treatment of stammering must try to eliminate or minimize any factors of this sort and try to build up more confident attitudes, to develop a sense of achievement and self-esteem and generally to promote a relaxed physical and mental state. It is obvious that these aspects of the treatment of stammering cannot be done by the speech therapist alone. The class teacher, as well as the parent, can contribute much to the development of a stable personality and healthy attitudes. There are specific issues on which the teacher's attitude can be important—the child will be helped if the teacher tries to see that the stammerer is not teased or imitated; patience in waiting for the child to say what he wants will help to avoid the stammer. Children who stammer should not be pressed to participate in oral work, although there are some stammerers who do not like being left out. It may be possible to reduce the amount of reading aloud by making greater use of silent reading and workbook activities. The stammer often disappears in activities such as drama, puppetry and singing.

The chief *defects of voice production* are those concerned with nasality, either excessive or insufficient. The characteristic speech of the child with cleft palate is the result of the inability to direct and concentrate the breath through the mouth, and this often continues after surgical repair of the palate. Children must therefore be re-trained to hear their defective tone and correct themselves. This is a matter for the speech therapist but the class teacher can co-operate by making sure that the child who has learnt to use normal tone continues to do so. Insufficient nasality and resonance occur in the child with adenoidal speech and again speech therapy may be advisable after tonsils and adenoids have been removed. Other defects of phonation such as husky speech, breathiness, high or low pitch, and intensity may be serious enough to warrant the attention of the speech therapist, especially if they do not improve in the course of normal speech and language experience in class.

Brain-injured children

Among the causes of mental handicap is damage to the brain sustained before or at birth, or during early infancy. One result of brain damage is cerebral palsy, which includes various types of motor disability. The most frequent are: *spastic paralysis* in which one or more limbs may be more or less seriously affected; *athetosis* in which there is an inability to control movements; and *ataxia* in which there is unsteadiness and inco-ordination due to difficulties in balance and posture. Children suffering from cerebral palsy range in intelligence from bright to severely subnormal. Most of them are provided for in schools for physically handicapped children, but some cases with only mild motor disabilities may be placed in an ESN school if their low intelligence and attainments warrant it. Special attention may be needed for them in connection with the development of co-ordination in physical activities, and the development of skills such as dressing, writing and using tools. Small apparatus requiring fine manipulation may need to be avoided. In some cases speech therapy will be required to develop clear articulation. They may also display some of the characteristics of children described in the next section.

Strauss's concept of the brain-injured child

In a book published in 1947, Strauss (7) drew attention to children who are brain-injured yet do not show the gross disturbances of movement characteristic of cerebral-palsied children. He claimed that they have characteristic disabilities in perception, thinking and behaviour and that special methods were required to overcome these. He therefore proposed a classification of subnormal children into two groups:

(i) *The endogenous group.* These are 'ordinary' subnormal children who are subnormal primarily because they fall into the group naturally occurring at the lower levels of intellectual endowment.

(ii) *The exogenous or brain-injured group.* These are children whose original mental endowment has been impaired by minimal injury to the brain.

Strauss's definition of the brain-injured child is:

A child who before, during, or after birth has received an injury to or suffered an infection of the brain. As a result of such an organic impairment, defects of the neuro-motor system may be present or absent; however such a child may show disturbances in perception, thinking and emotional behaviour, either separately or in combination.

Strauss does not include in the exogenous category children in whom there is severe motor disability, such as cerebral-palsied children.

Causes of brain injury. The common causes of brain injury are:

(i) *Occurring before birth.* Rhesus incompatibility; infection; very severe illness or trauma to the mother.

(ii) *Occurring at birth.* Very prolonged or difficult labour; difficulty of delivery or use of instruments; marked prematurity; precipitate birth; asphyxia of the infant.

(iii) *Occurring after birth.* Severe head injuries; meningitis or encephalitis (this can be a complication of any severe infectious disease accompanied by high fever).

The criteria for differentiating between the brain-damaged and non-brain-damaged are still the subject of much controversy (Sarason (5)). However, a diagnosis which will have the greatest possible degree of accuracy in the light of present knowledge depends on the discovery and evaluation of significant factors in the birth and early history of the child, the observation of the characteristic learning difficulties and modes of behaviour, and the detection of abnormalities in the nervous system.

Authorities differ considerably in their estimates of the incidence of the condition. Strauss estimates that approximately 15 to 20 per cent of all *defectives* come within the exogenous group; Fouracre (2) states that most studies of brain injury report an incidence of from 4–6 or 7 cases per 1,000 births of the general population. It is reasonable to suppose that 3 to 5 per cent of ESN children in special schools suffer from brain damage. The educational problems they present are often out of all proportion to their number. There can be little doubt that a proportion of the children excluded from special schools because their presence is detrimental to the education of other children come within this group. If a teacher has a child who shows some of the symptoms indicated below and whose case history is suggestive of possible organic damage he should, in the child's interest, ask for the opinion of a neurologist before any irrevocable decision is taken.

The characteristics of brain-injured children

The manifestations of brain injury are little understood at present but it is safe to assume that, as in any other group of children, there will be many individual differences. We cannot, therefore, detail the characteristics of the brain-injured child. The characteristics listed below are those which, from our observation of children in whom there is neurological evidence of organic impairment, would appear to be important in helping the teacher to recognize the condition.

Physical characteristics. In some brain-injured children there is evidence of slight muscular inco-ordination in the way the child walks, runs, manipulates and writes. Written work and art work may be untidy. Speech is often slightly defective.

Perception. Perception is the process whereby the mind organizes sensory impressions of the environment. The mind tends to select what is important and meaningful so that from the many stimuli impinging on our senses we ignore some and use others. Thus, in looking at a picture we see not just a collection of lines and colours but certain outstanding shapes which we identify as people, animals and objects. If it is a puzzle picture, in which the artist has cunningly concealed other shapes, we have considerable difficulty in ignoring the main shapes in the pictures in order to find the ones which do not stand out as wholes so clearly. This process of seeing patterns and wholes is basic to our ability to make sense of and act in our environment.

Some brain-injured children may have difficulty in organizing their perceptions in this way. They may, therefore, have difficulty in reproducing patterns, in appreciating the meaning of pictures, in learning to read, and in perceiving groups in number work. Moreover, their impressions of the everyday environment must, to varying extents, be distorted and this partly accounts for their unusual behaviour—their restlessness and distractibility. They may be particularly sensitive to stimuli which normal persons ignore, and therefore experience difficulty in concentration. In the classroom, their attention is focused for a while by one stimulus but suddenly switches to another usually quite unrelated. For example, Sylvia was performing successfully in a reading test when she suddenly remarked, 'Your hair is sticking up and you make me laugh.' Her attention was redirected to the reading, but after a short while she said, 'You send me. Will you tell your wife?' Further reading followed and then she said, 'I've had a drink of beer you know.' Reading tests with Sylvia are quite amusing and exciting!

Strauss claims that the perceptual disabilities of brain-injured children can be revealed by the disorganized way in which they do certain tests, such as reproducing specially designed patterns. Some tests have been designed to reveal the tendency of brain-injured children to be distracted by irrelevant details in the background of the patterns to be reproduced. The validity of these tests has not been fully established. We have found children who, although having neurological signs of brain damage, were not markedly abnormal on the tests.

Thinking. Since perception is disordered, it is inevitable that there should be disorders in thinking and concept formation. They are slower to classify and to see which things belong together, or to appreciate how known facts can be used in new situations. They are therefore poor at problem-solving, comprehension work and making generalizations.

Perseveration. There is a tendency to perseverate, i.e. to go on repeating an activity mechanically. A child who is asked to draw a circle may go on drawing circles across the page; a word or letter may be repeated several times; a movement in PE may be continued after the signal to stop. Their activity gets, as it were, 'in a groove'. There is thus the paradox that on the one hand they are distractable, while on the other hand they may become absorbed and oblivious to the environment.

There is also a tendency to repeat familiar and successful activities because these give a sense of security. These tendencies may partly account for the good rote memory which brain-injured children often have—remembering poems, tables, number facts, birthdays, and so on.

Behaviour. As we have noted, one of the characteristics of brain-injured children is extreme restlessness and distractability—an inability to fix attention because of being distracted by classroom noises, by children moving about, by sights and sounds outside the classroom. Their behaviour may also be characterized by extreme attention-seeking, hyperactivity, inability to delay gratification (what they want they must have immediately), talkativeness, over-familiarity and erratic, uninhibited outbursts.

It is difficult to know how far this behaviour can be attributed to the brain injury or to the child's attempts to compensate for his handicap or to the insecurity resulting from his disordered perception.

It certainly makes it difficult for the brain-injured child to be accepted by other children. As Lewis (3) suggests, the child's perceptual difficulties make it difficult for him to play group games. When he attempts to enter the group he cannot comprehend the pattern of the game. He therefore tends to hover on the periphery of a play group and not become part of it. However, he is impelled to seek recognition and will either disrupt the game or resort to seeking the company of much younger children or adults. Nevertheless, the rejection by his group injures his pride and can lead to difficult attention-seeking behaviour or to withdrawal and fantasy. These only serve to increase his isolation and social difficulties.

All these symptoms are not likely to be present in all cases.

Indeed, in the behaviour of some children who have neurological signs of organic damage, few symptoms are observable and occasionally these may include acute withdrawing rather than attention-seeking, passivity rather than hyperactivity. Nevertheless, a careful examination of their learning difficulties will usually reveal some of the abnormalities associated with the condition. The teacher should not jump to hasty conclusions since a diagnosis of 'brain injury' is exceedingly difficult to make. For instance, it is difficult to know whether some of the presenting symptoms are due to cortical damage, maladjustment or incipient mental illness. All brain-damaged children are likely to be maladjusted, but all maladjusted children are not brain-damaged. Even were a diagnosis of the condition certain, it is not easy to decide whether maladjustment is due to the injury itself or is caused by the child's attempts to live with his handicap. If we consider the symptom of distractibility, for example, the cause may be disturbance arising from inner-tensions and not the brain injury itself.

Treatment

What form the treatment of brain-injured children should take is still a matter for further study and experiment. There is certainly no one form which is suitable to all. The following suggestions should therefore be regarded as tentative and must be adapted to meet the needs of individual children.

We have seen that the brain-injured child often has disabilities in perception. These create learning difficulties which may need remedial treatment designed to help him organize his perceptions. Since he is easily distracted from a learning situation by apparently insignificant features, it may be important to exaggerate those perceptual clues which are important. For example, words to be learned and shapes to be coloured or cut-out should be outlined clearly. Colour should be used to highlight significant features; book illustrations should be limited. This help in perceptual activity is especially vital with young children since they are usually most distractible, and it is important to ensure that preventive measures are taken early if future learning is not to be hindered unnecessarily. The child's perception can also be aided by attention given to the improvement of the control of movement. In writing, for instance, tracing with finger contact or the holding of the child's hand by the teacher will help to focus the child's attention. In reading, a ruler placed under the line being read or the use of finger pointing will be useful. Such help must be given with discretion and gradually dispensed with as training and maturation make it less necessary.

Brain-injured children, particularly when young, are usually restless and distractible. Treatment should, therefore, aim at reducing restlessness and distractibility. Distracting stimuli must be reduced to a necessary minimum and only gradually re-introduced. This is particularly difficult in the class situation since the majority of ESN children require just the opposite, i.e. a stimulating, exciting environment. The brain-injured child can be placed temporarily away from the other children and be protected from too much stimulation, but this can so often lead to feelings of rejection and of being 'different'. The problem for the class teacher is certainly very difficult since it is often quite impossible to provide a stimulating atmosphere for the rest of the class and at the same time a more controlled, yet still interesting, one for the brain-injured child. In a large ESN school the brain-injured children, and those with somewhat similar behaviour characteristics, might be grouped in a small class. This, however, can create more problems than it solves. Medical treatment might be the answer to these problems. The use of pharmacological preparations such as *amphetamine* does, in some cases at least, control restlessness and distractibility and lead to improved behaviour and learning. For example, George is a boy whose behaviour in school was so disturbing, and whose educational progress was so poor, that his exclusion seemed almost inevitable. He was examined by two psychiatrists working independently and both found positive evidence of neurological abnormality. He is being treated with *amphetamine* and improvements in behaviour and learning are remarkable. His extreme restlessness, hyperactivity and distractibility have almost disappeared and he is responding to the same educational treatment that the rest of his class is receiving. It should be noted as a precaution, however, that such improvements could not be expected in all cases. We would also warn that improvements resulting from shielding the child from external stimuli may be illusory. The effectiveness of this method may simply be due to the isolation of the child from the disturbing influences of others rather than to any re-education of his reactions. It may be an expedient for reducing symptoms until the child by the natural process of maturation and adaptation learns to live with his handicap.

Educational treatment should also aim at improving the child's thinking. Efforts must be made to minimize perseveration, e.g. by not allowing the child to follow a particular activity for too long, especially if this is formal drill or is dependent on rote memory. The brain-injured child will readily escape into writing long lists of words, doing pages of mechanical sums or drawing repetitive patterns. Once he has been allowed to do this it is often quite impossible to get him to do any form of creative work or to use the facts he has learned to solve real life problems. Alan, a brain-injured boy, was very proud of his knowledge of number facts but because attempts were made to induce him to use these in problems he refused to do sums at all. As a consequence he concentrated on his reading and English and made remarkable progress. However, he then refused to do any letter writing or to attempt free written expression, although he was obviously capable of both. His perseverance was most creditable but his perseveration was disastrous.

Educational attainments of brain-injured children often show irregularity both between subjects and within one subject. John, for instance, has a good mechanical reading age and language ability but his comprehension is poor; in arithmetic his attainments are negligible. Margaret's results in art, drama and physical activities are the best in her class but, at fourteen years of age, she has barely made a start in reading and number. Her principal difficulty is an inability to associate symbols with sounds. Treating her has been made more difficult because of the emotional disturbance resulting from recurrent failure. However, she is beginning to respond to individual remedial education which gives her adequate support and encouragement and uses methods which are designed to overcome her disabilities in visual perception.

The educational treatment should aim at overcoming the irregularities in achievement. The danger here is, however, that the teacher may become too involved in the challenge presented and be disappointed with the slow rate of progress. Too much pressure on the brain-injured child to tackle his weaknesses frequently leads to truculence and open defiance. He certainly has his 'ups and downs' in behaviour and it is futile to press him when he is in an uncooperative mood. It follows, therefore, that teacher-child relationships are of the greatest importance. Treatment will only succeed if the teacher not only understands the child's intellectual and physical difficulties but also appreciates the many frustrations and confusions which will necessarily accompany the child's attempt to make adjustments to his personal and social environment. Optimism is essential because progress can usually be made. Indeed, with many brain-injured children, once a start has been made in acquiring a skill progress is often striking.

REFERENCES

1. BURT, C. *The Backward Child*. U.L.P., 1937
2. FOURACRE, M. H. *Learning Characteristics of Brain-injured Children*. Exceptional Children, Vol. 24, 5, 1958.
3. LEWIS R. S. *The Other Child*. Grune and Stratton, 1951.

PHYSICAL CONDITIONS

4. OLIVER, J. N. *Physical Education of ESN children.* Educ. Review, Vol. VIII, No. 2, 1956
5. SARASON, S. *Psychological Problems in Mental Deficiency.* Harper, 1952.
6. SHERIDAN, M. D. *The Child's Hearing for Speech.* Methuen, 1948.
7. STRAUSS, A. A. and LEHTINEN, C. A. *Psychopathology and Education of Brain-injured Children.* Grune and Stratton, 1947.
8. TANSLEY, A. E. *The use of test data and case history information as indications for the educational treatment of ESN children.* M.Ed. Thesis, 1951.
9. WALLIN, J. E. W. *Children with Mental and Physical Handicaps.* Staples, 1949.
10. WETZEL, N.C. *Physical Fitness in terms of Physique, Development and basal metabolism.* J. Amer. Med. Assoc., 116.
11. WORLD HEALTH ORGANISATION. *Juvenile Epilepsy.* W.H.O. Technical Series, No. 130, H.M.S.O.

FURTHER READING

CHESWORTH, A. and OLIVER, J. N. *The Physical Characteristics of Educationally Subnormal Boys.* Spec. Schools Journal, Vol. 45, No. 2, 1956.
WILLIAMS, J. M. *Some special learning difficulties of brain-injured children.* Forward Trends. Vol. 2, No. 3, 1958
GALLAHER, J. L. *Comparison of brain-injured and non-brain-injured mentally retarded children on several psychological variables.* Monographs of Society for Research in Child Development. Vol. 22, No. 2, 1957.
KEPHART, N. C. *The Slow Learner in the Classroom.* Merrill (Ohio), 1961.
TYSON, M. C. *Psychological study of Remedial Visuomotor Training.* Special Education, Vol. LII, No. 4.
STRAUSS, A. A. and KEPHART, N. C. *Psychopathology and Education of brain-injured children. Vol. 2.* Grune and Stratton, 1955
BOOME, E. J. and RICHARDSON, M. A. *Relaxation in Everyday Life.* Methuen.
MORLEY, M. E. *The Development and Disorders of Speech in Childhood.* Livingstone, 1957.
EWING, A. R. and A. W. G. *New Opportunities for Deaf Children.* U.L.P., 1958.
SCHONELL, F. E. *Educating Spastic Children.* Oliver and Boyd, 1958.

Books for Speech Training

BENNETT R. *Adventures in Words.* U.L.P.
MCALLISTER, A. H. *Steps in Speech Training.* U.L.P.
SANSON, C. *Speech Rhymes,* and *Acting Rhymes.* A. and C. Black.
COBBY, M. *We Play and Grow.* Pitman.
JONES, V. J. *Speech Correction at Home.* Blackwell.

V

AIMS, PRINCIPLES AND ORGANIZATION

WE have observed that the ESN child is one who, because of low intelligence and other causes, learns so slowly and unevenly that he is unable to cope satisfactorily with the usual educational demands of the ordinary school. He is not, however, so markedly different that his basic psychological, educational and social needs are in any way unique. He needs security and affection, recognition and self-esteem. He wants to feel that he belongs and that he is accepted in social groups at school, at home and in the community. Although his limited capacities may prevent him from reaching high levels of achievement, there is much that he can and needs to learn within his limits. The general aims of special educational treatment are therefore substantially the same as for any other children. Any differences that exist are chiefly a matter of emphasis to be placed on particular aims.

General aims

These may be considered under the two headings of personal adequacy and social competence.

(i) *The development of personal adequacy*. This involves:

(*a*) The growth of feelings of personal well-being through the maintenance of good physical and mental health.

(*b*) The eventual achievement of economic efficiency through vocational competence.

(*c*) The realization of any cultural potentialities the child possesses and the development of the desire and ability to use leisure time wisely.

(*d*) The acquisition of those basic skills and habits without which the other aims are impossible of achievement.

(ii) *The development of social adequacy*. This involves:

(*a*) The development of those abilities, attitudes and dispositions which make for good social relationships.

(*b*) The development of good citizenship through a growing aware-ness of duties, rights and privileges—at school, at home, in work and in the community.

These aims are listed for the sake of convenience but they are not, of course, mutually exclusive. Social adequacy is hardly likely to be achieved in the absence of personal adequacy; good social relation-ships are dependent on economic efficiency and vice versa; good citizenship is impossible without basic skills and these can only be raised to an adequate level if physical and mental health are good. Within these general aims there are subsidiary ones upon which the special school teacher must concentrate. These are:

(1) *The restoration and development of self-confidence.* Many ESN children, before admission to the ESN school, have experienced years of failure and frustration as a result of which their self-esteem has been seriously undermined. Lack of academic success, rejection by other children, faulty teaching and parental mismanagement lead to emotional disturbance, feelings of inadequacy and personality and conduct disorders. Children eventually find themselves in a vicious circle. The inter-play between causes and symptoms becomes more and more complicated and difficult to disentangle. The breaking of this vicious circle becomes one of the most important aims of treatment. It cannot be broken unless the school has established an organization and curriculum which will ensure progress and induce self-confidence in its pupils. Nothing succeeds like success, but success is not achieved without efficiency, knowledge, and under-standing.

(2) *The ESN child must be helped to know himself.* Each child must be able to realize, live with and, if necessary, compensate for his handicaps and limitations. It is essential to discover each child's strengths and weaknesses and to arrange his education so that through his own awareness of these he becomes capable of matching aspirations to abilities. This awareness is by no means easily achieved in a way which ensures the maintenance of a healthy mental life. Lack of awareness is usually disastrous while too acute an awareness of limitations leads to personality difficulties.

(3) *The development of good work habits.* The experiences of the backward child in ordinary school often result in the development of poor attitudes to work. Work that is too difficult results in bore-dom and poor attention. Lack of success may cause behaviour diffi-culties and an unwillingness to try. Careful attention to individual-ization of treatment, to curriculum content and balance, and to suitable organization are required if children are to develop the feeling of power to overcome difficulties and improve in self-directed application to work.

89

Principles of special educational treatment

(1) *Individualization of treatment.* Alice Descöeudres suggests five governing principles of special teaching. The fourth of these she calls individualization of teaching which she states is teaching which takes into account 'the needs of each particular type of mentality'. She goes on to say that attention to this principle will also tend to promote the harmonious development of the child. The application of this principle calls for skilful teaching which is based on a knowledge of children's development and of the way children learn, so that a careful observation and study of the child can lead to the choice of the most suitable learning experiences.

It might be thought that ESN children in the special school, comprising between one and two per cent of the school population, form a homogeneous group. However, the only criteria on which they are the same are that they have been classified as ESN and that they are boys or girls. In other respects there are wide individual differences. Although the group as a whole may have poorer physical development, there are as wide variations as in the whole school population. Although the average intelligence of the group is low, there are still considerable variations in intelligence. Moreover, children differ in the way intelligence manifests itself. Two children with the same IQ and mental age will often show significant differences in the kind of intellectual abilities. The same children are almost certain to display dissimilar personality development and capacity for learning. We may attempt to classify the ESN group into sub-groups, e.g. endogenous, exogenous; high, medium, low grade; severely subnormal, subnormal and psychopath. Such groups may suggest general indications for treatment but, in practice, are of little use because individual differences are so marked as to make individualized treatment necessary.

But individualized treatment should not be thought of as being synonymous with individual treatment. It is indeed very desirable that ESN children should learn in groups in which they learn to live together, to help one another and to share experiences. Treatment within the group should, however, take into account the fact that each child has his own growth pattern and should aim at ensuring that each member of the group is making the most of his capacities.

The teacher should, therefore, look upon his class as a collection of individuals each with particular characteristics and needs. To illustrate this let us consider some children in an actual class of 15 ESN children in a large school where grouping might be expected to result in reasonable homogeneity.

Child 1. Girl. Aged 11 years. IQ 70. Test results showed a marked verbal bias. She is very disturbed emotionally and there is neurological evidence of brain damage. Word recognition is at a 12+ year level but reading for comprehension is very poor. Number is particularly weak—some number facts have been memorized but she cannot apply these in solving the simplest of problems. She is restless and distractible, a disturbing influence in class, but usually popular with staff and children. Well cared for.

Child 2. Girl. Aged 11½ years. IQ 76. Test results show marked performance bias. Reading and spelling very weak; number within the normal range. Physical development normal. Amenable in school but too withdrawn. Lacks self-confidence to a marked degree. Broken home and very irregular schooling.

Child 3. Boy. Aged 11 years. IQ 75. Very undersized but physically active and wiry. Can be very aggressive and at times violent. Acute rivalry with brighter twin brother. Working much below capacity. Resents even mild correction and refuses help. He is beyond parental control and was previously excluded from school.

Child 4. Boy. Aged 11½ years. IQ 67 with verbal bias. History of epilepsy and still on phenobarbitone. Neurological and other evidence of brain damage. Personal habits offensive. Illegitimate and of mixed blood. Reading and spelling at 9-year level. Number very weak. Appears to be of average intelligence but functioning at much lower level. Mother is unable to control the boy.

Child 5. Boy. Aged 12½ years. IQ 62. Reading 7·4 years. Number 8 years. Making steady all-round progress. He is too fat and is very conscious of this. Very poor home but appears happy and contented and is always willing to give and accept help.

Child 6. Girl. Aged 11 years 10 months. IQ 70. Undersized but healthy. Attainments very poor but is making progress. Language development is very retarded. Very poor home background, parents subnormal, inefficient but well-meaning; Family Service Unit has done much to improve the conditions in the home. She is reasonably happy and contented and appears to have suffered little emotionally from the early deprivation.

Child 7. Boy. Aged 12¾ years. IQ 75. Very undersized; partially deaf (uses hearing aid); slight speech defect. At first very withdrawn and immature, but success in basic subjects has resulted in significant personality changes. Now outgoing and at times noisy and aggressive. Probably wrongly diagnosed on account of deafness and retarded language development.

Child 8. Boy. Aged 12¼ years. Verbal IQ 71. Performance IQ 48. Very restless and distractible but no definite evidence of brain damage. Defective vision. Reading age 7 years. Spelling 7·6 years. Number 5-6 years. Socially very inadequate. A problem.

These eight brief descriptions, which are by no means unusual, serve to demonstrate the range of individual differences in attainments, learning capacity, emotional development and aetiology present in this particular class of higher-grade ESN children. They surely indicate that mass teaching is quite unsuitable if these children are to be helped towards successful school achievement and better personal adjustment.

(2) *The use of appropriate methods of learning.* The various aspects of growth—physical, emotional, intellectual—should not be considered in isolation but as parts of a dynamic integrated process. We must ensure that our methods of learning and teaching will encourage total growth and are geared to the special needs and limitations of our pupils. We must strive to create a school environment which will influence each child's growth so that his personality is developed to its optimal level. The needs of the ESN child are, as we have stated, not markedly different from those of normal children. His interests are also very similar although they are perhaps more superficial and, for his age, more childish. In suggesting appropriate methods we are, therefore, more concerned with the way he differs from other children, e.g. his poor reasoning, his lack of experience, his emotional immaturity, and his adverse home influences.

(*a*) *Motivation*

The ESN child is often said to be lacking in drive, initiative and originality, and to be uninterested in school work. He often has a pre-special school history of truancy, petty delinquency and difficult behaviour. He is always aware of his failures and is constantly striving, often in ways which outrage the mores of his group, to achieve self-esteem, recognition and acceptance. His treatment must, therefore, be so organized and motivated that it develops feelings of power to overcome difficulties and gives a sense of self-satisfaction through accomplishment. The maintenance of good motivation is essential. It can only be achieved if he learns in a situation which gives him security and confidence. Good teacher-child relationships are vital all the time, and particularly when special educational treatment begins, since a willingness to overcome difficulties will only arise when previous faulty attitudes have been eradicated. Moreover, their replacement by favourable attitudes is necessary, and these can be developed only if the learning is successful and suited to the child's stage of development.

(*b*) *Learning Readiness*

The special school teacher must be expert in assessing, largely by means of observation, the child's readiness for learning. More positively he should be capable of planning activities which will hasten readiness.

Readiness for learning is not concerned solely with intellectual readiness. Emotional, social and physical factors enter into readiness in degrees which vary according to the nature of the learning to be undertaken. Furthermore, the child is continually 'getting ready' for the next stage in his learning. The learning and thinking that has gone on at one stage make him more capable of tackling more difficult learning and of acquiring more complex ideas at the next stage. The teacher must therefore ensure that children are not introduced to learning for which they are not fully ready. This requires a recognition of the fact that the various aspects of readiness do not always develop at the same rate. With young ESN children, it often happens that a child is ready for the beginnings of formal work in basic subjects except for the presence of a specific disability, such as a sensory handicap or a weakness in perceptual discrimination. An older ESN child may be ready in most ways for formal reading instruction yet be so emotionally immature or disturbed that progress is still impossible. In such cases the teacher must individualize treatment in such a way that the child can use abilities which are mature in order to overcome or compensate for the disability. For example, in the early stages of reading a child may have a particular difficulty in visual discrimination but be ready for reading as far as auditory and kinaesthetic abilities are concerned. The teacher might, therefore, use a kinaesthetic method, i.e. the child learns words by a tracing and writing method. Progress is thus made in reading, and incidentally visual discrimination improves. Another child may make a successful start to reading and quickly build up a basic sight vocabulary only to experience difficulty later when speech defects or poor auditory perception cause difficulty with phonic analysis. In such a case, auditory readiness must be developed by speech therapy and by training in auditory discrimination.

Readiness is a dynamic concept and it is not sufficient to think of it simply in relation to the early stages of learning. Piaget and Inhelder have shown how the development of logical thinking and social behaviour passes through several stages. These are not clearly demarcated and occur at different ages in different children but follow a remarkably similar seqeuence in all. In the beginning, the child's thinking is pre-logical and irrational, following which he passes through a stage of concrete operations when he can handle relationships between things he perceives, but cannot yet set up generalizations or hypotheses in the abstract. Later he is able to organize his knowledge and new experiences in relation to possibilities, reasoning and verification, and learn to generalize and establish laws. Piaget has shown how these various stages are present in all learning, e.g. in number, in the development of ideas of causality and of moral judgments. If these conclusions are valid, and observations of children would appear to substantiate them, then all teachers should be aware of their significance in teaching. Some of the practical implications for the teaching of ESN children are discussed in Chapters II and VIII. The special school teacher should realize that ESN children will pass through these stages of development at a much later time than normal children and are seldom likely to reach the last stage. In practice, teaching must be planned so as to anticipate and prepare for the next stage in development and learning, yet take into account the limits set by any handicaps the child may have.

(c) A practical approach based on meaning and usefulness

If good motivation is to be maintained it is important to ensure that the objectives we set for children should be obvious, tangible and possible of attainment. The ESN child is more at home in dealing with things he can see, touch and hear, or which are within his experience. Teaching which is related to practical human experience is more successful than teaching which involves abstractions, symbols and delayed gratification. The ESN child usually requires learning which can be quickly demonstrated as useful to him personally. A functional, utilitarian approach is essential. We shall see later (Chapter VII) that in the teaching of phonics it is important to demonstrate to the child how the learning of a particular sound is useful to him in reading for enjoyment and interest. If the child is making a model it is important, particularly in the early stages, that he should be capable of completing it fairly quickly even if he receives some help from the teacher to ensure a satisfactory result. The teacher will have to ensure that the various steps in making the model are clearly and simply defined. This may involve letting the child see the separate stages of the model demonstrated by the teacher, or leaving examples before him of the model in various stages of development. Many teaching situations have to be dissected in this way. Greater attention to particulars is required. For example, in pre-vocational training (Chapter XII) it is no use talking in generalities about the need for getting on with workmates and doing a good job, or the importance of punctuality. We must demonstrate by actual examples what these things actually involve. Thus, in regard to punctuality we must give practice in the estimation of the relationship between time, distance and mode of transport, to arrive at a given destination on time. Providing the child with first-hand direct experiences or, in their absence, ones which have meaning and purpose, is a *sine qua non* of teaching.

(d) Concept formation

This concrete approach to learning must, however, not be regarded as an end in itself. Our learning procedures must not result in the child being completely dependent on demonstration, imitation, or simplified learning situations. The 'concrete' should provide a base from which the child is enabled to reason for himself so that he can eventually plan his own means and ends. Many ESN children are quite capable of making *simple* generalizations and abstractions. But to achieve this they must be given ample opportunities to experiment, explore and discuss. The observant teacher will find innumerable opportunities every day for helping the child to see relationships. The child can be shown, or led to discover, likenesses and differences in sound, colour, texture, size and structure; his curiosity can be aroused; his interests can be expanded and enriched; he will respond to practical experiences designed to help him classify and order his environment. If he is nurtured in a class environment which gives confidence and security he will be willing to experiment. Indeed, he often shows quite an unexpected degree of insight and ingenuity.

It is often, and correctly emphasized that the ESN child must learn 'by doing'. But his 'doing' is not an end in itself. It should be leading to simple generalizations and the building up of concepts. For instance, in number teaching the ESN child with an elementary concept of five (i.e. an appreciation of the relationship between five and four, three, two and one; an understanding of the processes which can be performed with groups of up to five things of any size and quality; an ability to deal with any combinations up to five without the necessity of concrete aids) can, after further experience with objects, extend his five concept to six. This concept of six then contains all his ideas of five and becomes the foundation for other number concepts. In nature study or the study of the locality, the activities and experiences we provide are the material from which elementary but important concepts about living are formed. Each concept developed in this way prepares the way for further concept formation. As the number of concepts increases and as they are related to each other, the quality as well as the quantity of thinking develops.

Concept formation and language are very closely related. To continue the number example, the child's concept of six is associated with words about size, order, comparison, manipulation and application, e.g. many, few, first, last, more, less, add, share. If we are to help the child build concepts we must ensure, therefore, that we enable him to acquire the necessary vocabulary. The importance of special words is obvious in arithmetic teaching and should be recognized in other subjects of the curriculum. Our teaching must pay particular attention to the development of the ability to use the spoken and written word.

(e) Grading of work

Since the ESN child is a slow learner, the material to be learnt must be carefully graded to ensure continuing progress and feelings of success. Weeks and even months of patient work with a child whose confidence has been previously shattered can be vitiated by confronting him with work which is beyond his capacity. The observant teacher is quick to recognize when work is too difficult by the child's reactions—even though he attempts to conceal them. These reactions vary according to the child's temperament. The withdrawn child may revert to day-dreaming, nail biting, fidgeting and general tenseness. The outgoing child may make his feelings more apparent by resorting to stubbornness, truculence, defiance or, in extreme cases, by truancy and delinquency.

The grading of work for ESN children presents many problems to the teacher. Books which are suitably graded for very backward children are rare and the teacher must either be selective within a book or make his own individual materials. If systematic, orderly progress is to be achieved by all the children, then grading must cater for individual differences within the group. It is unrealistic to compel every child to follow every step in the overall grading for the class. The grading should be such that the slowest learner is catered for, and the quicker learner is given work which will extend him. This may suggest that ideally every child should have his own scheme of work, but in practice it means that the teacher has to select from within the general scheme for the whole class those exercises and assignments which best meet the needs of individual children. Thus in spelling, the slowest learner will probably have to adhere to the grading of the whole spelling scheme. Others will be able to omit some exercises altogether or use assignments which the teacher knows are of suitable difficulty.

The teacher should not prepare exercises or work units *in vacuo*. These should, at all times, be related to the children's developmental level and be changed and adapted in the light of teaching experience and the measured progress which the children make.

(f) Assessment of progress

Provision should be made, therefore, for assessing each child's progress. For this purpose, we recommend the use of standardized tests of attainment in word recognition, reading for comprehension, and spelling. For number there are no suitable tests and we have found it necessary to devise our own tests which are designed to estimate attainment levels within our own curriculum. It should not normally be necessary for these tests to be used more than once or twice in a school year. Provision should be made, however, for keeping detailed records, not only about progress in the basic sub-

96

jects but also about general development. How detailed these records should be depends on the child's age and how deviant he is. For very young ESN children a weekly note of progress in intellectual, scholastic, emotional and particularly social development is desirable. For disturbed children, progress should be assessed regularly and any significant incidents noted. In evaluating progress, the teacher should bear in mind that real progress has to be related to that progress which has been achieved previously. Thus progress in reading of one year in a school year in a child who has previously made no progress is usually more significant than the same progress in a child who during the previous year also made one year's progress. The teacher should also realize that marked progress is more difficult for the child working to capacity than for the seriously under-functioning child. He should also note any unevenness in progress and relate succeeding treatment to it. This unevenness may be apparent in various aspects of one subject, or between one subject and another. In reading, for instance, initial progress may well be rapid while the child is building up a sight vocabulary. A learning plateau may then occur because grading is faulty or because the child needs assistance in unlocking new words. Or again, progress in mechanical arithmetic may be encouraging but in problem arithmetic disappointing, suggesting the need for the increased use of number knowledge in real-life situations. The teacher's aim in such cases should be to achieve steady, balanced progress by careful modification of curriculum content and educational method.

The keeping of records of each child's progress is essential for efficient, individualized treatment. Each special school should therefore keep some kind of cumulative record card which should take the form of a condensed case history together with information, measurements and assessments which will help the teacher to understand each child and to adapt educational treatment accordingly. In addition to records kept by the teacher each child should be encouraged to keep a personal record of progress. The form this record takes will vary according to the developmental age and to subject. It must always be understood by the child and easy for him to keep. Its purpose must be to maintain motivation and to encourage each child to compete against himself. We find these child-kept records a great help in teaching, but if used unwisely they can lead to the opposite of the desired effect, viz. unhealthy child-child competition, flagging interest and deteriorating work habits. This can be obviated if the tone and group feeling of the class are good.

(g) *Consolidation*

Grading of new work and record keeping are very helpful in ensuring orderly progress, but we must also ensure that the progress is real. The teacher in his keenness to achieve optimum motivation and feelings of accomplishment must not lose sight of the importance, particularly with ESN children, of frequent repetition and adequate revision. How to provide these and maintain real feelings of progress is a constant problem, the solution of which calls for ingenuity, understanding, careful planning and hard work. Consolidation of previous learning is essential since without it new learning cannot be integrated and made meaningful. The teacher must, therefore, make adequate provision for drill. However, drill which is based on a philosophy that drudgery is good for the soul will not succeed. *It must be interesting, purposeful and have meaning for the child.* It should provide additional practice in old learning by presenting it in new ways, e.g. in games and play, or by application in other activities. (Chapters VII and VIII contain examples of the application of this suggestion.)

(*h*) *Active methods*

The learner will learn more quickly and efficiently if he is intellectually as well as emotionally involved. With ESN children, particularly older ones, positive intellectual involvement is not always easy to obtain. What we teach must be interesting and vital. Its use must be clearly demonstrable and we must teach it with methods which excite interest, arouse curiosity, and encourage active participation. This principle is obvious but is so often forgotten. We still teach things because tradition says we ought. There is still a tendency to think that if a class is active or if children are allowed to organize and use their own ways of finding out, we shall be regarded as cranks, and inefficient ones at that. Yet there is ample evidence in schools and from research to show that at all levels of learning, knowledge acquired through self-directed activities is more lasting and useful. This is certainly true of ESN children and Descöeudres includes it in her five basic principles when she says that we must use 'the natural activity' of the child. '*The child must do things with his body, his hands and his brain.*' He must be allowed to move about, to inspect, to discuss and to give or seek help under conditions of freedom compatible with the maintenance of good discipline, and without undue interference with others. Under such conditions the child is no longer the passive receiver of instruction but an active, interested, exploring learner. Under such conditions attention sharpens and concentration deepens.

(3) *Co-operation between various professions.* In diagnosis, treatment and research, co-operation between teachers, doctors, psychologists, administrators and social workers is vital. Unfortunately, in the past each discipline has tended to isolate itself and to concentrate on its own aspect of treatment. We are fortunate to work in an establishment

in which treatment is based on co-operation between disciplines. Consequently not only is child-centred treatment a reality but each member of the professional team learns from the others.

Doctors, in addition to being concerned with ascertainment procedures and biennial medical examinations, should see children regularly to check health and sensory abilities; should ensure that appropriate treatment is provided by themselves or consultants; should have regular contacts with other workers and see something of what they do. Psychiatric treatment of the ESN child is woefully inadequate, yet there are some indications that such treatment can have far-reaching effects. Chemo-therapy is known to be very beneficial for children who are epileptic, or for certain children who present behaviour problems. Segal and Tansley[1] have demonstrated the value of hydroxyzine (Atarax) in reducing symptoms of maladjustment. The value of this and other preparations in reducing symptoms such as restlessness and anxiety has been demonstrated in many countries. Their use, under proper medical safeguards, can make educational treatment possible in children who might otherwise be ineducable, particularly on grounds of inexpediency.

The psychologist can make a contribution by providing a detailed picture of the child's personality, by discovering any anomalies in development, perceptual and conceptual difficulties, intellectual strengths and weaknesses, emotional abnormalities, and by investigating learning difficulties generally. He should, however, be capable of suggesting lines of approach for teachers to follow and of carrying out treatment himself.

Perhaps the most neglected aspect of treatment is the social. Yet it is the most important of all. The need for social workers will be stressed later. It is sufficient at this point to emphasize their contribution to treatment not only as gatherers of case history information, but also as experts in family rehabilitation, parent guidance and community education, and as liaison officers between various statutory and voluntary social agencies. In any school for ESN children there will be children who are on probation, in the care of Children's Departments or whose families are receiving help from welfare agencies. Occasionally the various workers do not make contact with one another or with the school. Often their efforts overlap. The appointment of social workers attached to special schools could avoid duplication, ensure co-operation and lead to greater efficiency and economy.

If the various experts are to work as a team, there has to be one person who will act as convenor and as co-ordinator. The person

[1] Jl. Men. Sci. Vol. 103, No 432 July 1957.

best placed to do this is the head teacher. He should be sufficiently experienced to decide which children need particular help or investigation, to interpret the team's findings, and to make the necessary arrangements for the recommended treatment to be carried out. The choice and training of head teachers is thus of supreme importance.

(4) *Parent education and guidance*. In the last section, we suggested that the social worker should be responsible for parent guidance. This is so important that we include it as a principle of treatment. The efforts of teachers of ESN children are often nullified by bad home conditions and parental neglect or ignorance. This is particularly applicable in relation to the child who attends a residential school because his home is considered unsuitable. At the end of treatment he returns to the same conditions that were responsible for his being removed from his home in the first place. It is surely desirable that, while he is away, efforts should be made to improve his parents' knowledge and attitudes as well as the condition of the home. It may well be that the parents will need residential treatment themselves, such as that provided by a number of voluntary bodies for training ineffectual mothers. In some cases, it will be impossible to make improvements because of subnormality or character defect in the parents. But other parents, including those who provide good homes, need advice on how to promote the development of their handicapped child. There are many difficulties that can arise because of the child's handicaps or because of wrong attitudes and methods in the home. A social worker would be of great assistance. Lacking such a person, the school staff must undertake some of this work of educating parents since it can have such a beneficial effect on the child's adjustment to school.

The curriculum

The curriculum we select must serve our aims of developing personal and social adequacy. It must be adapted to individual needs and potentialities and have relevance to the child's present and future status in society, and the needs of that society. The organization of curriculum content may be viewed from three angles—the *logical*, the *psychological* and the *social*. The content might be selected in some *logical* sequence. It may be decided that within a given subject there are discernible elements of knowledge which need to be taught in a definite order. For example, in number we might decide to teach so many addition facts, then so many subtraction facts, and so on. Alternatively, we might also consider it logical to teach all four processes at once. In practical work we might, by analysing the techniques involved, fix a logical order of teaching them. This logical approach has dominated our educational thinking in the past and, in consequence, our curriculum has been subject-centred. Teachers have tended to think and teach in terms of subjects and their internal logic rather than in terms of the child's *psychological* needs and capacities at any stage. Child psychology, with its emphasis on the child as a growing organism, is replacing our preoccupation with subjects by an awareness that the logical analysis of a subject may not be the most important factor in improving the child's learning of it. It is more important to understand how a child learns and relate curriculum content to the process. Instead of fitting the child to the curriculum, the curriculum must fit the child. The increasing complexity of society has also forced us to plan the curriculum to meet those *social* requirements which prepare the child for living.

In any curriculum, all three aspects must be considered, but the emphasis placed on them will vary according to the age and abilities of the child. With ESN children it is necessary to stress the psychological and social. The curriculum must be specially designed to assist total growth as well as to develop basic skills and knowledge. It should not be a mere 'watering-down' of the curriculum designed for a normal school. To segregate children and provide such a curriculum is a travesty of special educational treatment.

How then should the special school curriculum be organized? Should it be split into subjects or should greater stress be placed on correlation between subjects as in projects, centres of interest and units of experience? There are dangers inherent in both. If the curriculum content is compartmentalized into subjects, it is less easy to provide those broad experiences and real-life situations which are so necessary. The importance of social education may be overlooked. If correlation is emphasized, the basic subjects are likely to suffer because of difficulties of control and continuity; teaching may tend to become subservient to the project and not related to the individual. We must therefore aim at a compromise which, whilst offering opportunities for vital experiences, creative expression and the development of social awareness, at the same time allows efficient teaching of the basic subjects and helps each child to learn more effectively.

We may therefore think of the curriculum as composed of two closely linked and interdependent parts:

(1) A central core of language and number; (2) a periphery of additional useful knowledge about the environment, creative and aesthetic activities, and practical interests. As the core develops, so the periphery widens, and as the child achieves command of the essential tools of learning he realizes their usefulness. The interplay

between core and periphery becomes more sensitive and apparent. In practice, this concept of curriculum building means:

(i) The teaching of the basic skills must be well-planned and controlled but should also be related to the peripheral subjects whenever possible. The amount of control will vary but will normally diminish with increasing attainments which make independent study more possible.

(ii) The periphery subjects can be integrated or correlated and used at all levels to encourage the development of basic subjects. There is no need for detailed syllabuses which so often result in an atomistic, subject-centred approach to learning. What is wanted is an approach which emphasizes the relationship between the various elements in knowledge and results in broad rather than detailed experiences.

The Timetable

From what has been written so far it will be obvious that we are opposed to any method or type of organization which frustrates the teacher's objective of making her treatment child-centred. The teacher must be free to organize the class and its work in the way likely to achieve the desired results. There are, of course, some limitations imposed by the necessity to deal with specialization and the efficient use of available space. Outside these limitations, and providing the teacher is aware of the importance of keeping an appropriate balance between core and periphery activity, she should be free to arrange her timetable, and if necessary, experiment with it. In forming the timetable the head teacher should make some provision for group and school activities and for using the specialist interests and abilities of the staff, e.g. in club activities for older ESN children.

Organization within the special school

(1) *School organization.* The internal organization of the special school will depend on its size, the quality of its teaching staff, the age-range of the pupils, the staffing ratio and the educational ideals which motivate it.

The size of the school and the age-range of its pupils will be largely determined by the child population in its catchment area. In a densely populated area, it is often possible to have schools for ESN children which are large enough to warrant the provision of specialist teachers in practical subjects, and a remedial education department within the school. In addition, it might be easier to arrange the necessary medical, psychiatric, psychological and social services. However, the majority of special schools are all-age (i.e. 7–16 years) and usually do not have many more than 100 children on roll. This size and age-range may limit the breadth of the education provided unless the staffing ratio is favourable and the teachers are versatile. There are many educationists who are opposed to larger ESN schools because they feel that increasing the size much beyond 100 leads to an impersonal approach and does not give each child the feelings of security and belongingness which are essential for successful treatment. There may be some substance in this, but if local conditions make a larger school (say up to 200) possible, it can be more effective in some directions and lose none of its intimacy if the staff, and particularly the head teacher, are well selected. An all-age, mixed school of some 200 children can be a happy, well-run but not over-organized, and progressive one. We do not wish to be dogmatic about optimum size of school but there is plenty of scope for experiment in this field. We have no information about the influence of size upon the ultimate success or failure of leavers. Indeed, we have little reliable and valid evidence to show whether segregation into special schools is itself as beneficial as we believe it to be. Such evidence could only become available after research which compared the results of two groups of matched children, one in a special school and the other with similar staffing and provision in ordinary school.

The organization should take the following considerations into account:

(a) The smaller the school the more generous should be the teacher-pupil ratio. The Ministry of Education suggests an average size of class of 20 children. In a small school of 60 pupils the staff, including the head teacher, would be three or four. This is quite inadequate, particularly in view of the fact that such a school is usually all-age and mixed.

(b) The younger the children the smaller should be the class. This is of paramount importance if the teacher is to provide a stimulating environment, keep records of each child's reactions and give adequate attention to promoting learning readiness and individualization of treatment.

(c) The more heterogeneous the class the smaller it should be. A class which has a wide range of age, attainment and general development, and which includes children with additional handicaps, should not exceed 15.

(d) Some provision should be made for extra-remedial work for certain children, viz. those with dual or multiple handicaps or serious learning difficulties.

(e) The system of promotion should be flexible. Each child should be in that class which will best further his total development. Promotion should therefore be based on a comprehensive picture of the child in his school setting. Consideration must be given not only to age, ability and attainment, but also to social and emotional maturity. It must also take into account teacher-child relationships and the class regimen. An over-insistence on any one criterion can result in a slowing-up of development even when individualization of treatment is efficient. However, promotions should not be too frequent since the ESN child needs 'my teacher'. Nevertheless it is undesirable for a child to have one teacher for the whole of his special school life. He must have opportunities to meet and get along with other adults and groups of children.

Promotion must not lead to a break in the continuity of treatment. When a child moves into another class the new teacher must make liaison with the previous one in order that she may be fully conversant with the child's progress and needs. This again is an obvious principle but is often neglected. A continuing, full and systematic recording of total progress should, however, obviate any such break.

The system of promotion need not adhere too rigidly to a normal class organization. For some subjects cross-classification, i.e. the grouping of children roughly of similar attainments in a given subject irrespective of their class placement, can be advantageous. This means that the whole school, or a large part of it, will have to do a particular subject at the same time. The children move to the group or set which is appropriate for them and are promoted to the next set when their attainments in the subject warrant it. We do not recommend too much use of this type of organization because it can have a restricting influence on timetable flexibility and can be unsettling for children who need the security of a familiar teacher. Teaching based on carefully graded individual assignments should make it unnecessary. Although it is designed to give greater homogeneity in ability and attainment it can result in too much heterogeneity in other characteristics, such as age and physical development. However, school circumstances are sometimes such that it is worth trying.

One further suggestion is worthy of mention: that in a school with senior children it is usually desirable when organizing the oldest class to include all those children who will be leaving school during the year, even if at first, the roll is over twenty. This will ensure that every leaver will have an opportunity of working through the leavers' programme (see Chapter XII). It also reduces the size of lower classes during the first term when the class teacher's organizational difficulties can be most severe.

(2) *Class organization.* We recognize that the application of the

principles and methods we suggest places great strain and responsibility on the class teacher. To get each child working up to a reasonable level with a measure of freedom calls for the highest teaching skill, great knowledge, good organizing ability and hard work. The following suggestions should be helpful to those teachers who are willing to try:

(*a*) Organize the class in small, carefully selected groups rather than in serried rows.

(*b*) Have a plentiful supply of alternative activities, e.g. a wide range of supplementary readers, free access to art and craft materials.

(*c*) Pay particular attention to the preparation of material and the planning of work.

(*d*) Allow the brighter children to help the duller ones.

(*e*) Avoid rigidity and do not be afraid of following suitable leads which come from the children.

(*f*) Encourage the children to participate in planning activities and to help with class organization.

(*g*) Allow as much freedom as possible within well-established limits. Be firm when these limits are transgressed.

(*h*) Be sensitive to the children's reactions. When interest in an activity begins to flag replace it by another, preferably of a different kind.

(*i*) Have several periods each week when the class is engaged, as a whole, on one activity, e.g. story, drama, or music.

(*j*) Do not be too reluctant to admit failure with an individual child and to ask for another opinion.

(*k*) Try to obtain parental interest and co-operation.

FURTHER READING

BURT, C. *The Backward Child.* U.L.P., 1937
BURT, C. *Causes and Treatment of Backwardness.* U.L.P., 1952
DESCOEUDRES, A. *The Education of Mentally Defective Children.* Harrap, 1928.
DUNCAN, J. *The Education of the Ordinary Child.* Nelson, 1942.
GOLDSTEIN, H. and GEIGLE, D. M. *The Illinois Curriculum Guide for teachers of the educable mentally handicapped.* Interstate Publishers, Danville, Illinois.
HIGHFIELD, M. E. *The Education of Backward Children.* Harrap, 1951.
INGRAM, C. *The Education of the Slow Learning Child.* Harrap, 1953.
KIRK, S. A. and JOHNSON, G. O. *Educating the Retarded Child.* Harrap, 1951.
MORRIS, R. *The Quality of Learning.* Methuen, 1951
PIAGET, J. and INHELDER, B. *The Growth of Logical Thinking.* Routledge and Kegan Paul, 1958.
SCHONELL, F. J. *Backwardness in the Basic School Subjects.* Oliver and Boyd, 1942.

VI

LANGUAGE

SCHOOLS give considerable thought to the ways of achieving good standards in reading and writing, but important as reading and writing are, it must not be forgotten that they are only subsidiary skills in language. Children's ability to express themselves orally and to comprehend what is said to them is more important. After they have left school, ESN children may make little use of their reading and writing but will certainly make daily use of language to communicate with others. At work, they often need to comprehend oral instructions. When they have difficulty about how to do a job or about getting on with workmates or superiors, the ability to follow instructions or to express themselves may help to overcome the difficulty. An ability to maintain a conversation is also important if our leavers are not going to be left out of social groups at work or club. There are, in addition, those increasingly numerous occasions when people need to make contact with welfare and official agencies. In these interviews, people need to understand what is said to them and to explain their own situation or point of view.

In school itself, language is fundamental to much that we do. This is most obvious in the basic subjects. Readiness for reading demands a varied vocabulary and an ability to talk in sentences. Both remembering words in reading and spelling and good comprehension in reading are promoted by understanding the words used and being able to relate them to meaningful experiences. Written English is almost completely dependent on oral English because children, and many adults for that matter, write as they talk. Moreover, even though we make the education of ESN children as practical as possible, emphasizing learning by doing and the use of concrete and pictorial aids, there still remains much learning that requires the comprehension of verbal instructions and explanations.

Finally, we must note the link between thinking and language. A greater facility in using words is a means to more effective thinking, and an increasing understanding of experience is reflected in a widening vocabulary. In short, language is of first importance since it is so much a part of mental growth.

Language development of ESN children

Ordinary children of normal intelligence and from a good home background usually arrive at school age with language sufficiently mature for them to be able to use speech as a means of getting on with other children and to make progress in pre-reading and pre-number work. Where the ESN school has a class for children younger than seven or eight, many of them are likely to be considerably retarded in speech. Some may have severe defects of articulation and others may use a small vocabulary and brief sentences like those of a two- or three-year-old child. They may be content to use one- or two-word sentences to convey their meaning—for example, 'Look—gone' meaning 'I've rubbed it out. It's all gone.' These children benefit from the attention of a speech therapist especially if her work can be carried over to the classroom. Others while not so retarded may have difficulty in finding and combining words, their immaturity and emotional reluctance being one of the chief reasons for their backwardness in expression. They often have recourse to gestures or to action rather than words. These children need a great deal of speech stimulation through play, through listening to adults and talking with them, and through the experience of stories and rhymes. They are usually capable of understanding much that they cannot say and while language needs to be kept simple, they are not helped by being indulged with baby talk.

With older children, the difficulties are in knowing what to say, or if they know what to say in finding ways of saying it. A small vocabulary is one of the chief weaknesses. The lack of a word, or the frequent inability to call it up when needed, results in hesitations, new starts and roundabout ways of saying things. Thus a boy describing the purchase of a model kit at a model shop said:

> 'Well I bought a . . . well I went into town. I went into this shop up in town with all those toys with yachts and I asked him has he got a . . . models of . . . big book of ships . . . drawings . . . and he said Yes and I bought one. So then he said Would you like this . . . all pieces of wood with like a shape of a boat that what I just needing. I said Yes and it come to 7/6.'

Sometimes the failure to find a word is filled in by expressions such as 'Whats it', 'Thing um e bob', 'What do you call it?' or by descriptive gestures. The greater frequency of this with ESNs points to the need for not accepting these substitutes and for plenty of practice in expression, especially in relation to activities.

Expression is often lacking in order, sequence and selectivity. A rather extreme example occurred when a boy was describing his Bonfire Night.

> 'Well, before we started our fireworks we went to the shop to go and buy some fireworks for 2/6 in a box and me Mum let them off me Dad was at work see and when they finished I went into see TV . . . when I watched TV I went to my friends house and he had a big bonfire. He had some fireworks he had 40 hundred and he had a lot of money he did . . . he might come to this school and you can ask him.'

The difficulty in knowing what to select to say is a common enough weakness in expression. It is fairly characteristic of the infant child; it occurs in adults. Getting children to talk needs to include getting them to talk more effectively—talking with a purpose such as describing a process or event to an audience of other children so that they understand.

The ESN child makes less use of different parts of speech in his oral expression. Sentences are mostly strung together with 'and' or 'then'; other conjunctions, although used, are not used so much. There is less use of adjectives and adverbs. There are sometimes confusions in the use of words such as prepositions and pronouns. For example, a boy describing how he cleans his shoes said: 'You get the duster and rub . . . when they go outside they put on their shoes and give them another polish . . . You put the tin and duster back.' He switched from thinking of himself doing it to thinking of the other boys doing it at the residential school he attended.

Errors in usage are, of course, frequent. Many of these are indeed the common and accepted forms in the child's environment, a large number of them being in the word forms 'to be', 'to do', 'to go' and 'to come'. The possibilities of cure are reduced by the fact that what the child hears out of school is in continual opposition to what he hears in school. Certain other errors such as *he catched, he runned*, and *he buyed* are common in the normal development of speech and usually disappear as the child matures. Sometimes these and other immaturities in pronunciation persist with much older children and should be looked for and remedied.

Finally, we must not forget that language is concerned with communication and this involves listening as well as talking. ESN children are often poor at remembering messages, and listening to instructions, stories and other forms of the spoken word. Attention

needs to be given to promoting listening and to reproducing what
has been said.

The causes of poor language development

The reasons for poor language development can be summarized in
four groups and a consideration of these suggests what factors have
to be taken into account in providing the conditions in school for
improvement.

(i) Poor background of speech and language at home.
(ii) A limited background of experience.
(iii) Emotional and social factors.
(iv) The limitations of the ESN child's thinking.

(i) *Poor background of speech and language.* Children are learning
English in the years before they come to school and continue to be
influenced all their school lives by the English they hear out of
school. On average, ESN children start talking rather late and most
of them have less encouragement and stimulation to talk at home.
It is not only, of course, that the limited vocabulary and poor
expression of the parents gives children poor models to imitate.
More important is the fact that few parents will be conversing with
children, telling them stories, answering questions and giving them
the experiences of listening and talking that many average children
have in their homes. Language is acquired not just by imitation but
in this interchange of talk which stimulates thinking and creates the
need to find and practise techniques of expression. The difference
that a better verbal background makes is sometimes demonstrated
by subnormal children who come from good homes. Their vocabulary is often surprisingly extensive even though their low intelligence
still limits their use of it.

It follows that the ESN school needs to make a special effort to
make up for this deficiency by giving children as much opportunity
as possible to talk with adults.

(ii) *Background of experience.* It has been said that an interesting
environment favours the acquisition of nouns, interesting activities
favour the acquisition of verbs and that the other parts of speech are
relatively more dependent on the quality of the child's thinking.
Certainly, interesting experiences are soon registered as gains in
vocabulary as even children's experience of television shows. Children who are taken on holiday or for day trips, or who have plenty
of toys and activities at home, are more likely to acquire a better
vocabulary than children who live a very restricted life as so many
ESN children do. Teachers who have taken children on school
journeys or to school camps know how much children gain in voca-

bulary from seeing new places, as well as in spontaneity of expression about the things that excite them. But it is not only the experience itself that matters. The crucial thing is the use to which experience is put. Experiences must be worked over in talk, question and answer, as they are in good families, if children are to get the maximum benefit from them.

(iii) *Emotional and social factors.* In infancy, speech develops in the encouraging, approving atmosphere of a home, the close relationship with mother being particularly important. Any disturbance in this relationship or in the normal family pattern is likely be to reflected in poorer language development, as it frequently is in the case of deprived children. Later in childhood, insecurity or emotional disturbance may result in the child who is timid and silent, or in more serious cases, in the child who will not talk. The language programme should include attempts to help these children to a better adjustment so that they can gradually become able to participate in classroom talk. Since verbal expression is so easily influenced by emotional conditions, it is important for all children that the atmosphere of the class should be encouraging so that children feel able to ask questions, seek help, and make suggestions without fear of disapproval or criticism. The personal relationships in school exert a subtle influence in this matter and the nearer relationships are to those of a good family the greater is the likelihood of improvements in verbal expression.

Social relationships within a class are also important. Children who are unsociable, or who are not accepted by others, miss the interchange of ideas and chatter on the way to school, in the playground or in play generally. Missing this, they miss the practice in talking with others that the normally outgoing child has, and miss also the extension of general knowledge and interests that come from sharing experiences with others. Children not only learn to co-operate in mixing with others; they also learn how to use speech for getting on with others. As Watts says, 'It is certainly through quarrelling that the majority of children first realize the need to make themselves understood.' It is important, therefore, to help the isolated children to be drawn into the group. Indeed we need to make much use of co-operative and group efforts so that all children have increased opportunities for purposeful communication in social situations.

(iv) *Limitations of thinking.* As we noted in a previous chapter, ESN children are limited in the ability to think and reason about their experiences. They have a poor capacity to generalize from experience and so develop the concepts which are summed up in words. This is especially so when they are dealing with words for abstractions rather than for things. Hence there is value in drawing their attention to words which stand for a 'family' or class of words, e.g. fruits, tools, vegetables, seasons, instruments, and in giving them practice occasionally in using words to describe the uses and compare the appearance of things. Limited intelligence also means that there is a reduced awareness of significant relationships in their experience such as those involving the use of prepositions, adverbs and comparatives. Relationships of cause, result, time and place which would find expression in the appropriate adverbial clauses are slower to appear in the speech of ESN children and are less frequently used. It is not just that they do not happen to have the words for ideas which they perceive in an undefined, non-verbal way. They do not connect things in their experience in a way that calls for the use of these parts of speech. The practical implication is that incidental opportunities should be utilized to help children pattern their experience and to find words to talk about it. Intelligent children do this for themselves with a minimum of adult guidance in their ceaseless exploration and discovery of their environment, whereas ESN children need help. Just as the development of number concepts and processes cannot be left merely to chance, so in the field of language concepts and relationships need to be more consciously defined and verbalized. This does not mean of course that there should be a lot of artificial lessons on language. Language skills are only acquired and practised as children find a need to talk about their activities. Opportunities for this arise in every part of school work. Although the method is informal it will not be aimless, for the teacher will be trying to lead children on to greater fluency of expression partly by example, partly by practice, partly by definite guidance.

Aspects of the language scheme

It is clear from this brief summary of the chief factors affecting the development of language that active methods of learning are required. Children do not extend their vocabularies or their ability to speak and write English by sitting down in desks ploughing through work books and writing exercises relating to vocabulary and usage. These may play a part at some stage, but in the first place children learn by talking about what they have seen or done, by discussing what they are going to do and how they are going to do it.

First hand experiences are the most effective for they evoke stronger feelings of enthusiasm and interest and these feelings create the impulse to express. In a residential school, the ESN child who was surprised to find a swan's egg floating on the pond needed no prodding to fetch his trophy and show it off to everybody. 'It's addled,' he said, 'and it smelt. Mr. X blew it. Look at the two holes. He did them with a skewer.' At a camp school, a child from a town school surprised her headmaster by changing from a silent uncommunicative child to one who was continually chattering with her delight in the new experience. Language growth can also be promoted by visits to museums, old buildings, the zoo, shops, and, with older children, to factories. In addition, an effort needs to be made to create in the classrooms a stimulating environment. Some school buildings are dull places and children whose lives outside school are often a little drab need more colour and interest in the school. Such things as an aquarium, pets, frequent changes of pictures, collections of nature specimens and other things are most desirable to arouse curiosity and to promote talk. They should result in children adding to their store of words and ideas, and should increase the opportunities for expressing these ideas to others.

It is not, of course, *what* is in the classroom, or the number of times children go out on visits that matter, so much as the activity of the class in relation to them. The teacher should stimulate and guide the child's thinking about his experiences. For example, what children notice on a nature walk might well be limited to the suitability of trees for climbing. If the teacher points out the little oak seedlings growing in the wood, several of the class will be looking for more, and having collected some will be ready to hear again a simple account of the process of germination and growth.

But one cannot always be providing first-hand experiences. There is a limit to the number of times one can go out on visits and to the number of real things one can have in the classroom. Ordinary children increase vocabulary and general knowledge from reading but children who cannot read well can still gain much from pictures and books in the classroom. There is an increasing supply of well-illustrated information books which help to stimulate talk and to increase knowledge. Even non-readers enjoy referring to illustrated reference books. Making scrapbooks or interest books, either individually or in groups, can be the source of useful talk and discussion. A good supply of old magazines on a variety of topics is a useful source of pictures. Films, film-strips and wireless can also extend children's experience and the range of things about which they can talk. Children certainly learn a good deal from television and, whatever the educational value of their favourite programme, it at least provides experiences which can be talked about. We could probably make more use of it in school.

Stories and drama

One time-honoured way of learning about the world and, at the same time, of growing in knowledge of one's mother tongue is through hearing stories. Not only do stories increase the vocabulary for things but also for the emotions—love, hate, fear, beauty, good, wicked, gentle, kind—and of common phrases and expressions. Watts has calculated that the most common nursery rhymes introduce children to about 400 common words. These rhymes should be used at the junior ESN stage for although many children will have heard them in the infant school, they may have been too immature to learn from them. The same applies to folk tales, fairy and bible stories. It is surprising how much some of the older children enjoy stories which would seem too young for them, presumably having missed them at an earlier stage. Since ESN children are later than ordinary children in reaching a point at which their own reading enables them to extend their vocabulary, there is all the more reason for reading to them as much as possible, even in the later age groups. A good background of stories also stimulates the imagination and is needed if we are going to make use of story-telling, whether oral or written, or story-making in puppetry and drama.

Drama in various forms offers many possibilities for the development of speech and language. With younger children, speech will occur naturally in the course of ordinary make-believe play—playing houses and shops. This can be developed as children go through the school into the free drama (as described in Chapter IX) in which children make up stories or dramatize stories that they have been told. Drama, at first, will consist largely of mime and action; speech should be allowed to come naturally rather than trying to force it. Trying to make a script for the play in order to benefit reading and writing is likely to inhibit the spontaneity of the drama and may not benefit expression very much.

Simple forms of puppetry (as described in Chapter IX) can be a useful means of bringing-out the shy child who is diffident about expressing himself. Some informal play amongst the children, allowing the puppets to speak to each other, can lead to simple puppet stories. A puppet theatre concealing the children using the puppets can easily be rigged up with some chairs and cloth and is as satisfactory as a more elaborate theatre. The first stories may be very meagre ones, needing much prompting and suggestion from the teacher. A short puppet play by the teacher is often needed to give children the idea of combining action and speech. Much depends, of course, on the children's background of stories and whether they have seen puppets on television or elsewhere.

Telephoning, using either toy telephones in the younger classes or real ones with older children, always stimulates expression. An amusing example of the difficulties is illustrated by a quotation from an article by Stapleton and Renfrew about speech work with a group of reception class children.

Telephone games were used but in these the children had to be helped out constantly at first by the adult. One day the boys had a free choice of activity and decided on 'cowboys'. This resulted in their jumping happily round the room yelling, so we devised a shooting, a telephone to the doctor and the ambulance, and a ride home to tell the family. As usual, the children played with the telephone dial, put the receiver to the ear and kept smiling blankly.
Adult: Ask how your friend is.
Child into telephone: How your friend is.
Adult: Tell him what you did.
Child into telephone: What you did.

A similar problem is often shown by leavers who are asked to phone back to school when they are out on an 'assignment'. It is not unusual for the boy to make the call correctly and then be unable to find words to talk into the telephone when he gets through. Using children to receive messages on the school telephone is of course excellent practice.

There are few children who are not familiar from radio or TV with the technique of an interviewer interviewing a well-known personality, and older children often enjoy dramatizing such interviews. With a model microphone in front of them, or better still the microphone from a tape recorder, they can interview several children from the class about a visit they have just made or about a football match they have just played in. In the later years of school, mock interviews for jobs (or other real-life situations) can be dramatized, helping to familiarize children with the situation as well as giving practice in language techniques. They are often more ready and able to see the faults in their interview when it is played back on the tape recorder. Other radio panel games may be utilized according to the age, ability and interests of the children: Quizzes, Twenty Questions, Brains Trusts.

In these activities, a tape recorder has been found a most valuable aid. Whereas one might expect many of our slower children to 'dry up' when confronted by the microphone, the reverse is often true. Children who are usually silent are often really keen to hear their voices played back. There are innumerable uses for the recorder in relation to language development. Apart from the dramatic situations just described, it can be used to record News Time, to record

114

accounts of visits, etc., which can be referred to later on. 'Programmes' can be recorded. Different classes or groups of children can contribute items to the programme which is later played to the whole school or to parents or visitors on an open day. Recorded 'programmes' or messages can be exchanged between schools or classes.

There may also be a place for using the recorder in later age groups as a means of enabling children to recognize some of the errors and weaknesses in their expression—for example, in a mock interview for a job. This needs judicious handling since it may deter children from expressing themselves freely on a subsequent occasion. Indeed, one has to consider how to use the tape recorder with individual children. The child whose stammer is brought on by an 'emotional' situation may be upset by hearing himself on the tape. The shy, quiet child may not be able to talk spontaneously into the mike and will be relieved to be offered the suggestion of reading something or even to contribute an item to a programme with percussion instruments—anything to avoid his being and feeling left out.

Getting orderly expression

What we are concerned with in language work is not, of course, just the acquisition of new words nor the stringing of words together. There are, indeed, quite a number of children who can talk 'nineteen to the dozen' and might be said to be fluent of speech. Often what they are saying is rather aimless chatter. In trying to improve expression, we are aiming at improving the relevance and the effectiveness of speech. Apart, therefore, from informal talk, there may be occasions when children talk about something of which they have some knowledge—their pets and how they look after them, or how to perform some simple process. This type of expression can be assisted by having things actually in the classroom to talk about, or a process can be mimed at the same time as it is described. Relevance and sequence can be developed by getting children to describe actions which have been performed in front of them. Various aspects of schoolwork, such as practical subjects, nature study, P.E., will suggest other things which can be so described. Many children enjoy retelling stories, and these give practice in getting sequence. If, as often happens, there is a tendency for the stories to be told unselectively as a long rigmarole, miming or dramatizing the story before telling it may help to bring out for the child the essential features of the story.

Conversation

The most useful skill in language to which this work will be leading is the development of the ability to converse. It is, after all, the main use of language in life after school and the child who has learnt to talk to others and to listen to what others have to say is better prepared for getting on with his fellows. Speech starts by being very egocentric—the statement of personal wants and feelings. The youngest children in ESN schools are often still in this stage. The first form of conversation is dispute—as Chesterton said, 'People quarrel because they have not yet learnt to argue,' and few could doubt that ESN children remain longer in this stage than one would wish. A teacher who encouraged his class to take responsibility for the care of materials and certain routines in the classroom found, as one might imagine, that at first they had little capacity for reasonable discussion about who was to blame when things went wrong. Discussion consisted of allegations and counter-allegations rather than of a consideration of facts and evidence. It would seem important for children to argue, converse and discuss in the classroom so that they get practice in putting their own point of view and hearing somebody else's. Such discussions must, of course, be about things which mean something to them personally. With those who are slow to contribute to discussion, there is value in the small conversation group of six to eight children, in which the teacher can help to bring the quiet ones into the conversation, can open up new topics when conversation flags, and can unobtrusively suggest better ways of saying things. News Time can, for example, be taken in this way with a small group gathered round the teacher. This encourages a conversation rather than a series of statements by individual children. Practice in conversation is also given when the staff have school meals with the children. With older children, discussion groups as described in Chapter XII provide valuable training in expression as well as preparing for school leaving.

Correction of errors

The correction of errors in oral expression is difficult. Adequacy of expression and clear communication of meaning are the first priority. It follows that the correction of particular errors should not be so stressed that it has an inhibiting effect on spontaneity. The fact that grammatical errors occur in what otherwise is a clear and adequate communication is of secondary importance. It will be recalled that the normal infant school child continues to make errors (wrong tense; singular verb with a plural subject) even into his seventh and

116

eighth years. With practice, and from hearing the correct form often enough, he gradually learns what is correct. The fact that many children do acquire a better form of speech for use in school does suggest that progress can be made. This is also illustrated by the more correct speech of deprived children brought up from an early age in a Children's Home. One form correction can take is to repeat the child's sentence or phrase in the correct form, making the repetition in a neutral, not a critical way. As with marking written work, there should be selection of what to correct. It is best to confine correction to casual talk rather than spoil the child's contribution to discussion, his story-telling, dramatization or News Time.

FURTHER READING

BEASLEY, J. *Slow to talk*. Bureau of Publications. Teachers College; Columbia University, 1956.

BERNSTEIN, B. *Social Structure, Language and Learning*. Educational Research.

BRUFORD, R. *Speech and Drama*. Methuen, 1948.

CUTFORTH, J. A. *English in the Primary School*. Blackwell, 1952.

GULLIFORD, R. *Teaching the Mother Tongue to Backward and Subnormal Pupils*. Educational Research, Vol. II, No. 2.

RENFREW, C. E. *Speech problems of backward children*. Speech Pathology and Therapy, April 1959.

SCHONELL, F. J. *Backwardness in the Basic Subjects*. Oliver and Boyd, 1942.

SMITH, A. E. *English in the Modern School*. Methuen.

STAPLETON, M. *Experiments with a Tape Recorder*. Special Schools Journal, March 1957.

STAPLETON, M. and RENFREW, C. E. *Come and Talk*. Special Education, Vol. 48, No. 2, March 1959.

TAYLOR, E. A. *Experiments with a Backward Class*. Methuen, 1949.

WATTS, A. F. *Language and the Mental Development of the Child*. Harrap, 1944.

VII

READING, SPELLING AND
WRITTEN EXPRESSION

The importance of basic subjects

IT is often suggested that the ESN child is not aware of his failings and that the aims of treatment should be the fostering of happiness through compensatory activity. The implication is that ESN children can be happy because of this lack of awareness or because they can develop other skills and interests. Except with children who are very low-grade or mentally ill, there is little evidence for this assertion. The great majority of our children are very much aware of their failings, particularly in basic subjects. Indeed many of their behaviour problems and personal difficulties can be attributed to their feelings of inadequacy in these subjects. Other problems are exacerbated by these same feelings. It seems to us that reading is the subject in which failure causes the most disturbance, for it is the skill which lends itself most easily to the making of comparisons between child and child in school. The older the child the greater the effects of his obvious failure; emotional strains are more pronounced; behaviour and attitudes deteriorate more rapidly. The educational and psychological treatment of the ESN child will therefore have little chance of success unless it engineers and maintains feelings of success in overcoming reading difficulties. This is possible if we bear certain basic principles in mind so that the best conditions for learning are available.

Some basic principles

This is not the place to deal with the psychology and teaching of reading in every detail. There are already many books for further study. The following points, however, are of special importance in relation to the teaching of ESN children.

118

The importance of reading readiness

ESN children do not become ready to respond to the formal and systematic teaching of reading until very much later than ordinary children. Research into readiness for reading has shown that children's success in reading at later stages is often delayed by introducing them to instruction before they are able to benefit from it. Yet even today children are introduced to formal reading lessons before they are ready with the result that they become frustrated, bored, puzzled and lacking in confidence. It is then often more difficult to teach them when they do become ready to learn. It is essential, therefore, that teachers of young children and of ESN children up to 11 years old should be aware of what readiness for reading entails and how readiness can be promoted. The following summary indicates the main factors which should be assessed:

(a) *Mental maturity.* Learning to read requires the association of meanings with the correct printed symbols. The child must therefore have an adequate background of experience and language so that he understands the meanings of words and ideas in his reading. He must also be mentally mature enough to make the necessary discriminations between letters, sounds and word shapes. A mental age or about six or six and a half years has often been taken as a rough indication of the stage of mental maturity at which children can succeed on the beginning stages of formal, systematic reading. This is, of course, only a rough guide because much depends on other factors in the child. On the one hand, there are children with mental ages of six or more who are backward verbally or still too immature in personal and social development to make progress. On the other hand, there are some children who can make progress with apparently lower mental ages. In assessing mental maturity, the teacher should take note of the child's response to verbal instructions, his understanding of stories, his language development generally, and his ability to use instructional materials and to plan activities purposefully. She should also realize that intellectual development cannot be isolated from such things as memory, attention, concentration, emotional development and social background and experience.

(b) *Background of experience* is highly important in providing interests and knowledge upon which the teaching of reading can be based. It is also important in influencing the child's language growth and the extent to which stories and books are likely to appeal to him. The majority of ESN children come from unstimulating homes and their background of experience is meagre. It is, therefore, essential that the pre-reading programme should attempt, in every possible way, to make up for this limitation.

119

(c) *Personal characteristics.* We have already mentioned some of the emotional difficulties of young ESN children and the importance of remedying these before formal learning is attempted. These difficulties are usually reflected in the child's social behaviour and may result in isolation—self-imposed in the shy and timid, group-imposed in the restless and negativistic. Since learning has to take place in a group setting, readiness for group participation must receive adequate attention from the beginning. Moreover, learning to read demands qualities of persistence, concentration, self-reliance and independence and these depend partly on the child's feeling of security and his relationship with the teacher. There are many ESN children who need help in acquiring these attitudes and feelings before they are ready to tackle the difficult and for them sometimes frustrating task of learning to read.

(d) *Specific abilities*

(i) *Visual readiness.* Serious defects in visual acuity are likely to have been discovered but should the child show signs of eye-strain, e.g. frequent blinking, watering, inflamed eyes, head held to one side when looking at pictures, an investigation must be arranged. However, visual perception and discrimination are the important elements to consider, e.g. the child's ability to interpret pictures, to match and compare shapes and patterns. Until these are sufficiently developed and refined so that the child can see likenesses and differences in shapes, letters and words, the beginning of reading may need to be delayed.

(ii) *Auditory readiness.* Hearing deficiencies are more easily over-looked. If the child's speech suggests inaccurate hearing of sounds, or if he is inattentive, does not respond to or frequently misunderstands directions, or assumes a peculiar posture when spoken to, the possibility of some degree of deafness should be considered. But hearing can be quite adequate and the child may still be poor at discriminating sounds, e.g. three and tree, ball and bell. As we point out later, it is important to recognize this in introducing phonic work, but it is also important in the early stages of reading.

(iii) *Motor readiness.* In learning to read, the child has to acquire the habit of moving the eyes from left to right along the line, to fixate at certain points to look at the words, and then to move to the beginning of the next line. Some children seem to have greater difficulty in acquiring these habits and may need additional practice in achieving controlled left-to-right movements. This is sometimes one aspect of a generally poor co-ordination shown in poor hand-eye co-ordination and general clumsiness. Such children may also have difficulties in writing, and since writing is often used in the early stages in reading the weakness may affect his progress.

120

(*e*) *Health.* If the child is physically below par, he is unable to participate fully in school activities. Recurrent illness, tiredness, and listlessness affect his span of attention, his interest and the amount of effort he makes. Since poor physical conditions are frequently present in backward children it is essential to watch this aspect carefully.

Readiness is thus a complex matter involving the interaction of many factors. In addition we must ask the question—readiness for what? If we emphasize phonic methods at an early stage, then auditory perception and discrimination and intelligence are important. If we use a great deal of writing, motor co-ordination is an important factor. Whatever the method, each child's weaknesses must be noted so that he can be given experiences which help him to overcome them. Tests of readiness are used in the U.S.A. but as no English tests are available, teachers need to rely on their own observation—which can be just as effective. However, a number of teachers have used readiness tests in junior ESN classes and have found them useful, if only to increase the understanding of what to observe. Available tests are:

Monroe, *Reading Aptitude Tests* (16).
Gates, *Reading Readiness Tests* (10).

Some teachers have found it advisable to keep fairly regular records of each child's progress through the readiness programme. These records show any irregularities in maturation and development and demonstrate individual differences. There can be, of course, no given time in which the programme should be completed. Rather should it be looked upon as a period of becoming more and more ready for higher levels of activity—a period of growing into reading.

Importance of good teacher-child relationships

By the time the ESN child has been admitted to a special school he is almost certain to have experienced several years of recurrent failure in the ordinary school. Even in the apparently insensitive child this failure will have given rise to feelings of personal inadequacy, frustration and antagonism towards school in general and reading in particular. In some children these feelings manifest themselves as aggressiveness and stubbornness, in others as withdrawal, apathy and hopelessness. The first task of the special school teacher is to replace these feelings by ones of co-operation, mutual trust, optimism and enthusiasm because little permanent learning can take place in the presence of emotional stress. The first few weeks and months in special school are therefore crucial. If the new child is to be made to feel that he can overcome his learning difficulties, the teacher must be sensitive to and plan to meet his needs as an individual. In many cases this is difficult. It is often difficult to determine the causes of the child's backwardness. It is not easy to differentiate between symptoms and causes. The child's emotional disturbance may be caused by reading failure or be the cause of it. It is more likely that these two may be symptoms of other causes, e.g. parental pressure, ill-health, irregular attendance and so on. We suggest, therefore, that the teacher should concern herself with building up good relationships with the child, with making her learning procedures appropriate, and with the development of good motivation.

The importance of good motivation

Experience has shown us that learning failure is very often largely due to poor motivation. Children taught by a teacher using motives in a sensible, individualized way will always learn more quickly and better, even if the method used is faulty.

The various kinds of motivation which can be employed in teaching reading can be considered in relation to five types of motive which have been suggested by Dolch (5): the play motive; the story motive; the utility motive; the mastery motive; and the please-the-teacher motive.

The *play motive* is used when we devise apparatus and games by means of which words, phrases and other aspects of reading can be practised in a way that draws upon the enjoyment of play. Thus a basic sight vocabulary or the words coming in a new book can be practised by playing *Snap* with words, playing *Dominoes* or *Lotto* with words and phrases instead of numbers. Word families (such as play, stay, day; or play, played, playing) can be learned as a card game of collecting families of words. Many teachers have invented gadgets with lights which flash when words are correctly matched; or have devised racing, football, or fishing games, the aim of which is to give an interesting motive for the rather dull process of consolidating learning. This is undoubtedly a motive which has a place in learning to read, especially in the early stages of acquiring a basic vocabulary, or with an older child whose previous experience of reading has produced an antipathy to reading books and for whom reading has to be motivated in an enjoyable way to ensure subsequent success. Too great a variety of reading exercises and games can, however, lead to confusion and can distract the learner from the aim and purpose of his learning. The play motive is best viewed as a means of providing activities which lead to a point where other motives—such as the story or the mastery motive—can begin to take effect.

The *story motive* can be a powerful one at all stages of reading. The sooner we can get children on to reading simple stories the better and we need to look at the simplest reading materials to see whether they have sacrificed the story element in order to achieve a 'scientific' vocabulary control. Both are important. As the reading age approaches seven, the story motive can be extremely useful. It is sometimes a good method to read for or with the child the first two or three pages of a story about adventures, smugglers or pirates. Once interest is aroused, children are often eager to read on independently. There are still some books on the market which consist of rather disjointed snippets of reading; it is difficult to see how children can be expected to feel any urge to read them except to please the teacher. On the other hand there is an increasing supply of simple books with good stories. (See Appendix B.)

The *utility motive* is again one which, in varying degrees, can be used at all stages of reading. In the pre-reading period reading should be related to the activities of the children, such as reading and writing labels in the classroom. When a beginning has been made, children will see the usefulness of reading if it can be related to their interests and hobbies. This is, of course, most effective with older children. It is surprising what difficult passages can be read or puzzled out when the child wants to read instructions about how to make a model, to read a letter that has been written to him, or to find information about football, pets, aeroplanes, etc. At the later stages of school, the utility motive can work through the need to read instructions or follow directions in connection with practical work or real-life situations.

It is the *mastery motive* that probably has greatest importance in the teaching of backward children. As we said earlier, most children *want* to learn (even though their failure has made them cover up with an attitude of indifference or hostility). Once they have tasted success, and if the material is graded to ensure its continuation, the desire to master reading is the chief motive for progress. Children need little encouragement to note that they are going on to a new book, or to make a record of the number of supplementary readers they have read. It is often not easy to harness this motive satisfactorily. Too much emphasis on achievement can lead to anxiety both in teacher and pupil. This can be avoided to some extent by adequate preparation for the next stage. It is essential that the teacher should be thoroughly aware of the stages in the learning process and be able to anticipate those parts which are known to be difficult with ESN children, e.g. phonic readiness, blending and syllabification, reading for comprehension. When success is in the air and children are keen to get continued signs of progress, there is often the need for tact and skill in holding them back. For example, children often want to go on to the next book before they have consolidated at the previous stage. This is often a very real problem. To achieve the adequate consolidation of previous learning and at the same time maintain the child's feelings of mastery and success calls for great skill and understanding on the teacher's part. It depends largely on the judicious use of appropriate supplementary published or teacher-made material, i.e. books, cards and written exercises.

The *please-the-teacher motive* will be in operation if there is a good teacher-child relationship but it needs to be supplemented by the other motives we have mentioned. In addition, as the child begins to experience success in his reading, he should become personally involved, setting and accepting his own standards.

Reading as part of language development

Reading should be looked upon as one aspect of an integrated programme of language development which also includes speaking, writing and spelling. In the development of reading skills the child's speaking and meaning vocabulary should always be well ahead of what he is reading. The words and ideas that the child is reading should always be well-based on experiences and language which he understands and uses. Furthermore, reading should be a skill which the child can see is useful for getting information and for giving him enjoyment. The teacher must guard against over-emphasizing recognition skills at the expense of comprehension. In brief, reading should not be thought of as an isolated skill.

The reading method[1]

The majority of ESN children appear to be visually ready for reading before they are auditorily ready. It is thus suggested that in the early stages a visual method should be used, i.e. the beginnings of reading should concentrate on the acquisition of a sight vocabulary of meaningful words. However, ESN children are poorer at making those phonic generalizations which lead to better word recognition techniques, and it is important that the reading programme should include specific provision to overcome this difficulty.

A reading programme for backward children

A sound reading programme for backward children should consist of four parts: the development of reading readiness; the acquisition

[1] Now published as *Racing to Read* and *Sound Sense* reading schemes. (Pub. E. J. Arnold and Sons Ltd., of Leeds.)

of a sight vocabulary of meaningful useful words; the development of independent reading aided by the use of phonic analysis and other word recognition techniques; the development of speedy, relaxed, silent reading for content and ideas. Through such a programme the child should grow into reading at his own rate.

The reading readiness programme

The pre-reading programme should not be regarded as a period of waiting for the child to reach a stage of mental maturity required for a successful start with reading but as a period of development in which the various aspects of readiness are encouraged and hastened. Since the majority of ESN children have been reared in unstimulating environments, the readiness programme must provide for a wide variety of experiences to make good deficiencies. These experiences must be so used as to encourage mental activity, language development, sensory activity and appropriate emotional and social responses. The main lines of approach will be:

(i) *To encourage intellectual activity*
The classroom should offer a plentiful supply of materials for group and individual play. Sand, water, paints, modelling materials such as plasticine and clay, tools, toys, house and doll play materials are needed to allow activities at different levels of maturity. Some children may still need play at a pre-school level; others may be capable of constructive and creative work nearer to their chronological age level. Opportunities should be provided for collecting, naming, labelling, arranging and classifying; for the making of picture books, scrapbooks, individual and group models; for story listening and telling, miming and dramatization. There should be trips and excursions as well as many things in the classroom which stimulate curiosity and discussion.

The aims of these activities are:

(*a*) An increase in knowledge and interests.

(*b*) A wider vocabulary and increased powers of expression.

(*c*) Improved work habits—a readiness to settle to difficult tasks and to persist.

(*d*) Improved social relationships—the sense of being 'at home' in a classroom which establishes the security and confidence needed as a basis for learning.

(ii) *To develop an interest in books and in reading*
For this purpose, the classroom should contain a good supply of picture books about a wide variety of interests. These should include books which are published as pre-readers as well as many books which are not specifically school books. If children are to appreciate

reading as something which is desirable and worthwhile, it is vital that they should begin to enjoy looking at attractive books and enjoy hearing stories read from them.

They should be encouraged to read labels, names and advertisements and to appreciate other uses of reading. As they make their own picture books, they can themselves use labels and captions. They can also be encouraged to learn new words in the classroom, such as those on weather charts, or labels and captions referring to pets or to the places where toys and materials are kept. Pictures they have painted can have sentences attached; birthdays can be recorded; models, nature specimens and collections can be labelled.

The aims of these activities are:

(a) To emphasize that reading has a purpose and is related to interests and activities.

(b) To promote perception and discrimination of letter and word forms.

(iii) *To develop the specific skills known to be essential in reading*

Many of the activities we have already mentioned, such as arranging, classifying, labelling and looking at pictures, will be promoting visual discrimination. Some other activities which develop visual perception are:

(a) Graded sets of jigsaw puzzles, i.e. starting with a few pieces and going on to those with twenty or more pieces as the children feel confident enough to do them. Certain reading schemes provide jigsaws related to the scheme.

(b) Drawing and tracing pictures, patterns and shapes.

(c) Matching games—matching colours, shapes and patterns. Later simple words and picture matching can be introduced.

(d) Putting a series of pictures in the right sequence.

Auditory discrimination and memory can be improved by emphasizing good articulation and attentive listening and by the use of rhymes, jingles, songs with repeated phrases or action sequences, word games, repeating rhythms and sounds and the carrying out of simple instructions and requests.

Motor development and co-ordination will be improved incidentally by many of the activities we have mentioned. Drawing, painting, modelling, and other art and craft activities are needed to develop hand-eye co-ordination. For encouraging left-to-right eye movements Marion Richardson writing patterns, or following picture sequences as in picture strips are useful. Provision for this type of activity is made in books of the *Getting Ready for Reading* (13) type.

(iv) *Personal and social development*

The whole atmosphere and activity of the junior class should be leading children to a stage at which they can apply their emotional energies to the task of learning. This is not achieved by coercion but by providing the experiences suited to their less mature stage of emotional and social growth. They need to feel that they belong to the class group, that they are approved of and accepted by the teacher. There must be opportunities for expression and successful achievement in many directions.

The acquisition of a sight vocabulary

There are divergent views on the methods to be used in the teaching of reading, and particularly in the initial stages. The method which is described below is one which has been arrived at through our experience with backward children and by a critical analysis of what the reading process involves and how it appears to develop. As we shall see later, the results achieved certainly suggest that the method has much to commend it.

In the early stages of the development of the method, and towards the end of the reading readiness programme, the children used to make their own books about topics which interested them. The teacher discussed each child's interest with him to ensure that he had sufficient knowledge to make a small book about it. If further knowledge appeared to be necessary, it was discovered by discussion, reference to pictures and models and, if possible, by direct experience such as a visit to a farm, a railway station. The teacher, or the child, made a book with pages of half imperial size sugar paper, interleaved with tracing paper. She then asked the child to tell her what he wanted to put in his book. Suitably modified to meet the demands of vocabulary control and the need for words of different shape to assist discrimination and memory, the child's sentence was printed in black crayon using letters about three-quarters of an inch in size. On the early pages, only one three- or four-word sentence was given per page, the number of sentences gradually increasing on later pages and in later books. Having made certain that the child could 'read' what she had written, the teacher asked him to draw or paint a suitable picture on the opposite page. The child was also taught to trace over the words with his finger or with crayon, at the same time saying the words. This process was repeated on succeeding pages, the tracing being dispensed with when the child was ready to do so. An important feature of the method was the fact that further practice was given with the words, the teacher making sentence and word cards for each child and encouraging the reading of these cards independently of the books. In this way, individual words were learned by sight to the point of immediate recognition. Each child also had a word ladder of his own sight vocabulary and later a word dictionary with a thumb alphabetic index.

This approach to the beginnings of reading, supplemented as it was with a variety of well-known word games and exercises, was quite successful with even low-grade ESN children. Reading did become an ego-involved activity, comprehension was assured from the beginning and classroom organization was helped by the variety of work involved, i.e., painting, modelling, writing, matching, etc. However, it involved an enormous amount of preparation on the teacher's part. Also, since we aimed at an initial sight vocabulary of 100–150 words, motivation was difficult to maintain, particularly with older children. Making books was quite exciting in the early stages but later the children began to feel that they were not really reading unless they could use published books. Using these too early upset the vocabulary control we knew to be necessary and did, in practice, lead to inefficient teaching and learning. We therefore decided to print in school some books based on the children's vocabulary and interests which would maintain a suitable increment of words for each book and control the amount of repetition.

To determine a meaningful vocabulary 300 of the children's individual books were analysed. From this analysis 125 words which occurred most commonly were selected as the basic sight vocabulary. Later a further 75 words were added in order that the sight vocabulary should be big enough to lead into phonics. These 75 words comprised a number of nouns useful for interest value, e.g. helicopter, rocket, and words selected from various word counts of children's vocabulary, e.g. Dolch (6), Dale (4), Burroughs (3). A series of twenty-one books was then written based on the 200 selected words. By compounding known words, e.g. sea and side to make seaside, and by adding common endings such as 's', 'ed', 'er' and 'ing', another 109 words were obtained. The original scheme was consequently modified and organized around the new books which were printed by the older boys in the school. All our non-readers, when ready, start systematic work by making their own reading books, but the first 15 words learned are those occurring in the first reader which is called *My House*. Thus when the child is given the printed book he is able to read it with a minimum of help from the teacher or other children. The vocabulary used is given below and the average repetition in the books is 109 for each word.

A Basic Sight Vocabulary

a	about	afraid	after	all	am	and
animal	are	as	ask	at	back	ball
be	bed	before	big	black	blue	boat

128

box	boy	Brenda	but	by	came	camp
can	car	caravan	Carol	cat	catch	cave
children	chimney	climb	clothes	cloud	come	could
cow	cross	dark	do	dog	doll	door
down	duck	elephant	fall	farm	fast	father
feed	field	find	fire	fish	flower	for
friend	frock	from	garden	get	girl	going
green	had	has	have	he	helicopter	help
her	here	him	his	holiday	horse	house
I	if	in	Indian	is	it	Jesus
jump	keep	let	light	like	lion	little
look	lost	make	man	map	Mary	me
men	mill	moon	money	monkey	mother	my
net	no	none	not	of	off	old
on	our	out	over	park	Peter	pilot
play	pool	pretty	put	red	Richard	ride
river	rock	rocket	roof	round	Ruff	run
said	sail	sand	saw	says	sea	seat
see	shall	she	sheep	ship	side	sit
sky	sleep	sun	stairs	stop	swim	swing
Tabby	some	tea	tell	tent	the	their
them	take	they	three	time	to	two
walk	there	was	water	wave	we	went
were	wall	wheel	where	white	will	window
with	wet	would	under	up	us	yellow
yes	wood	zoo				
	you					

Sentence and word cards, matching and word games are still used when necessary, but the grading of the books has reduced the need for their extensive use. They are used principally as a means of introducing new words to be encountered in the next book, and for consolidation of previous learning. Each child keeps an alphabetic list of his own sight words and a list of the books he has read.

Each book contains exercises and suggests activities designed to consolidate learning, to add meaning to what has been read, and to test comprehension. While the child is reading a book or doing exercises and activities in connection with it, he is preparing for the new vocabulary of the next book. This preparation consists, in the case of the early books, of making a book containing the new words, studying any difficult word by tracing it in sand, making it in Plasticine or writing it on the blackboard. With later books additional attention is given to arousing interest in new ideas to be introduced. For example, for the books dealing with holiday experiences, the children dramatize situations such as playing on the sands, fishing in pools, being rescued from dangerous situations, or going round a lighthouse. Pictures, films, film strips, actual outings, talks and discussions enrich the children's understanding of experiences to be used and ensure that the child's meaningful spoken vocabulary keeps abreast of his reading vocabulary.

This plan of making books based on the vocabulary used by the children seems the best answer to the perennial problem of finding a reading scheme suited to the early stages of reading with older ESN children. Many of the published schemes have too little consolidation of the recognition vocabulary at each level. Moreover, the usual reading schemes are mostly suited to the interests of younger children and few, if any, of the series for older backward children have a sufficiently gentle gradient of difficulty. There are many very useful series that can be used once a reading age of about seven has been achieved. The problem is to get the older backward reader to this stage, and the method outlined here is, we believe, the best type of solution.

However, some observations about reading schemes should be made.

(1) To give adequate practice at each level, a scheme should be selected that provides a great deal of supplementary reading material for each stage or main book.

(2) Additional reading material or apparatus can be made to supplement this.

(3) After the basic sight vocabulary has been acquired books from several schemes can be used to give adequate practice at each level. The differences in vocabulary are mainly in names and common nouns which usually cause less difficulty than the small words (here, there, is, was, he, your, go, play, etc.). The doctrine of vocabulary control is sometimes advanced as a reason for using one scheme throughout. But one can rarely get sufficient practice at each level from one scheme. Vocabulary control is, of course, important but there should also be variety and interest in the reading programme once a successful beginning has been made. Experience shows that schools which have a wide range of books and supplementaries available get good results.

(4) As far as possible in the early stages, children should learn as many as possible of the new words in a book before they start it, so that their progress through the book can be quick. Nothing is more demoralizing than to be on the same book for two or three terms.

Reference to studies of vocabulary

If books are specially written for the school or class, help in choosing the most useful vocabulary can be gained from some of the vocabulary studies which have been published. For example, Dolch (6) has presented a vocabulary of 220 simple words which occur most frequently. These words make up 50–70 per cent of most reading matter. Dolch (4) has also prepared a list of 1,000 most frequent words; Dale (4) a list of 769 easy words and Gates (11a) a list of 1,500 words. These sources should be consulted in deciding on a vocabulary to be used in the preparation of reading material for the use of backward readers, or in preparing other reading material such as reading games and exercises.

Many vocabulary lists have been prepared of the most frequent words in reading and writing but only a few lists of the frequency of words in children's speech. Burrough's study of the vocabulary of young children compares the words obtained in samples of the spoken expression of five- to six-and-a-half-year-old children with their occurrence on other word lists. There is, as far as we know, no comparable list of the speech vocabulary of ESN children.

The main value of such lists is that a knowledge of them provides an indication of the words of greatest frequency. These should form the highest proportion of words in reading and spelling. However, the fact that a particular word does not occur on the list does not mean that it should not be used. If it has high interest value or relates to the experience of the particular group of children it should obviously be included.

One outcome of studies of word frequency has been the attempt to find ways of assessing the difficulty of reading materials so that books can be graded. These attempts have been based on an examination of such factors as the average sentence length and the number of difficult words. A readability formula which is quite useful for assessing the difficulty of the language used in books for the early stages of reading is that of G. Spache (17). Several samples, 100 words in length, are taken at random through the book. The average sentence length of each sample is calculated; the number of words in the sample which do not occur on Dale's Easy Word List of 769 words is counted. From these figures an index of difficulty can be calculated. The results obtained need to be used with some caution, particularly on books for older readers. The formula tends to overvalue short sentence length as a factor in reading ease since it was derived from reading materials for children of 6–9 years where sentence length is carefully controlled. In materials for older readers it is the proportion of unfamiliar words rather than length of sentence which makes for difficulty. A formula such as this has many limitations but a quick check with it is one way of getting an impression of the vocabulary load of books.

The development of recognition skills

When the child's sight vocabulary has increased to about 100 words we encourage him to begin to make associations between frequently occurring letters and their most common sound. The alphabetic word-books help for this purpose. With some children these associations are not easily made and it is often better to wait for this stage of development to come naturally rather than risk the recrudescence of former feelings of frustration. Nevertheless, if progress is to be maintained, the child must eventually be able to perform this operation. The difficulties can usually be overcome by using the tracing-writing-saying technique regularly and systematically. It is surprising how often 'the penny seems to drop' after a period of failure and despair even in children in whom some perceptual difficulty is suspected. When the sight vocabulary is nearing the 200 mark, we prepare for the beginnings of systematic phonic work. The child's attention is drawn to words which have similar visual pattern and sound and to words which rhyme. For instance, when the child can read the word '*old*', and knows the letter sounds of *c, s, t, g* and *h*, he is asked to read *cold, sold, told, gold* and *hold*. He is asked to put letters in front of known words such as '*it*', '*at*', '*in*' to make new words which he writes and then reads to the teacher. When the child can experience a measure of success in this type of exercise, he is usually ready for the next stage in the reading programme.

Intelligent children if provided with opportunities for suitably graded, extensive individual reading require little help in the development of word recognition techniques. They are able to make their own associations and generalizations about words and apply them to the process of recognizing unfamiliar words. They are also able to use context clues to assist in the making of intelligent guesses at unknown words. Backward children are usually deficient in these abilities and require a systematic programme of word recognition exercises if reading progress is to be maintained. This programme must be viewed as an integral part of the overall plan for reading development. It should not be a rigid, isolated, elaborate course in phonic drills or word-form study but an interesting, integrated, controlled attack on the analysis and synthesis of sound units which will lead to continuing improvements in reading for content and ideas.

(A) The teaching of phonics

We have already stressed that readiness should be looked upon as important at all levels of learning. Readiness for learning word recognition techniques is no exception. Research results suggest that children are in general unable to profit adequately from phonic training until they have a mental age of seven. Arthur (1), for instance, in 1925, concluded that the teaching of phonics to children with a mental age of five and a half years was largely a waste of time; children with mental age from five-and-a-half to six years gained something from phonics, but the increased efficiency at mental age six-and-a-half to seven years was so great as to suggest that the mental age seven was the best. Dolch and Bloomster (7), Garrison and Heard (9) and Miles Tinker (18) agree that a mental age of seven is needed for the best results. Our observations with ESN children show that these conclusions do not apply in many cases. Some children with mental ages of nine or ten appear to be unable to tackle phonics while others with mental ages of five-and-a-half to six years can be surprisingly successful. With ESN children, there appears to be a higher correlation between phonic readiness and a mechanical reading age of seven. It was for this reason that in the books mentioned earlier the sight vocabulary was enlarged to result in a reading age of six-and-a-half to seven years before phonic work was started. However, teachers may not know a child's mental age or reading age and will need some practical way of assessing phonic readiness in the classroom. The following abilities, which can be observed or tested informally in the classroom, appear to be necessary before systematic phonic work is possible.

(i) To be able to give the more usual sounds for the common letters.

(ii) To discriminate between letter sounds. For example, in such exercises as the following:

(*a*) Which of these words is out of place? man, mill, met, cap (beginning sounds).

(*b*) Which of these words is out of place? cat, hat, foot, fire, hit (ending sounds).

(*c*) Listen to these words. Baby, boat, boy, box. Which of these do they start with, c, p, b, t?

(*d*) Tell me a word which begins with t (i.e. the letter sound as in the game 'I spy').

For these activities it is better to use words which are in the child's sight vocabulary, if possible.

(iii) To detect rhymes, e.g. to select the non-rhyming word in a set of rhyming words or to give a word, either spontaneously or from a given choice of words, which rhymes with another word or group of words.

(iv) To blend sounds, i.e. letters, phonograms or syllables. The child who is unable to put sounds of a simple word together is unlikely to make satisfactory phonic progress. Very often the backward reader is able to hear individual sounds but is unable to remember them in sequence and synthesize them into words. Where this deficiency in auditory memory and blending is particularly marked it is advisable to ensure that the child learns to blend sounds before he is presented with the visual symbols. The sounds used should be chosen from words he already knows. These same sounds can then be applied to unknown words which are meaningful. Sounding initial letters and left-to-right blending should be stressed from the beginning.

The development and use of phonic knowledge is a vital part of the reading programme and requires good systematic teaching. The following suggestions will help teachers to ensure that their teaching of phonics is reasonably sound and takes its proper place in the reading programme.

(*a*) New sounds should be introduced in words which are known by sight, or in words included in simple sentences which help the child to make intelligent guesses from context clues. From these words he should be encouraged to make a generalization about the phonogram's sound, e.g. from *man, cat, has,* infer the sound made by the middle letter. He should then be asked to apply this generalization to words which he cannot read but which can reasonably be expected to occur in his spoken vocabulary. Reference to vocabulary studies is useful in this context. This application should then be consolidated by a variety of interesting written exercises and oral practice. The following exercises are useful: putting words into sound families, e.g. finding words which belong to the same family; finding the 'stranger' in a list of words; putting in missing letters; choosing the right word, either for rhyming or comprehension; word squares; and putting jumbled words or phrases in the correct order to make a sentence.

(*b*) New learning should be integrated immediately into reading for meaning by using it in passages to be read and understood. In this way the usefulness of the new knowledge and skill is demonstrated to the child.

(*c*) Teach only those phonic elements which are likely to be most useful in maintaining reading progress and language development; for example, teach the phonic elements which will help the child to progress on the next book of a scheme.

(*d*) Any new words containing phonic elements which the child has not studied should normally be treated as sight words. Throughout, a balance should be maintained between a visual and auditory approach. Phonically irregular words should be introduced gradually.

(*e*) Avoid class teaching and cater for individual differences. Every child, competing against himself, should be allowed to go ahead at his own rate. The more efficient the teaching the bigger will be the spread of attainment.

(*f*) Avoid too many rules.

(*g*) Pay particular attention to clear articulation and correct pronunciation, but without over-emphasizing individual sounds to the detriment of good blending.

(*h*) Do not over-emphasize the teaching of phonics at the expense of other word recognition techniques, and of reading for meaning.

(*B*) *Structural Analysis*

The method of structural analysis is described in detail by W. S. Gray (14). It involves the identification of parts of unknown words which form meaning units. The child is encouraged to look for '*root*' words in inflected, derived or compounded words. For example, in inflected words using *s*, *ed*, *ing* and in derived words using *er*, *ly*, *ment*, *age*, *ful*, *ish*. It also involves the identification of *pronunciation* units, i.e. syllables such as *ight*, *tion*, *ous*, *ation*, *ection*, *ture*. Phonic and structural analysis used in conjunction are very useful in helping the child to develop his own rules for word attack and recognition. We have already seen how this combination can be used, even towards the end of the reading readiness stage. When the child can read '*call*', structural analysis will give *calls*, *calling*, *called* and *caller*. Phonic analysis will give *tall*, *ball*, *wall*, *fall*. A combination of the two gives *taller*, *tallest*, *walls*, *balls*, *halls*, *falling*, *falls*, *fallen*, and so on. A judicious application of these two techniques leads to a rapid expansion of both reading and spoken vocabulary and is a great help in overcoming blending difficulties.

Context clues. Even backward children derive considerable benefit in learning unknown words from the use of context clues and graded written exercises. With the former, teacher-made material is essential but wisely selected supplementary readers are also useful. With the latter, comprehension and multiple choice exercises are effective.

The development of rapid reading for comprehension.

Although for the sake of convenience we deal with this topic in a separate section of the reading programme, we would stress that reading for comprehension is an integral part of developmental reading *at all stages*. During the preliminary stage of building a sight vocabulary, the content must be restricted but ideas built around this content should, as we have pointed out, be expanded and enriched by discussion, direct experience and pictorial illustration. During this stage, when skill in word recognition is promoting growth in reading power, a wide variety of interesting, easy, attractively illustrated books is essential. The choice of books should cater for the children's individual interests and reading levels. Backward boys show particular preference for adventure, mystery, detective and travel stories. Backward girls seem to prefer adventure stories which centre round family situations, bible stories, fairy stories, and books about domestic animals. The provision of books about special interests and using a specialized vocabulary should not be forgotten. Children can often manage books which are a little too hard if they are really interested. In general, however, the range of difficulty should be such that each child has a choice of books which are just below his point of difficulty for word recognition. If this provision of books is to be satisfactory it is essential for teachers to acquaint themselves with children's books and to be able to estimate level of reading difficulty (see page 131). It is perhaps advisable also for one teacher in each school to become an expert in this field in order that book lists may be kept up-to-date and as comprehensive as conditions permit. The list of reading books in Appendix B may be useful to teachers. It is not a complete list and is only intended as a preliminary guide.

One of the aims of a reading programme is to ensure that word recognition, reading for comprehension and spoken vocabularies should develop eventually more or less at the same rate. With backward children, particular attention has to be paid to word meaning, comprehension and the development of ideas. It is important, therefore, to arrange for comprehension to be emphasized throughout. This can be done by judicious testing of understanding through oral and written exercises, discussing for content and richness of concept formation, paying particular attention to dictionary exercises and the giving of definitions, and encouraging children to ask questions and use suitably graded reference books. Such exercises as the following may be very useful: choosing antonyms and synonyms, following or completing directions, selecting phrases or sentences in answers to questions, rewriting a given passage in other words, selecting single words for given definitions and vice versa, changing tense, gender, number, comparative and superlative, classifying words according to the qualities, uses or actions they represent (e.g. groups such as things we wear, eat or drink; things in the home, country, or town; things which are alive, have been alive and are now dead, or have never been alive), sentence completion and story writing when certain significant words are given.

Writing plays an important part throughout the reading programme. It assists visual discrimination and memory and the association between visual and auditory patterns. It encourages the child to realize the relationship between reading and writing in communication. However, it is also of great use in expanding vocabulary and inculcating habits of clear and concise expression.

Spelling

We recommend that the beginning of the systematic teaching ot spelling should coincide with the teaching of word-recognition skills, i.e. phonic and structural analysis. There is little doubt that spelling weakness is a common complaint with backward children. The causes of this weakness may be many, but the principal one is inefficient teaching, e.g. too many words to be learnt at a time, too much attention to rules; insufficient attention to individualization or group work, which results in a failure to provide for the wide range of attainments and abilities in a class; not enough revision, particularly of words of persistent difficulty; lack of understanding on the teacher's part of what spelling involves and failure to give the child a definite technique for learning words.

The learning should make use of several modes of perceiving the word—visual, auditory, kinaesthetic (speaking and writing it) and should utilize the association with meaning. With children who have special difficulty, tracing the word with finger contact should also be used. The following suggested method has, in our experience, given the best results.

(*a*) The teacher prepares a set of graded assignments, each of not more than 15 words. The words of the set are selected because of their frequency in written usage and are arranged so as to coincide with the words used in word recognition, and to maintain a balance between phonically regular and irregular words. These assignments should make adequate provision for revision.

(*b*) The class is given a spelling test and from the results the children are grouped in pairs according to spelling attainment. Each pair is then given the most appropriate assignment for their level of attainment.

(*c*) Each child copies out the assignment ready for word-study with his partner. The learning process then adheres to the following pattern.

(i) The teacher ensures that the assignment has been copied correctly and that each child knows the words and pronounces them as correctly and distinctly as speech development will allow.

(ii) Each word is now studied. The child looks at the word, says it and tries to memorize its visual form. Without looking again at the word, he tries to write it and then checks his effort against the correct version. He repeats this procedure until his spelling is correct. When he and his partner have completed the assignment in this way, they test each other by writing the words when asked. Oral recall is not encouraged since spelling is needed principally for writing, and oral reproduction adds an unnecessary difficulty. Moreover, writing the word and saying it at the same time assists visual, auditory and kinaesthetic memory.

(iii) When the pair are satisfied with their results they are tested by the teacher.

(iv) When the teacher is also satisfied, she asks the children to write sentences which illustrate the meaning of the word, or to give orally such sentences, or to answer comprehension exercises based on the word meanings. When this is completed, the whole process is repeated with the next assignment.

This method assists reading progress, helps to ensure that spelling keeps abreast of reading, hastens language development and provides the child with a technique for tackling words which gives security and an awareness of progress. The following results, obtained by a class (average IQ 65) which used this method, demonstrate that spelling need not be markedly behind word recognition.

Spelling Attainments of a class of 13-year-old ESN children

Reading Test: Burt Accuracy Test.
Spelling Test: Burt Graded Spelling Test

R.A.	S.A.	R.A.	S.A.
8·2	8·9	9·8	9·8
9·7	9·2	8·0	8·1
8·3	8·5	9·5	9·3
12·6	11·6	10·2	8·5
8·9	9·5	8·0	8·0
12·1	9·8	8·6	8·3
11·6	9·4	9·5	8·9
8·7	9·4	7·2	7·3
12·6	9·5	8·0	8·2
8·8	8·6	9·0	8·3

The persistent non-reader

Most special schools have pupils who have failed to respond to the usual programme in reading. These may include children who are so limited in ability and so incapable of applying themselves to school work that the lack of progress is hardly surprising. An attempt can be made to equip them with at least a small sight vocabulary of useful words which they will meet after leaving school. There are other children whose attainment in mechanical arithmetic, practical subjects, and other aspects of school work show that they are not of very low intelligence and that their failure to read must be due to other causes. It is imperative to tackle this problem for two reasons:

(1) Failure in reading can reduce the child's chances of adjusting to post-school life by sapping his self-confidence and making him more liable to frustration and inappropriate behaviour.

(2) Continued failure in reading is often a symptom of inadequate personality development, and this in itself needs treatment.

These children need remedial teaching either in a small group or individually. This teaching should include:

(i) A thorough study of the causes of the failure.

(ii) The use of methods and techniques selected to suit the individual difficulties revealed by the study.

(iii) A more therapeutic approach than is usually possible in the classroom setting. The approach usually needs as much attention to psychological factors as to purely educational ones, but above all the teaching must inspire the non-reader to new efforts and increased confidence.

The causes of failure

It is tempting to suppose that there must be some specific disability causing the continued failure: a weakness in visual memory; poor visual or auditory discrimination: or as M. D. Vernon (19) has suggested 'some fundamental cognitive incapacity'. (A useful survey of the many possible causes of severe reading disability is given in *Backwardness in Reading*, M. D. Vernon.) Certainly backward readers show many faulty reading habits as well as negative attitudes resulting from their failure. Thus non-readers usually have no consistent way of tackling words. They omit letters, they reverse letters and words, they guess from slight resemblances to other words, their knowledge of letters and sounds is confused; they seem unable to retain what they have learned. These characteristics may be symptoms of disabilities which prevented them from learning in the first place, but they may also be symptoms of the child's present uncertainty about how to tackle words and of his extreme lack of confidence or his avoidance of reading.

The causes of failure are usually cumulative. There was probably a premature start on reading or phonic work before the child was ready; emotional and personality difficulties might have interfered with learning. As soon as the child lagged behind, teachers, parents and the child himself might have become anxious. A succession of teachers probably tried different approaches and with each failure the child lost confidence still more, until finally he tackles reading with very low morale; or he avoids it. He cannot concentrate; he gives up. It is often this emotional situation which has to be tackled first as the following case illustrates.

Walter was admitted to an ESN school when he was fourteen years old with virtually no attainments in reading. He was listless and thoroughly depressed. For a term, he remained uninterested in school work and was often found roaming aimlessly round the school. His only interest seemed to be in pets and birds. At the beginning of his second term individual remedial teaching was started. He attended most unwillingly at first but his attitudes improved when he realized that his early sessions appeared to have no connection with reading. He talked to the teacher, spoke into the tape recorder and painted animals and birds. Towards the end of this term an attempt was made to start building up a sight vocabulary of words connected with his interest in birds and pets. This and several later attempts failed. His half-hearted efforts were usually accompanied by excessive sweating, blushing and disturbing shakings and involuntary movements. On one occasion he was given tests to discover any disabilities in visual perception and discrimination. He showed no signs of difficulty with shapes and patterns but when letters were introduced he flatly refused to co-operate. Anything which reminded him of his feelings of hope-lessness about reading was anathema to him. Nevertheless we felt sure that he was capable of reading. A successful beginning was not achieved until he was in his penultimate term at school. It took eighteen months of patient work to re-establish his confidence and induce him to tackle his difficulties.

The approach to the backward reader

Considerable ingenuity is needed to devise a stimulating fresh approach, and to overcome the unfavourable attitudes of the back-ward reader. In addition, the teacher needs to be observant of actual reading difficulties which need special remedies.

The improvement of attitudes. If the child is over-anxious about reading, one step in remedial work should be to reduce anxiety by giving continual encouragement, and by creating some initial success. A 'don't care' attitude often conceals an underlying desire to read and will often change gradually as some success is experienced. In another child a 'don't care' attitude can be a sign that the child has given up and begun to accept his failure. Such a child will be difficult to motivate unless he can be convinced that reading will be of prac-tical value to him when he leaves school, or of value in connection with some other interest.

Most very backward readers have more latent knowledge of words than would appear at first sight, and this can sometimes be used to start them on some simple reading material specially prepared for them.

The crux of the matter is motivation. The older non-reader needs to be persuaded that reading is interesting, that it can be useful to him and that he can master it. To do this there has to be a judicious combination of interesting work with a well-planned programme which starts from the point the child has reached in reading and takes him through the stages described earlier in this chapter—

establishing a sight vocabulary, developing recognition skills and techniques for quicker reading.

In the final analysis, motivation depends to a large extent on the relationship between the teacher and the non-reader. Knowledge of the child's special difficulties or of the most suitable books and methods can be less important than the stimulating, encouraging and optimistic attitude of the teacher. We said earlier that it is important in the normal reading programme; it is even more important in remedial reading.

Patience and understanding are essential because progress may be very slow or variable. Attitudes resulting from years of failure cannot be changed quickly.

Reading methods

Remedial teaching must take into account the weaknesses noticed in the child's attempts at reading. Thus, some children have got into the habit of trying to read words letter by letter, sound by sound and lack the confidence to try to read words as wholes. These children need to be encouraged in quick recognition of words by means of flash cards and similar devices using a look-and-say approach. Other children read carelessly, guessing from slight clues. These need to scrutinize words more carefully, and the Fernald (8) kinaesthetic or a phonic method might be considered for them. Others seem never to use the context clues or pictures to help them recall words and they can be helped to use such aids. (See Diagnostic tests, p. 248.)

The type of approach which the child has had previously should be taken into account. During years of failure in reading, 'everything' will have been tried. It is important, therefore, at least in the early stages, to avoid materials and methods which have been used unsuccessfully before. A fresh approach is needed.

An attempt should be made to discover what books have been used before and to find something different. It is often a good plan to avoid published books for a while and to make some special reading material, or to use the technique described earlier in which the child makes up his own book about something that really interests him. Often, of course, the child has no interests which can be utilized and an interest has to be created—for example, by taking him on a visit.

A fresh approach can also be made through a different method of learning to read. For example, the older backward reader has usually been 'barking at print' for several years. Methods using silent reading or writing can be a refreshing change. Silent reading can be brought in by preparing work sheets giving instructions to draw or make;

or by giving activities similar to those in published workbooks but preparing for the vocabulary of the simple reader that the teacher has in view. The Non-Oral method of McDade (15) suggests a type of approach which might be experimented with, especially with children who are held back by speech defect. It was used at one time in Chicago schools and has been reported upon by Buswell (2). Children did not learn to read orally at first, although they were well-prepared by talking about what they were going to read. Words were matched with pictures, objects and actions. Phrases and sentences related to the child's activities were read silently, emphasis being placed upon meaning and using the context. Something similar can be used with backward readers. Apart from matching words to pictures and objects, they can respond to flashcard instructions to perform certain actions. Written instructions can be given to place small detail pictures on a larger picture or flannelgraph. Backward readers have enjoyed the novelty of this approach and while it is not a method which can be continued for long, it does help to make a 'different' approach in the early stages.

Another method which the child may not have met is the Fernald Kinaesthetic Method (8). The essence of this method is the use of kinaesthetic memories, i.e. of the movements of tracing and writing words. The word is learnt by tracing over it with the finger or a pencil, writing it from memory (not from copy) and is finally written into the child's alphabetic word book. It can be used in connection with writing the captions for the child's own reading book (see page 127). or for writing a diary entry, story or letter. In this way the child acquires a basic vocabulary of words which he knows with confidence. It is a slow process in the early stages but can be useful in re-establishing confidence, especially with children who cannot retain words by visual memory. Although the rationale of the method is that it uses kinaesthetic memories, its success is partly due to the fact that it makes children scrutinize words carefully. This, of course, is what many very backward readers do not do.

The best remedy is *success*, if this can be engineered. If the backward reader can be taken on to some easy but interesting stories, even though he needs much help and prompting, he is more likely to feel that he is really reading. When this happens, it is often surprising how well some of the longer and more difficult words are remembered even though the small words continue to cause difficulties.

Sooner or later the very backward reader needs special attention to acquiring the technique of unlocking new words. Most of them are very confused in their knowledge of sounds and the approaches described earlier indicate the best methods of dealing with this.

Written English

We stressed in Chapter VI that the main aim of English is the achievement of as great a facility as possible in spoken expression since this is a skill which children will need every day in life after school. The main aim of written English with ESN children is similarly a practical one—the ability to write a letter for ordinary purposes. Although the aim is a limited one, this does not mean that work in written English must be narrow and strictly utilitarian. Indeed the more practice children have of writing in various ways in schools (diaries, stories, and accounts of things they have done), the more secure their writing skill is likely to be, and the greater confidence they will have.

It is important that this main aim of helping children to acquire the difficult skill of putting ideas down on paper should be kept to the fore and the subsidiary uses of writing not become ends in themselves. These subsidiary uses of writing are (*a*) writing words as an aid to word recognition, (*b*) written work as a means of checking reading for comprehension, (*c*) written exercises in connection with word study or spelling. These have a place but must not (as they sometimes are allowed to do) take up time and effort that could more profitably be devoted to oral and written expression. Children learn to express themselves by writing not by completing workbook exercises, inserting words to complete sentences or writing answers to questions read. These do, of course, practise some of the skills such as handwriting and vocabulary which are needed in learning to express ideas in writing, but there is less transfer to written expression than is usually assumed. Such work does not tackle the main problems in written expression which all children, and especially backward children have to face.

The first problem is that of knowing how to put words together to express ideas. This ability must be achieved first in speech; hence the importance that we have attached to spoken English. The second problem is having something to say. Written work should be about something that the child has done or seen, or for a purpose which he understands. As in oral work, children need experiences which can serve as a basis for expression. Apart from special experiences such as visits, ordinary everyday events will have to be drawn upon to a great extent. Some preliminary talk about them will be useful, for example, in connection with writing a daily diary. Informal talk will elicit some of the events and experiences which the children would like to write about and their expression can be helped by introducing some of the words and phrases that can be used. It is a well-established practice for written work to be preceded by preparation in which words and ideas are suggested by the class and noted on the board. This practice is sound so long as it does not mean that children are always being spoon-fed. The aim should be to develop gradually the ability to write independently so that they will be sufficiently competent when they leave school.

One class of senior ESN children whose attainments in written English were very poor, benefited from writing a class diary. The events of the week were discussed and the sentences suggested by the class were written up on the board with any modifications which the class agreed were needed. Finally, the weekly entry was written in the children's diaries. This method had the advantage that the children were getting practice in thinking what to say and how to say it. It also produced a piece of work which was well written and helped to raise their own standards. It was not the only type of written work which the class did during the week and was conceived as a step towards better individual written work. The practice of copying from the board is not to be recommended in general. There are too many backward readers who have to copy passages from the board which they cannot read and which have no personal significance for them. In this particular case the boys knew what they were writing and care was taken to see that each boy could read back what he had written.

The problem of finding what to say is not always solved by making extensive use of pictures in written work. Writing about a picture can easily become a brief list of things without interpreting or describing the picture as a whole. Much will depend on whether the picture is about something children know and understand and about which they feel keen and interested. It is preferable to use pictures which relate to recent experiences of the children rather than ones which may have little significance for them.

The problem of written expression is not only a matter of knowing what to say but of having an urge to say it. Writing is a labour to most people. How much more so for children who have difficulty in using the tools of writing, have difficulty with spelling and other techniques, and have generally little confidence in their ability to write. The average child can produce a tolerable piece of written work when it is expected but with the backward child we need to ensure at all times the maximum motivation for writing. This will depend on the pupils' interests and the types of activity going on in the class. The most effective writing will occur if the pupil feels a need for or realizes the purpose of writing. Writing something for a wall newspaper may appeal to one; keeping a record of what has been grown in the school garden may appeal to another; preparing something in writing which is later to be read into the tape recorder may suit another. It may be possible to stimulate the desire to write

144

through puppetry and drama (although one has to be careful not to spoil the drama by the intrusion of writing). In some cases, writing may come through the preparation of simple topic books.

Writing letters is perhaps the most effective way of giving real purpose to writing. In the residential school, there is the ready-made need to write home. In day schools, letter writing should not become a series of artificial exercises. Real occasions for writing letters should be sought and used wherever possible: for example, writing to a pupil who is in hospital, to a teacher who has left; to firms for materials and information, and invitations to a school event. Writing letters to another school often works well, although one cannot expect such an activity to maintain its interest over a long period. In younger classes, letters can be written to each other, posted in the class postbox and delivered by the class postman.

Free writing of stories, accounts of real or imaginary experiences, descriptions of things, scenes and events should be used from as early a stage as possible. In this the child should be encouraged to write with confidence and without fear of ridicule and excessive correction. The child's early efforts in creative writing may be extremely brief, but with patience, encouragement, aroused interest and feeling, judicious help and praise, more and more will be produced. In many schools, where free writing has been practised in conjunction with other forms of creative work, ESN children have exceeded all expectations in the length, content, variety and correctness of their written expression.

The correction of written work

Marking should be positive and selective. It should not discourage children who in any case may not be keen about writing and for whom there are so many difficulties in writing. Only those mistakes should be corrected which the child at his level of development can reasonably be expected to correct. Just as we would avoid continually correcting children's spoken expression lest we make them diffident about talking in class, so in written work we should be selective, choosing a few errors for correction. Marking should be thought of as something that encourages and helps them—not as a punitive measure for poor work.

As in oral expression, stress should not be placed on correctness of usage so much as upon finding something to say and saying it clearly. Interesting, adequate expression is more important than accuracy, although a balance between the two should be aimed at. We cannot expect in written work a standard of English much above that used in speech. When the backward child writes, he is talking rather than writing.

READING, SPELLING AND WRITTEN EXPRESSION

In the correction of spelling mistakes, we must distinguish between those words which the child should know (because he has learned them in his spelling assignments or used them in his reading books or because they are among the common words frequently needed in writing) from those which he is not likely to use much or which are beyond the stage he has reached in spelling instruction. If, however, we are dealing with one of those children who writes lines of nonsense words which only he can read back, we need to make a fresh start with him—simple writing of sentences probably in connection with his reading. Systematic work in spelling and a technique of learning words would be important in doing so.

Observation of children's oral expression shows that they have little idea of how to break up speech into units of thought and meaning. Until there is more evidence of pattern in speech, it is rather futile to have too high expectations for punctuation in written work. One useful technique however is to get children to read some of their written work aloud so that they can learn to sense where there should be a full stop and capital letter.

REFERENCES

1. ARTHUR in SMITH, B., ' What research says about phonics instruction.' J.Ed. Res., 51, Sept. 1957.
2. BUSWELL, G. T. Non-oral reading: a study of its uses in the Chicago Public Schools. Supp. Educ. Monog. No. 60, Univ. of Chicago Press, 1945.
3. BURROUGHS, G. E. R. A study of the vocabulary of young children. Oliver and Boyd, 1954.
4. DOLCH, E. W. Problems in Reading. Garrard, 1948.
5. DOLCH, E. W. Psychology and Teaching of Reading. Garrard, 1951
6. DOLCH, E. W. A Manual for Remedial Reading. Garrard, 1945.
7. DOLCH, E. W. and BLOOMSTER, M. Phonic Readiness. Elem. School Journal, Vol. 38, 1937.
8. FERNALD, G. Remedial Techniques in the Basic School Subjects. World Book Co., 1943.
9. GARRISON, S. C. and HEARD, N. T. An experimental study of the value of phonetics. Peabody J. of Ed., Vol. 9, 1931.
10. GATES, A. I. Reading Readiness Tests. Bureau of Publications, Teachers College. Columbia Univ.
11. GATES, A. I. The Improvement of Reading. Macmillan, 1935.
12. GATES, A. I. A reading vocabulary for the Primary Grades. Teachers College, Columbia Univ., 1935.
13. GRASSAM, Getting Ready for Reading. Ginn.
14. GRAY, W. S. On their own in reading. Ginn, 1948
15. MCDADE, J. E. Essentials in Non-oral Reading. Scott, Foresman and Co., 1941.
16. MONROE, M. Reading Aptitude Tests. Houghton Mifflin.
17. SPACHE, G. A new readability formula for primary grade materials. Elem. School Journal. LIII, No. 7, March 1953.

18. TINKER, MILES. *Teaching Elementary Reading.* Appleton-Century-Crofts, 1952.
19. VERNON, M. D. *Backwardness in Reading.* Cambridge Univ. Press, 1957.

FURTHER READING

ANDERSON, I. H. and DEARBORN, W. F. *The Psychology of Teaching Reading.* The Ronald Press, 1952.

BRISTOL UNIVERSITY INSTITUTE OF EDUCATION. *Survey of Books for Backward Readers.* U.L.P. 1957.

BRISTOL UNIVERSITY INSTITUTE OF EDUCATION (ed. T. PASCOE). *A Second Survey of Books for Backward Readers.* U.L.P., 1962.

CARLSON, B. W. and GINGLAND. O.R. *Play Activities for Retarded Children.* Cassell, 1962.

DALE, E. (ed.). *Readability.* (Five articles from Elementary English, Jan. to May, 1949.)

KEIR, G. *Teachers Companion to Adventures in Reading.* O.U.P., 1951

KIRK, S. A. *Teaching Reading to Slow-learning Children.* Houghton Mifflin, 1940.

HARRIS, A. J. *How to Increase Reading Ability.* Longmans, 1947.

MONROE, M. *Children Who Cannot Read.* Univ. Chicago Press, 1932.

RUSSELL and KARP. *Reading Aids through the Grades.* Bureau of Publications, Teachers College, Columbia Univ., New York.

SCHONELL, F. J. *Psychology and Teaching of Reading.* Oliver and Boyd, 1945.

SCOTTISH COUNCIL FOR RESEARCH IN EDUCATION. *Studies in Reading, Vol. 1 and 2.* U.L.P., 1949.

STONE, C. R. *Progress in Primary Reading.* Webster, 1950.

WITTY, P. *Reading in Modern Education.* Heath, 1949.

VIII

THE TEACHING OF NUMBER

WHEN she entered school Laura had a mechanical reading age of ten years which was equal to her chronological age. She was obviously quite proud of her attainments in the basic subjects and remarked, 'I know my tables.' Thereupon she recited her two times table ending with 'Twelve twos are twenty-four, twenty-four pence are two shillings.' She also 'knew' her ten times table and ended with 'Twelve tens are a hundred and twenty, a hundred and twenty pence equal ten shillings.' She was then asked, 'How many pennies make a shilling?' and replied without hesitation, 'Four.' She was unable to do the simplest calculation even with concrete aids. This is probably an extreme case but there are many children whose knowledge of number consist of facts learned by rote and others who can work quite difficult sums on paper without being able to apply even simple processes to real life number situations.

We believe that most experienced teachers of ESN children feel fairly happy about the methods of teaching reading but are not so sure of the best way of going about the teaching of arithmetic. Recent developments in the theory and practice of number teaching, notably the discoveries of Piaget, provide the basis for re-thinking the approach to the teaching of number with ESN children. This chapter shows how these new ideas can be incorporated into a number scheme.

What is number? Number is concerned with the quantitative relationships within and between groups, and the number system is designed to help us put order into the numerical situations we meet in our everyday environment. Arithmetic is a way of thinking about and using number. Arithmetic teaching is therefore concerned with the application of the number system to the arrangement, manipulation and measurement of quantities and the development of the ability to deal with number relationships symbolically and by abstraction, i.e. in the absence of concrete objects.

Certain principles are fundamental to number teaching. These are:

(1) It is necessary to understand how the child's ideas of quantity develop and to study the stages in the process. For instance, when can we expect a child to have developed an understanding of simple groupings, such as those up to 10, so that he is ready to pass on to more complex groupings needed for an understanding of the decimal nature of the number system? An appreciation of the importance of number readiness is fundamental to sound arithmetic teaching. The work of Piaget and his disciples is of supreme importance in this connection. Reference will be made later to the implications of his findings, particularly in connection with the early stages in the ESN child's development of number concepts.

(2) Arithmetic teaching must be so devised as to make apparent to the child from the beginning the importance of number relationships. This pre-supposes an awareness on the teacher's part of the importance of equipping the child with an adequate meaningful number vocabulary with which to express and encourage the development of numerical ideas (see page 154). It also emphasizes the close consideration which must be given to the teaching materials used. It is not sufficient to surround the child with varied attractive objects to count and arrange, with shops, post offices and the like. Number relationships are not necessarily learned from number situations posed in a social setting. Yet it is an appreciation of these relationships which is essential for the successful application of number to social situations. We do not wish to detract, however, from the desirability of providing, as soon as children have begun to acquire simple concepts, many challenging practical experiences, since these do give ample opportunities, with wise teacher direction, for the expression and use of quantitative relationships.

(3) The teacher must understand the decimal nature of the number system and the inter-relatedness of processes. Teaching must be so systematic and graded that the child also becomes more and more aware of what the number system is and how it can help in ordering the quantitative aspects of his environment. An understanding by the child of the number system and number operations is essential if meaningful learning is to be achieved.

Other important factors in teaching number to ESNs

We have previously discussed the problem of individual differences in ESN children. In any ESN group there will be wide variations in arithmetical abilities. Nevertheless there are some generalizations which can be made.

(*a*) ESN children are slow to see relationships, particularly when these are expressed in symbolic rather than concrete ways. Furthermore, they have the additional difficulty in making the transfer of knowledge to practical situations in money, time, measurement. For this reason they have a tendency to use fingers and counters as props for a long time and lack the confidence, even when they are ready, to dispense with them.

(b) The majority of ESN children come from environments which are not likely to offer them the opportunities of assimilating the elementary ideas of number which much younger children from better homes acquire even in their pre-school years. Children coming from better-class homes have, on the average, a much larger store of number ideas and experiences than those from poorer areas. This means, therefore, that children coming from homes devoid of stimulation start school with disadvantages. If these are exacerbated by dullness, as with ESN children, the early school experiences in number are unlikely to be interesting and exciting unless the school is capable of individualizing treatment from the outset. This is rarely found because schools are often quite unaware of the basic principles of number readiness and are therefore too prone to start normal teaching too early. It is sometimes neglected because of school conditions, though seldom can these be an acceptable rationalization for inefficient teaching.

The backwardness of the child coming from a bad home and further handicapped by intellectual retardation is thus likely to become cumulative. He lags increasingly behind his peers and becomes a more difficult teaching problem as time goes on. His attitudes to number lessons become antagonistic or apathetic; his work habits deteriorate, and in many cases emotional 'blocking' results. He becomes conditioned to the fact that he cannot keep up and teachers regard him as a 'case'. At this stage he is either neglected because his teacher (and he may have had several teachers by now) is unable to find time to help him, or he becomes the subject of teaching by expedients. His real needs in number work are not understood; he has a watered-down version of what the rest of his class are doing, is left to amuse himself with games, sticks, counters and the like, or to help in the class shop or post-office. He is 'drilled' and 'talked at'. He suffers from a common failing of the teaching of backward children—over-explanation.

In planning the arithmetic curriculum and in selecting teaching methods for ESN and other backward children, we must take into account the preceding generalizations. Our experiences with many sub-normal children suggest that the following principles are also of vital importance (some of them are, of course, equally applicable to all children):

(a) The substance and method of our teaching must be related to the child's individual psychological, educational and social needs. Methods should be selected so as to capitalize on abilities and minimize or correct weaknesses.

(*b*) What we teach must be meaningful and purposeful and, thereby, interesting to the child. Good arithmetic teaching needs no extraneous 'tricks' to make it vital—it is self-motivating.

(*c*) Our methods must be concerned with developing insights into the nature of the number system and how it is used in the study of the organization and arrangement of number groups, i.e. quantitative relationships. The majority of ESN children are capable of understanding and applying sufficient of the simpler of these relationships to deal eventually with the necessary arithmetical situations they are likely to meet in post-school life.

(*d*) Informal diagnosis followed by appropriate treatment is a *sine qua non* of good arithmetic teaching. This is particularly important in the emotional field since progress will be impossible until earlier bad attitudes and lack of confidence have been replaced by feelings of success, interest and enthusiasm.

What should we teach?

The majority of ESN children can be equipped with sufficient arithmetical knowledge to be able to cope with the arithmetic they are likely to need after leaving school. Research has shown that the arithmetic needed in adult life is not extensive and that nearly all the numerical problems which adults have to tackle are concerned with money and time. Our curriculum for ESN children must therefore concentrate on these and be strictly utilitarian. It must not be a watered-down version of the curriculum used with normal children. It should be specially designed both in content and arrangement to meet the children's needs, and our teaching methods should be so devised that it can be taught with understanding and continuing success. The following curriculum has been shown to be very satisfactory.

A. The Essential Minimum
Section 1 (*a*) Notation and Recognition of numbers to 20.
          (*b*) Number facts to 12 ($+$, $-$, $\times$).
          (*c*) Money to 1/– including 6d and 3d.
          (*d*) Telling time to hours.
Section 2 (*a*) Notation and Recognition to 100.
          (*b*) Number facts to 20 ($+$, $-$, $\times$).
          (*c*) Money to 2/6 including 2/– and $\frac{1}{2}$d.
              Making up an amount from various coins.

(*d*) Telling time to nearest 5 minutes.

Section 3 (*a*) Money to £1.

(*b*) Telling time to minutes.

B. *Additional desirable content*

Section 4 (*a*) Number facts to 100—mechanical and problem.

(*b*) Money to £10. Wages, deductions, personal and family budgeting.

(*c*) Time in social situations, e.g. at work, in travel, and leisure; estimation of time.

(*d*) Linear measure. Yds, ft, and ins, to ½ins applied to home, garden and hobbies.

(*e*) Weight. Pounds and ounces related to shopping, gardening and cooking.

(*f*) Capacity. Pints and gallons related to week's supply and cooking.

Section 5 (*a*) Number facts to 1,000 excluding compound multiplication and long division.

(*b*) Weight. Tons and Cwts—coal supply.

(*c*) Linear measure to $\frac{1}{16}$in.

(*d*) Simple banking, hire purchase and use of Postal Orders.

(*e*) Simple graphs and their interpretation.

The Importance of Number Readiness

Most teachers are agreed that formal teaching of the basic subjects should not be attempted until the child is psychologically ready. However, whilst educational literature contains many references to reading readiness little has been said about readiness for number. The recent work of Piaget (2) on the way a child's concept of number develops has important implications for the beginnings of number work. He demonstrated by developmental studies that each child in acquiring number ideas passes through a series of stages the sequence of which is always the same although the length of time taken for each stage differs from child to child. He postulated three stages which he described as *pre-operational*, *intuitive* and *operational*. In the first stage the child is unable to appreciate the simplest of quantitative relationships and uses crude perceptual approximation in making judgments. He has no idea of what Piaget calls '*conservation*' or the invariability of a quantity. For example, even though he can count by rote in correct sequence he is unable to appreciate that, say, six balls close together are equal to six balls spaced out, although, by simple comparison, he has previously realized that the groups are identical. He does not see that six balls remain six balls irrespective of their arrangement. He is perceptually deceived and not yet able to analyse logically his numerical experiences. He has little idea of number.

In the second stage, the child is able to appreciate conservation but is still not able to rationalize what he thinks is right with what he actually sees. He is still groping to equate what he suspects is intellectually acceptable with the apparent inconsistency of his perceptions. For example, he now says that six balls are six balls whether close together or separated in groups but he still tends to believe that six balls spaced out are more than six balls close together. When questioned he will give the right answers, or answers which suggest correct assumptions, but he is unable to give acceptable explanations. Piaget calls this the 'intuitive stage'.

In the third stage the child is able to assume constancy however the material is arranged, and to give satisfactory explanations. He now understands what is meant by a quantity and its measurement in units. His thinking is sufficiently flexible for him to appreciate different arrangements of elements within a given group and the inter-relatedness of arithmetical processes. For instance, he realizes the complementary nature of number combinations; he understands that if $3+2=5$ then $2+3=5$, $5-2=3$ and $5-3=2$. In short, he is intellectually ready to begin to study logical number with real understanding.

Piaget and his collaborators explored other areas of the child's thinking in relation to number, e.g. cardinal and ordinal aspects and the relationship between these; the ability to make a series and relate it to other series, and to classify. We cannot discuss these other areas in the present book, but all teachers of young and subnormal children should study Piaget's work in some detail. We have mentioned the experiments on conservation because we feel they are the most important. Our experiences suggest that children who are not at the 'operational' stage in this are not ready for *formal* number work. They cannot take for granted that a given quantity has a nature all of its own, that no matter how we rearrange its constituent elements it nevertheless remains the same quantity. It is, of course, true that many children not at the operational level are able to count with one-to-one correspondence, and to carry out simple numerical operations even in the abstract. However, these operations are not based on real understanding—they are more the result of memorizing than true learning. They are mental habits rather than mental operations. The child is not capable of reversible thinking, e.g. the child may know that $5+4$ make 9 but he is unable to manipulate this piece of information to discover that, in consequence, $4+5$ also make 9. In studying the development of ESN children through these stages, we have found that children who are fully aware of conservation are capable of reversible thinking—the quantitative relationships within groups and the complementary nature of numerical processes are understood.

If, as we believe, the growth of number readiness follows the pattern so strikingly demonstrated by Piaget, is there anything teachers can do to foster it, or is it purely a matter of maturation? If there is a definite pattern in the development of these concepts, can the teacher so arrange her teaching and provide such experiences that the emergence of these concepts can be hastened?

The development of number readiness is obviously related to maturation but our work with ESN children convinces us that, because of their lack of adequate pre-number experiences, the stages of readiness can be hastened. The principles upon which the readiness programme is based are as follows:

(1) We must understand how number concepts are developed and, by observing the child's reactions, appreciate how to prepare him for the next stage.

(2) We must provide experiences which will help the child at his level of development to develop ideas of quantity and to appreciate relationships by experiment, estimation and checking.

(3) We must equip the child with the vocabulary of number so that he can express his ideas and use language to fix, integrate and expand them.

He must be taught the meanings of *more, same* and *less, long* and *short, heavy* and *light, fast* and *slow, high* and *low, first* and *last, beginning, middle* and *end, before, after* and *next*. This can be done by experiment and discussion (it will be a part of number lessons for several years). Ideas of *sameness* and *more* are appreciated before the meaning of *less*; *longer* is understood before *shorter*, *first* and *middle* before *last*. It is also important to develop flexible thinking in the use of these comparative terms. For instance, the children should be encouraged to do exercises such as the following:

> Find the longest stick for the tallest child.
> Put the heavy weight by the middle boy.
> Put the smallest book on the highest shelf.
> Find two sticks which are the same and fit them next to the longest stick, etc., etc.

In the junior ESN school teachers should stress these aspects of number readiness with the majority of their pupils. Whenever a suitable opportunity arises to point out the use of language in defining relationships in groups, mass, length, space or time the wise teacher will make use of it. Children should be encouraged to talk about and discuss their developing number ideas as they arise. Many opportunities will occur in free play and craft lessons. If we choose simple materials for use in a readiness programme, we can manipulate them so as to encourage the type of thinking we know is necessary for the development of number concepts. The correct patterns of thought do not ensue, with backward and ESN children particularly, from surrounding the child with things to count, measure and weigh or from providing a wide variety of presentations of number in social situations. Indeed such practices might well lead to faulty thinking and confusion. What is needed is a definite programme of exercises and experiences, posed in play situations when possible, which is so designed and presented that it predisposes the children to make judgments at their levels of development. The making of judgments will be encouraged by situations and problems which call for a preliminary rough estimation followed by confirmatory activity.

The following exercises have been found to be of particular value in the development of number readiness.

Exercises emphasizing constancy or conservation of quantities[1]

Materials used include wet sand, clay, plasticine, containers of various sizes, wooden rods and blocks, cardboard strips, home-made weights and scales.

(1) To get a rough indication of the children's level of development make two identical mounds of sand (e.g. sand pies). If the children agree that the mounds are the same, change the shape of one and ask if the two quantities of sand are still the same. Now ask individual children the reasons for their answers and discuss them. The way in which the shape is changed can be varied to increase or decrease the difficulty of the exercise, e.g. the mound can be knocked over, spread out evenly, re-formed into one shape or a number of shapes.

(2) Let the children work in pairs. One of the pair takes a handful or any rough measure of sand. The second child is asked to take the *same* amount. The two children then check as follows:

(*a*) by weighing on opposite sides of scales.

(*b*) by weighing both amounts separately using unit weights and pairing the two lines of piles of sand.

(*c*) by making paired lines of sand pies using a plastic egg-cup.

---

[1] We are indebted to Mr. A. A. Williams, Deputy Head Teacher, St Francis Residential School, Birmingham, for his contribution to this Number Readiness programme.

In making their comparisons the children may need to be reminded of the purpose of their activity since they tend to forget this in the excitement of the play situations. It is often desirable to let two children do these exercises watched by others. The spectators derive considerable benefit from the mental activity stimulated by the physical activity of the two children doing the exercise. Indeed we have had many examples of the spectators developing much more awareness of the purpose of an exercise than the doers. In organizing lessons teachers should make use of this and remember that activity can be physical or mental or both. Watching others work has its usefulness!

Large cards or plywood boards marked as indicated below are useful for 'pairing exercises'.

....	sand			sand
....	sand			sand

The children assume 'sameness' when two lines are identical. Where inequality exists younger or duller children should be asked which of the pair has *the more sand*, the term *less* being introduced later. When (*b*) or (*c*) result in equal lines or piles one line can be altered, i.e. spread out or concentrated, and a test for constancy made.

In making their comparisons the children may use counting, but it is not suggested by the teacher at this stage.

Exercises designed to develop cardinal relationships (i.e. for comparing size of groups)

(1) Using counters, shells, or beads (what Piaget calls discontinuous quantities) the child is again asked to take what he considers to be, by rough estimation, the same number as his partner. The children then check by pairing. The child with more is then asked to make his group the same as his partner's. Again tests for the assumption of constancy should be made, e.g. one group can be spread out more than the other and the child is asked whether the two groups are still the same.

(2) Using cards with dots placed in a random fashion, three or more for each number from 3 to 9, the children play the following games:

(*a*) Finding 'pairs' from jumbled cards.

(*b*) Starting with a hand of five cards children compete to find five matching cards from the pack.

(*c*) Teacher makes a pattern with counters, etc., and children seek cards with the same pattern.

Variations of these games suggest themselves. We recommend, however, that at least in the early stages of development counting of dots should not be encouraged. We want children to acquire the ability to estimate since estimation will be important throughout number work. However, later on, when counting with one-to-one correspondence has become operational, cardinal exercises in classroom situations can be used; for instance, such exercises as: 'Bring enough bottles of milk so that each boy and girl in your group may have one.' 'How many more chairs do we need?'

Exercises designed to develop ordinal relationships, i.e. the ability to put things in order according to size.

(1) Picking out smallest and largest, or shortest and longest from groups, beginning with examples where the discrimination is easy. For example, the teacher can select the tallest child and the shortest child in the class and ask the children who is the tallest and who is the shortest. The teacher will then select two children who are not so different in height and later several children can be put in order of size. The same exercise can be repeated using other materials—books, trees, rods, etc.

(2) Placing cards in sequence according to length of lines and size of shapes drawn on them.

(3) Placing rods, blocks, cards, Plasticine, balls, etc. in order of size or to complete a series.

(4) Making double series such as dolls with sticks, footballs and players, cars and garages, and so on.

(5) Making stairs with blocks of different sizes.

Other exercises which are of value

Graded exercises which ask the children to classify objects are useful since classification plays an important part in number, e.g. putting all the counters of one type or colour together, all the rods of the same length. The apparatus we use includes sets of cards containing common elements in their patterns, e.g. find the cards with squares or circles, straight or wavy lines, dots or crosses. Classification exercises are also included in the language development programme. We also include exercises which ask the children to make or complete from a range of alternatives a given pattern when only part of it is given. For example, give the child a length of cardboard or wood and ask him to select from other lengths two which will make the same length. Alternatively, supply one part and ask him to find the other. Variations of this type of exercise to develop ideas of putting together and separating out suggest themselves. In the readiness programme the child can thus use arithmetical processes—putting together and taking apart—and see their inter-relatedness without having the ability to use arithmetical terms, symbols or signs. When these are introduced the child can then understand that they are conventions and a form of shorthand which he can use to help him express and manipulate number situations and operations simply, quickly and accurately.

These pre-number lessons should be arranged so that each child has the opportunity to move with reasonable freedom from one aspect of the programme to the others since the various sections are not mutually exclusive but part of an integrated plan. The teacher should keep suitable records of each child's progress bearing in mind the three stages of development mentioned previously, i.e. pre-operational, intuitive, and operational, and the different skills being learned, i.e. conservation, cardination, ordination and classification. The child must be given opportunities to experiment and discover, to estimate and check, and eventually to liberate himself from irrational thinking. Throughout the number readiness programme teachers should encourage discussion and the asking of questions.

It will be found that once this programme has been satisfactorily completed the child should be ready to begin a systematic study of the number system. This study will now be based on real understanding and on ability to apply relational thinking to quantitative situations because the child can assume constancy. He will realize that the symbols he will be asked to use represent quantities which are invariable. The figure 5 will represent a group of five things whose value will remain the same irrespective of how they are arranged. He will be able to appreciate the inter-relatedness and complementary nature of processes and have elementary ideas of part-whole relationships. If he is to be taught through a counting approach his counting can now be relational, i.e. he will be able to use his counting to compare two or more groups of objects; if by a structural or mensural approach, i.e. using rods, he will be helped by his experience during the readiness programme.

How shall we teach?

When the teacher is reasonably sure that a child is ready to start systematic number work (with many ESN children this will not be reached until they are about nine or ten years old) it will be necessary to bear in mind certain important principles. These must include the following:

(a) As stated earlier, the teacher must understand the number system as a logical system. From the system she must decide which parts are going to be useful as a basis for the development of those essential attainments which the ESN child is going to need in the affairs of his daily life (i.e. the essential minimum curriculum).We suggest that the ability to deal relationally with groups of up to 20 is almost sufficient. If the ESN child studies each number from 1 to 20 and he knows all the addition, subtraction, and multiplication facts within 20 and can apply them to social situations, he is well prepared for the future. In practice, we find that if the child's number thinking is truly relational at this level of 20 he is usually capable of further advancement if time and circumstances permit.

(b) In studying a particular number, all the facts (with the exception of division which we do not stress) and the relationships between them should be taught, i.e. the child should appreciate the complementary nature of addition and subtraction. He should also appreciate how a new group is related to those he has learned previously. This ensures an understanding of the relationship between cardinal and ordinal number, e.g. when a group has a sixth element it is bigger than a group of five of the same element.

(c) As soon as a concept of a number has been formed it should be used in practical, everyday situations. For example, when the child really knows the meaning of six he should use this knowledge to deal with sixpence, six inches, six hours, six boys—six of anything. This is a very essential principle. We find that giving a subnormal child many varied groups of five things to count will not develop a concept of 'fiveness'. He needs to use one particular type of object (counters, pencils, cubes or rods) with which to study his groups, the teacher guiding his thinking to discover the quantitative relationships. Introducing different qualities in the objects he handles (e.g. varying size, shape, colour, texture) interferes with the quality of his arithmetical thinking. Once the concept is established it can *then* be applied to practical situations.

(d) *Number symbols and signs should be introduced only when the child understands the quantities and processes for which they stand.* For example, when the child appreciates that the addition process is simply the putting together of two groups to make another group equal to the two groups together then the + sign can be introduced as a shorthand sign for 'putting together'. When he understands that if a group is separated into two groups and one is taken away he is subtracting, the − sign can be introduced. Similarly, multiplication must be understood as the putting together of equal groups and

159

division as the separating out into equal groups, before the signs are used.

(*e*) Mental and oral work should be emphasized in the early stages, the child checking his answers with whatever apparatus the teacher decides to use.

(*f*) The teacher must remember that the development of number readiness does not end when the child is ready to begin formal work. The child is always getting ready for the next stage in understanding. This 'getting ready' is essentially a process of integrating previous learning to a level that anticipates the new learning that logically follows. For example, in the addition process the ESN child needs much practice in the simpler stages. He needs an understanding of the importance of ten and of the use of zero as a place holder before he starts using carrying figures. Or again, the difficulty of dealing with money has to be anticipated by a thorough study of the composition of twelve. This integration can take a long time with ESN children whose understandings develop slowly. Very careful attention must be paid, therefore, to the grading of new learning situations because it is the quality rather than the quantity of the child's thinking that is of real importance.

(*g*) Even when due attention has been given to the gradual building of understanding, frequent revision is necessary since the ESN child's powers of retention are usually poor.

(*h*) Drill will be essential but it must always follow understanding and its purpose made obvious to the child.

(*i*) When problems are introduced the teacher must ensure that the vocabulary used is at the child's reading level. In our reading programme the basic sight vocabulary of 200 words does not include such words as *how, many, altogether, cost, long, what, time, away*. These have to be taught if the child is to develop independence in reading problems.

The study of groups 1–20

No matter which method or what material is used in teaching the groups 1–20, the teacher has to bear in mind that the outcome of teaching must include ideas of notation, enumeration, operational processes, the ability to compute accurately and quickly, and apply these to problems. These objectives are best achieved when the children study the structure of each number in a way that brings out the fact that arithmetic is concerned with processes of re-grouping. The provision of re-grouping experience is, therefore, fundamental for real arithmetical learning. This experience must be so arranged that the child by actively observing, arranging and considering arrives at an understanding through generalization.

Study based on counting

We recommend that in studying groups by a counting approach only one type of material should be used at first in order to avoid confusing the child. The method might follow the pattern outlined below:

The children are told that they are going to learn the story of, say, seven. They are given 7 counters of the same colour in the first instance and we assume, for this example, that they have previously studied the structure of the groups 2 to 6. They will have been taught the symbols 1 to 6 and be able to write these. They will also have been introduced to $+$, $-$, $=$ and $\times$ signs and be more or less aware of their significance.

First of all, the children work independently, perhaps in small groups, with the seven counters and, if they are able, under the heading 'The story of Seven', they write down as many as possible of the number facts within the group seven. The teacher then joins the children and by questioning and discussion guides the children's quantitative thinking about the 7 group. For example, the children will probably have arranged the number facts in random order. The teacher may then help the children to arrange these in more logical sequences and in ways which emphasize relationships. She might ask the children to arrange the facts so as to point out that addition and subtraction are complementary processes, e.g. $3+4=7$, what do $4+3$ make? $7-4=$? $7-3=$? She might get the children to arrange the addition and subtraction facts in order, e.g. $6+1, 1+6, 5+2, 2+5$; $7-6, 7-5, 7-4$. She will probably ask questions such as:— 'How many groups of two can you get from seven?' 'How many threes or fours or ones?' She may put a number of counters less than seven on the table and ask the children to pick up sufficient counters from spare piles to make her group up to seven, and ask the children to check their estimations. She will certainly revise the groups 2 to 6 and encourage the children to see the relationships of the group seven to these. Using previously prepared cards based on the group seven she will leave the children to do set work.

In any class there will be individual children or groups of children who are studying a variety of number structures. The teacher will be kept very busy moving from group to group. She may not be able to keep every group fully occupied with number work. We find that organization is greatly helped if alternative activities are made available, e.g. reading, craftwork, so that the children are working purposefully all the time. There will be children in the class whose number attainments are sufficiently good for them to be applied to practical situations and then the teacher will make use of her shop, post office, measuring exercises, and so on. Other children will be occupied with exercises to drill the number combinations they have previously learned.

When the child has studied several numbers by using counters, the teacher has to ensure that his knowledge is applied to real situations. We suggest that a study of numbers to 5 should be completed before this happens. There can be no hard and fast rule about this. Some may decide to transfer the child's knowledge to practical situations immediately each group is learned. Others may decide to continue the systematic study of numbers to a later stage. Much will depend upon the individual child's rate of learning and the degree of motivation which can be maintained. In this connection, it is important to remember that the ESN child usually needs a long period of practice before number relations are sufficiently understood to be useful in practical application. Too long a period of study using concrete material may therefore lead to flagging of interest and not allow the child the feelings of success which accrue from the realization that his knowledge of the most elementary number facts can be useful. The child who has taken a long time to understand groups to six is very pleased to realize that he can use sixpence, six inches, or six hours and solve problems involving the number six.

If the beginnings of number are to be based on counting it is vitally important for the teacher to realize that she must try to encourage her children to acquire more and more mature ways of counting. The method of 'adding on', for instance, has to be taught or ESN children will, when adding 5 and 4, continue to count from 1 to 5 and on to 9 to get the correct answer. Practice in the speedy recognition of group sizes is very useful in this respect, care being taken to ensure that a particular group is presented in a variety of configurations or patterns. This encourages the children to see groups within groups and to 'add on'.

Study based on a mensural approach

For the past four years, after much experiment, we have rejected the exclusive use of counting in favour of one which combines counting and a measurement or structural approach. We suspected that counting did not emphasize sufficiently the relationships within and between groups and the relative importance of the cardinal and ordinal aspects of number. We felt that it was difficult to wean the ESN child away from the props used in counting and to induce independence of thought and action in number situations. At first we used the material described by Stern (3) in her book *Children Discover Arithmetic*. However, we were not happy about the rods she used because they were segmented. This, particularly with the older ESN child who had previously failed on traditional methods, enabled the child to fall back on counting rather than use estimation of lengths. We now use the Cuisenaire (1) material which consists of sets of coloured, unsegmented rods measured in centimetres to represent the numbers 1 to 10. The material is supplied in boxes containing 241 rods giving 50 ones, 50 twos, 33 threes, 25 fours, 20 fives, 16 sixes, 14 sevens, 12 eights, 11 nines and 10 tens. The rods are coloured in number families, e.g. 2, 4 and 8 are the red family, 3, 6 and 9 are the green family, 5 and 10 are the yellow family, but these colour families are rarely needed with ESN children.

In the first place the children use the rods as play material with which to build models and make patterns. During this play, they are encouraged to build stairs, match lengths (e.g. in building a wall), learn the colours, and compare lengths using various rods. This informal activity leads to an incidental appreciation of sizes and relationships. For example, in building the wall of a house, children may discover that two yellow rods are equal in length to an orange one. At this stage no attempt is made to associate a particular length or colour with a number name. When children appear to be ready for systematic number work (and readiness includes the ability to build a staircase by putting the rods in serial order) we begin to teach the association between colour, length and number name. This is done in the following way: the children in the group are asked to pick up two rods of very dissimilar length indicated by the teacher. Each child holds the rods behind him and is then asked to produce the long or the short rod estimating length by feeling. This is continued with two rods not so dissimilar, with three rods and so on. Ideas of long, short, middle, big and little are developed in this way. The next step is a repetition of the above but the children are asked to produce the rods by colour name, there being no reference to size. The final step is to give the rods their number names by reference to the stair and the children are asked to produce the correct rod for a given number. This sounds a difficult operation for ESN children to perform. In practice we have been very much impressed by the speed with which ESN children of 9, 10 and 11 years of age are able to achieve it.

When the child knows the number names of the rods, he begins to study each number in turn using the Story of a Number approach. For example, to study the number seven he takes the black seven rod and makes combinations of other rods that equal seven.

Touching the rods he says the combinations, 'four and three make seven', 'five and two make seven', and so on. He says the subtraction facts. The teacher questions him about the numerical relations within seven, e.g. $7-3$, $7-4$, how many 2s can you get out of seven? The child writes the combinations in his book under the heading 'The story of Seven', the number symbols being introduced as the numbers they represent are studied.

When the study of the numbers 1 to 10 has been satisfactorily completed by this method, we introduce graded exercises in addition, subtraction, and multiplication. These exercises include the 45 addition, the 45 subtraction and the multiplication facts to 10, omitting zero facts since we emphasize at this stage the use of zero as a place holder in the decimal system. We also include oral and written problems to encourage the child to use his number knowledge in everyday situations. The written problems have to be specially prepared on cards to suit each child's reading level. The children are encouraged at all times to work independently both with and without the Cuisenaire rods. To encourage the children to work without aids we give individual weekly attainment tests to be worked without the rods. The teachers graph the results of these tests and from each child's graphs we are able to observe speed of learning, individual difficulties and degree of retention of previously known facts. These graphs have demonstrated that this mensural approach to number teaching does result in better attainments with the majority of ESN children.

The process is continued by the study of each number from 11 to 20. As each number is studied, its use in arithmetical situations involving chiefly money and time is demonstrated and practised.

The Cuisenaire material seems to offer many advantages in the teaching of the number system. The important ones are:

(a) A mensural or structural approach does help the children to see numerical relationships more readily and to develop relational thinking. For example, the child is able to see that a four rod and a six rod together are the same as a ten rod whereas he has difficulty in seeing that four dots and six dots make ten dots.

(b) Relationships can be estimated and easily checked from the beginning of number learning.

(c) Each number can be studied in detail as a separate entity and its place and significance in the number system made meaningful because cardinal and ordinal aspects are taught simultaneously.

(d) The decimal nature of the number system can be demonstrated readily.

(e) The inter-relatedness of arithmetical processes is made obvious.

There are some disadvantages, however:

164

(*a*) The material is rather small for some young children who should be using the rods in the number readiness programme.

(*b*) There is a danger that the material might be used simply to improve computational skills without due regard being given to the use of these skills in real life situations, e.g. using real money and articles.

(*c*) The use of discontinuous quantities can easily be overlooked.

It is essential that the children should appreciate from the beginning that one of the most important facts about a number is that it contains a definite number of the same unit which separates it from the one immediately preceding it. For example, ten consists of ten units similar to the one which separates it from nine. For this to be of use in life the child must be able to count the ten units. The knowledge that ten, as a part of the number system, consists of ten units is useless unless it can be related to ten external objects. We believe, therefore, that in the study of groups to 20 some relational counting must also be taught using the unit rods in the first instance. However, relational counting must not be over-emphasized nor carried on for so long a time as to be detrimental to the economical ways of solving problems which the Cuisenaire material facilitates.

With a secure knowledge of groups up to 20, we find that our children have a firm foundation on which to build more advanced concepts. Many are able to go well beyond our Essential Minimum and some even beyond our Additional Desirable content.

Some additional suggestions:

(*a*) Teachers are very often tempted to surround the children with a wide variety of number games—number wheels, number jigsaws, fishing games, darts, cards, number lotto and the like. Such games should be used with discretion. They will rarely teach number facts; their usefulness as a means of motivating drill is often doubtful; they can be used quite indiscriminately and not as a part of a *systematic* teaching programme designed to develop number concepts.

(*b*) Practical work is essential but should be well-organized and used intelligently. Shopping, measuring, and weighing activities look very impressive but unless these operations are really meaningful they can be a waste of time particularly with ESN children who are less able to extract generalizations from a variety of practical experiences.

(*c*) A successful beginning to number must not be marred by lack of system later. The work, at all levels, has to be well-graded and essentially practical. This means that the teacher must not rely on published schemes which are largely unsuitable. A series of graded assignments prepared by the teacher and printed on cards is far preferable.

REFERENCES

1. CUISENAIRE, G and GATTEGNO, C. *Numbers in Colour.* Heinemann. The Cuisenaire material is obtainable from The Cuisenaire Co., Crown St., Reading, Berkshire.
2. PIAGET, J. *The Child's Conception of Number.* Routledge and Kegan Paul, 1952.
3. STERN, C. *Children Discover Arithmetic.* Harrap., 1949.

FURTHER READING

ADAMS, L. D. *A Background of Primary School Mathematics.* O.U.P., 1953.

BRIDEOKE, E. and GROVES, D. *Arithmetic in Action.* U.L.P., 1939.

BROWNELL, W. A. *Arithmetic in Grades 1 and 2.* Duke Univ. Press, 1941.

BRUECKNER, L. J. and GROSSNICKLE, F. E. *How to Make Arithmetic Meaningful.* Winston, 1947.

LAWRENCE, E., THEAKSTON, T. R. and ISAACS, N. *Some Aspects of Piaget's Work.* National Froebel Foundation, 2 Manchester Square, London, W.1., 1955.

MATHEMATICAL ASSOCIATION. *The Teaching of Mathematics in the Primary School.* Bell, 1956.

SCHONELL, F. J. *Diagnosis and Remedial Teaching in Arithmetic.* Oliver and Boyd, 1957.

SCOTTISH COUNCIL FOR RESEARCH IN EDUCATION. *Studies in Arithmetic* (2 vols.). U.L.P., 1939.

WILLIAMS, A. A. *Number Readiness.* Educ. Review, Vol. 11, No. 1, 1958.

IX

CREATIVE WORK

THE educational and social limitations of educationally sub-normal children are so obvious that a great deal of time and effort is devoted to ensuring that these children acquire certain basic skills (such as reading and number) and habits of behaving (social training), which have obvious practical value in life after leaving school. The benefits derived from creative and expressive activities such as art and craft, drama, music, movement and dance are not so obvious and there is sometimes a tendency to think of these rather as relaxation after the more serious work of school is done. Our view is that they provide experiences which are essential for the full development of pupils. Creative work is, in essence, a form of play and just as play provides children with the variety of experiences needed for all-round growth so creative work in school helps to foster development on a broad front. The freedom, activity and satisfaction of creative expression are often the means by which the child achieves balance and harmony in his own process of growth, and the child who achieves that, even partially, is more able and ready to learn.

Creative work helps emotional growth

The relaxed, happy atmosphere of classrooms where children are encouraged and helped to find some means of expression frequently provides evidence of personal and emotional growth. Every teacher is familiar with the child whose personality is revealed in the tiny cramped drawing at the bottom of the paper, or in the drawing that is tight and neat but devoid of detail and vitality; or the child who is at first unable to join in free drama or music and movement, remaining on the edge of the group. Creative and expressive activities enable such children gradually to unfold and to 'let themselves go'. As they do so they gain in confidence and become more capable of

167

participating in life at school and more generally alert and responsive. Most educationally subnormal children, especially on entry to
the special school, need feelings of achievement and success to
counteract their loss of confidence and sense of inadequacy. Many
children are able to achieve success, or have it contrived for them,
in one or other of the creative activities. On this foundation, other
successes, perhaps in academic subjects, can be based. At the least
it is a valuable compensation for failures and difficulties in other
aspects of schoolwork. Apart from this, there is the relief and
relaxation obtained from touching and handling materials, of moving
about and doing. We have all experienced this relaxation after
periods of effort or frustration and difficulty, when we achieve
release from tension by means of games, hobbies or the vicarious
emotional experiences of film and novel. For this reason, backward
children should have the means for creative work readily available
in the classroom. As one teacher remarked, 'If Billy has reached a
point of frustration and fatigue with his reading, I tell him to go and
finish his painting or his model and come back to the reading later.'
There is much to be said in favour of formal work being closely and
genuinely linked with creative work.

There are few special schools without some children whose emotional and personal difficulties mark them out as difficult or problem
children. They range from children whose emotional difficulties are
expressed in an active and aggressive way to those who are extremely apathetic and withdrawn. The special school has as much
responsibility for dealing with these problems as it has for specific
learning difficulties in basic subjects. Creative and expressive activities
are perhaps the chief components of what may be termed a therapeutic curriculum. Pent-up feelings of hostility or frustration find a
safe outlet, for example, in free drama. The fact that such outlets are
achieved in a situation watched and controlled by a tolerant teacher
seems to make emotional release all the more effective. The therapeutic values of painting, music and drama are being increasingly
recognized in other fields of work concerned with mental health.
There is need for further experiment along these lines in special
schools.

Creative work requires thinking

But creative work is not only concerned with emotional aspects of
growth. Creation involves thinking as well as feeling. The child who
models, paints or dramatizes some aspect of his experience is certainly learning more about it. He becomes more observant, he thinks
about what he observes and becomes more ready to interpret similar

experiences later. In expressing what he has experienced he assimilates and organizes his impressions. Since ESN children are more limited than normal children in verbal expression there is all the more need for them to have alternative means of expression. Descöeudres, describing her methods with backward children over thirty years ago, made the same point. She believed that art 'stimulated the intelligence', that it compelled the child to see properly and then to express his thoughts in a form that is tangible and precise. 'Drawing', she said, 'should be looked upon primarily as a form of speech.' The simple and spontaneous drawings of the young or mentally immature child serve just this purpose. In his drawings of people, houses, boats and trains, he is going back over what he has observed about them and learning their essential features. In making pictures about stories he has been told or about events he has witnessed or taken part in, he is familiarizing himself with them. It is a form of learning for which the old teaching maxim, 'expression checks impression', is not inapplicable.

Thinking is also involved in the choice and use of materials. The possibilities of the media have to be thought about and turned to advantage. Making a picture from different colours and textures of paper or cloth requires choice, planning and the trying of alternatives. In group painting or dramatization, discussion of the various possibilities is needed. Purposeful thinking will often be provoked if the creative work is an extension of work in some other aspect of the curriculum. For example, the basic reading scheme prepared by the school as described in Chapter VII was printed by the senior boys. For technical reasons we were unable to illustrate these books and therefore encouraged the boys to illustrate the books themselves with pictures and models about the central themes in each book. Apart from the interest and satisfaction obtained by this method, there was the valuable impetus to find out something about the topics and to consider the ways of representing them.

One of the outstanding characteristics of educationally subnormal children is their poor concentration. They are often distractible, and lacking in persistence, especially on entry to the ESN school when they are suffering from the effects of failure in the ordinary school. The quality of concentration is related to level of intelligence but factors of interest, and expectation of success or failure are also influential. Within limits, the ability to concentrate is learnt in the repeated experience of absorbing and satisfying activity. Play in general, and creative work in particular, provide conditions for the development of this trait; materials and occupations suited to the child's level of ability and to his interests often sustain attention for surprisingly long periods, even with a mentally retarded child. Many

ESN children have had too few play opportunities. Creative work, broadly conceived, can go a long way to make up for this lack, giving them some taste of the satisfaction of absorbing continuous effort. It is rather out of fashion to talk of training the attention but work with failing children does suggest that habits of work developed in creative work may be transferred to other areas of the curriculum.

Creative work promotes other learning

Since ESN children are in general rather more clumsy in both fine and large movements, an additional value of creative work is that it improves motor co-ordination. Poor co-ordination is due to a basic neuro-muscular weakness combined with lack of practice and exercise and its effects are often cumulative. Children avoid what they cannot easily do, especially as they grow older and become more aware of their limitations compared with other children. ESN children need more, not less, of those activities which will help co-ordination to improve. Art and craft, movement and dance are among the means of helping them.

A class where creative activities are encouraged, especially if these arise naturally in connection with other work, is bound to be one where many aspects of learning can be acquired incidentally—learning to share materials and tools, and to look after them, learning to co-operate with others and to experience the satisfaction of group participation. Language and expression will also be afforded opportunity for development in talking about what is going to be done and how to do it, and in discussing results. There are also the incidental, but by no means insignificant gains in vocabulary from describing tools, processes and materials, or in comprehension from following instructions. Children also become more aware of the qualities of beauty in form and colour, movement and sound through creative work. In this the attractiveness of the whole school environment plays an important part.

Finally, it is worth stressing that these activities often help to bring about good teacher-child relationships through mutual participation in an enjoyable and satisfying experience—singing, acting or making together. Moreover, creative work can lead to a greater understanding of the child since the child's expression often reveals what experiences he has had, what he has made of them and how he feels about them. These activities may provide other situations for seeing the child in a new light. This understanding is essential in teaching all children but is especially necessary with handicapped children.

The teacher's function

Many of the values of creative work which have been mentioned depend for their achievement on the personal involvement and full participation of the child. This raises the question of the extent to which the teacher should give help and make suggestions. How far do we leave children to express themselves spontaneously? How far do we advise, suggest or actively help? There is no clear-cut answer since the age, ability and previous experience of the children have to be taken into account. But some suggestions can be offered for guidance.

In the first place, the teacher contributes by providing the variety of materials or the suitable conditions needed, and in the second place, by giving help and advice about their use. It is sometimes thought that modern views about the teaching of creative work reduce the teacher's contribution to a very passive one while the class gets on with self-expression. This is not a correct interpretation. It is obvious that help with techniques of handling different materials can be a means of releasing and facilitating expression which would otherwise be hindered. For example, it is necessary to offer advice about the use of paint and brushes, modelling materials, or of making and arranging properties and effects in drama. Advice of this kind can stop short of suggesting *what* should be done since this so often produces a stereotyped imitation of the adult's suggestion. An understanding of children's development is also required in order to be aware of the uses to which children are likely to put materials at different stages. The cue for advice is often given by the children themselves. For example, at early stages of development children are satisfied with their schematic representations of the human figure, but there comes a stage when they are dissatisfied and want to make their drawing 'more like'. It is then that help can be given, not by telling them how to do it but by drawing their attention to the proportions and details about which they are dissatisfied. Instead of sketching suggestions on the board, which will probably be slavishly copied, it is better that children should be encouraged to observe and find their own way of drawing or painting. There are some children who have no confidence in their own ability and need rather more help to get started. The solution will often be one of providing some new medium about which they have not had the chance to develop unfavourable attitudes. For example, they can make pictures with different kinds of materials if they believe that they cannot make pictures with paint, or they can use various ways of stencilling if they lack confidence about free pattern work. It often happens that some limited and unobtrusive help by the teacher establishes a feeling of success and achievement which enables a child to go ahead without help. The criterion of successful intervention by the teacher is whether the child is enabled to work more freely and spontaneously afterwards.

Another important contribution of the teacher is to ensure that children have some ideas to express. The prolific productions in the art class after Bonfire Night, or Christmas, testify to the importance of vivid experiences. Few ESN children have a sufficient store of these and one task of the teacher is to make good this deficiency by visits, the use of pictures and the selection of stories. Another, and perhaps more important, task is to help them to use their everyday experience, and to become more observant of things and events in their own environment. At younger ages there should be discussion of birthdays, pets, their house, family, toys and play. As children grow older, there should be discussion of the wider environment, bringing in not only the perpetual favourites—fire engines, trains, aeroplanes—but also topical news—explorers, space travel. Often the ideas to be expressed will be derived from other aspects of school work, such as stories or records of visits. The teacher will have to make suggestions as well as ensure an atmosphere in which children feel encouraged to express themselves. We are more likely to provide that atmosphere if we realize fully that it is the *process* of creating, not the *results*, that matters most. Perhaps most important of all are the enthusiasm and inspiration of the teacher.

Art and Craft

Teachers who are not themselves specially skilled and experienced in art and craft should not therefore feel that they are unable to help children get benefit and enjoyment from these activities. Many of the techniques are of a simple kind and a knowledge of a variety of them is easily acquired. What is more important is that the teacher should have a real appreciation of the value of art and craft in the development of children and in the learning of backward children in particular. Backward children have a great need of practical and pictorial means of learning and expression, and therefore creative work should take place as the need for it arises in teaching reading, nature study, religious education and other subjects. Every teacher of ESN children should be able to use art and craft work in this way. It is only at later stages of the ESN school, when children are becoming more critical of their efforts, that their waning interest may call for that extra touch of inspiration and enthusiasm which can be given by the person who is specially interested and experienced.

The following suggestions are not intended as a scheme but as an

172

indication of the range of materials and activities which can be drawn upon to suit different ages and abilities. Selection will be determined by the interests, capacities and previous experience of individual children.

Activities for the younger children

When the reception class caters for children of five years to eight years, it is usual to find that their abilities are comparable with those of normal children aged three to five years. Their programme, therefore, will be basically the same as that for normal children in nursery schools and the reception class of the infant school. They need ample opportunity to develop and exercise the impulse to draw, paint and construct in as many ways as possible. Since their hand co-ordination is poor, it is desirable that they should have practice in making large hand movements such as using chalk on blackboards and painting with big brushes or crayoning on large sheets of paper. Some of the children, because of low ability, physical handicaps or lack of experience may be unable to do more than apply paint in daubs to the paper. This is a stage which all children go through, and it is important that they should not get the feeling that their painting is 'not much good'. The teacher's appreciation and encouragement will help them to continue and is especially important with those children who are already feeling uncertain of themselves or beginning to be aware of parent's anxiety for signs of progress. A wide variety of materials and activities should be available: work with coloured paper, torn or cut to make simple decorations or pictures; finger painting; clay, although many will not be beyond the stage of enjoying the feel of moulding and kneading it.

One of the needs at this stage is for materials which can be worked and used in different ways. It is interesting, for example, to see the different uses to which sand, clay or even a bag of bricks are put by children at different stages of development. It is important that in equipping the class with educational toys and large apparatus some of the simple material preparing them for creative work in later classes should not be forgotten.

Activities for older children

Picture making

Up to 11 or 12 years of age, picture making is a main interest of children. These pictures tend to be representations of things which interest them, the spontaneous carefree expression of their experience. The teacher may need to do no more than encourage, express

173

approval or suggest improvements indirectly by such remarks as 'Do you think . . ?' or 'Have you noticed . . ?' Many children will need more stimulation by way of actual experiences or by discussion with the teacher of what they are going to paint. There should be many pictures in the classroom—on postcards, in books, magazines or newspapers. This is not to suggest that they copy, but that they should have a means of filling out their concepts of what they are painting. The young child from the average home normally has ample opportunity for browsing over pictures, and the indirect results are often noticeable in his painting. Since ESN children have a more restricted range of experience, the use of pictures is helpful in extending and enriching the content of their pictures. Many of their pictures will, of course, be based on their own experience of home and neighbourhood, and here the teacher can help them to think more clearly and in greater detail.

In painting pictures, it is best to apply paint directly rather than to sketch first in pencil or charcoal. Pencil should be avoided since it usually results in small shapes and details which are unsuitable for painting. Moreover, children get discouraged immediately by the realization of the inadequacy of their sketch. Those children who are at a loss without the support of a sketch should be urged to sketch with a brush. Powder or poster paints are the best media since they are easy to use and give a bold, not a watery, effect. There should be a choice of brushes of different sizes and of various kinds of paper. Kitchen paper is usually the main standby but sugar papers in different colours are to be recommended. For example, a dark paper can be used for a night scene, or blue for one of sea and sky. Coloured papers make for richer colour effects. For example, a dark paper throws up light colours, a blue paper makes more subtle effects. Another variation is for the children to paint shapes which have been previously cut out, e.g. one class was provided with differently shaped birds cut out of newspapers, and the children vied with each other to produce the most decorative and richly coloured birds; another class painted shapes representing the buildings in a street (houses, shops, church, school, factory), the buildings being finally assembled as a frieze. They were prompted to go and look at the streets in their own environment and include the results of their observation in the paintings.

Another variant is *montage* in which the picture is made up from many types of material—sweet papers of many colours, wrapping papers of different colours and textures, wool, pieces of cloth, feathers, shells, etc. There is hardly any limit to the materials which may be used as long as there are suitable adhesives available for the different materials. One of the advantages of this method is that the various materials may be tried out by being placed on the paper before they are stuck. A similar technique is that of making picture mosaics with coloured papers torn from advertisements in glossy magazines, or from old paintings which are no longer needed.

Variety at this stage can be introduced by means of group work. Group or collective pictures are worth while since they provide another way of encouraging co-operation as well as a situation where the less able child can share some of the satisfaction that the rest of the class more easily achieve. The group painting which is worked on by several children at the same time, or the frieze depicting a country or street scene to which all the children contribute figures they have drawn, painted and cut out, often produces an outstanding effect. In the frieze, there is no reason why each child should contribute the same thing, as sometimes happens. The frieze is more interesting and satisfactory if it reflects the individual interests of the class.

Modelling

There is no doubt that children enjoy modelling, and various ways of doing this should be used from time to time. Plasticine has its uses but also its limitations. It tends to lead to small models which are hard to work and does not provide the best practice in co-ordination. Clay is a more satisfactory material to use at all ages. It is easy to work, responding and yielding easily to pulling and pushing with the hands. Moreover, mistakes can easily be put right. Children enjoy making a coil or thumb pot; models of people and animals can be dried and when painted in bright colours and varnished look very attractive.

Modelling with wire makes an interesting change but is much more difficult since it requires a clearer idea of the nature of the material and what can be done with it. Even so, some older ESN children have used it to good effect in making aeroplanes, insects and animals. Wire is frequently used as a framework on which a surface is built up with bandage or strips of paper and plaster, the model being finally painted. A collection of wire animals made in this way gives obvious satisfaction to children.

A collection of scrap materials can be useful for making models. Cardboard boxes, match-boxes, spools and reels, packaging material and so on, can be used to build up trains, ships, lorries and houses. Individual models can be made or group models of streets, villages, harbours and castles can be constructed to illustrate centres of interest. Boys particularly enjoy using wooden boxes and timber off-cuts for some crude but, to them, satisfying woodwork.

CREATIVE WORK

Children, especially boys, love using tools to carve, whittle and scrape away at materials. A start on this can be made by making a small totem pole from a short branch of trees such as beech, apple, or cherry. Interesting designs and patterns can be cut away on the bark with a penknife and then be embellished by bright poster paint. Branches or driftwood picked up on walks can often be whittled to suggest faces or figures. Balsa and other soft wood can be carved to make model canoes, aeroplanes, people and animals. Stone carvings are not beyond the capacity of some ESN children. Soft stones, such as sandstone or chalk, which yield to probing with an old kitchen knife or a 6-inch nail are the most suitable. An alternative to stone is plaster of paris if the almost inevitable mess can be tolerated. Leather-hard clay can also be used. Soap is expensive and salt carvings have the disadvantage of impermanence, but both might be considered for an individual child. Some boys may manage carving in harder stone. One group did so, making chisels for themselves in metal work and mallets in woodwork.

Puppetry

Puppetry has much to commend it if only because it is a useful way of getting children talking, dramatizing, or making up stories. It is often a way of drawing out the quiet, withdrawn child. It also acts as a focus for other art and craft activities such as painting scenery for a play, and sewing simple costumes (even boys will rise to this). Glove puppets are the easiest for backward children to handle and simple ones can be made from potato or matchboxes, or by stuffing a stocking or paper bag on which a face can be drawn or attached. Puppet heads can also be made from papier maché fairly quickly. The more complicated procedure of making puppets with strips of paper and bandage glued together on a Plasticine base, which is later removed, is not usually the best one to start with, because ESN children need something tangible for their efforts which they can use quickly. Another variation is that of shadow puppets. Puppets are cut out from strong cardboard and their shadows are projected on to a screen by a light, which the boys will enjoy rigging up. These puppets are fixed to a strong piece of wire so that they may be moved by a child from below the screen. The limbs of the puppet can be attached by clips so that a certain amount of extra movement can be obtained. Added effect may be achieved by shadow scenery such as trees or houses cut out in card. A satisfactory effect can be made fairly easily and, since backward children often need quick success, it is a pity that this technique is not used more.

Printing and Pattern making

An interesting range of activities is suggested by the possibilities of printing. Many children discover for themselves that pencil shading on paper which covers a coin produces an imprint of the coin. There is a subtle satisfaction in obtaining a representation so easily. The same technique can be extended to rubbings of the barks of trees with cobbler's heel or wax crayons. Materials collected on the nature walk can be used in various ways. Leaves may be painted over and then used to print a pattern, or the same leaf may be stencilled round with fairly dry paint which is applied round the edge with a bandage. Prints from other common objects, such as feathers, can be used in a pattern in conjunction with potato and stick prints. A simple technique is to arrange string on a square of soft wood or card. When an interesting shape has been made, the string is fixed with glue and painted, and a print then taken. A simple form of a woodcut can be obtained by drawing with a pointed tool on soft wood, such as a piece from an orange box, the resulting picture being printed off, using ordinary powder paint or printing ink.

Pattern-making can be done in so many interesting ways, combining stencilling, printing, brushwork and other techniques, that it is a pity to limit it as sometimes happens, to the drawing of squares which are to be filled in with the brush or with potato prints. Many ESN children need no encouragement to escape into this kind of repetitive activity and something freer not only provides a more interesting effect but is of greater educational value.

Drama

In Chapter VI we stressed the important role which drama should play in a comprehensive programme for language development. We now look at drama in more detail to discover its educational value in a wider setting. As we have previously suggested, all creative work has an intellectual content since it is the result of the child's awareness of and thinking about his experience. However, it is the use of drama as a means of fostering personality development which we wish to emphasize now. Experienced teachers of educationally subnormal and backward children realize that with many children the emotional development is often as retarded as the intellectual. With others it is out of step with other developmental processes, as in the case of the adolescent boy or girl who is too immature emotionally to know how to deal with physical problems. We believe that drama, the 'doing of life' as Peter Slade defines it, can do much to minimize the difficulties, both personal and social, which arise from emotional retardation and disturbance.

The aims of drama may be summarized as follows:

(1) *To develop personality through spontaneous dramatic activity.* Watching children at play one realizes how characteristic is their love of make-believe and dramatic play. One observes the fundamental and dynamic part which emotion, movement and rhythm play in their activities. One is struck by their imagination and by their complete absorption in dramatic play as it arises spontaneously in the absence of self-consciousness. One sees the wide range of individual differences in play ranging from the intensely personal play of very young children and those older ones who are withdrawn and timid, to the group activity and gang play of the older or more out-going children. Creative drama should be based on these forms of play and develop from them. It thus grows out of, and meets the psychological needs of the child as an individual and as a member of a team. It is child-centred. It does not limit itself to the end of term play in which the teachers can demonstrate what they can do with ESN children. It takes its place as an integral part of the school's programme for child development.

(2) *To provide opportunities for the imagination to develop through improvisation, for the development of increasing sensitivity and appropriate reaction to the environment.* In our drama we encourage the children to use their imagination in both real life and imaginary situations. For example, we ask them to show us what they would do if a wild animal ran into the room, how they would feel if they were lost in a wood or if a spider were crawling over them, or if they had lost money they had been given for mother's shopping, etc. We make use of rhythms (on a drum, tom-tom, tambourine) and music to suggest dance forms, animal movements, dramatic situations and emotional states.

(3) *To provide opportunities for emotional re-education and for the improvement of social behaviour.* Many ESN children are socially deprived, having been wrongly handled in their up-bringing. They have often been denied opportunities for normal play. In many cases their lives have been almost devoid of love, affection and security. They have not experienced feelings of success and self-esteem, and have had little chance to build up happy social relationships and ideas of acceptable behaviour. From our knowledge of child development and the case history material we possess, we use our drama so as to give children who need it the opportunity to 'live through' their early years. We mime and act baby situations, we pretend to be babies, feel like, walk and cry like babies. We act family outings, tea parties, quarrels with brothers and sisters, street play, games, helping in and around the house.

With older children, we find that giving opportunities to compose their own plays allows us to provide outlets for their aggressiveness, negativism, destructiveness and feelings of antagonism towards authority and other children. As Peter Slade points out blowing off steam 'offers continual opportunity for playing out evil in a legal framework'. The last three plays developed by our senior boys have all been particularly aggressive, the themes being based on piracy, espionage and escapades of prisoners of war. However, good has always triumphed over evil. We have been especially impressed with the strong group feeling that has developed even in the most egocentric boys. Sociometric surveys made at the beginning and the end of a term's drama sessions have revealed the benefits which derive from the work. The dominant, histrionic leader becomes less dominating; the isolate begins to make contact with the group. The withdrawn, fearful child gains considerably because his bottled-up aggression is brought out into the open. He is no longer afraid of his aggressive impulses since they are accepted, and he gradually becomes more relaxed and enters the team.

(4) *To enrich and make more meaningful other areas of the curriculum.* If the principle of 'learning by doing' is accepted, drama in all its forms becomes an essential part of the educational process. There are many occasions in history, geography, religious education, arithmetic and reading when simple dramatizations can make learning more exciting and vivid. Our reading scheme uses drama extensively. The children are asked to make up plays about the stories they read, to improvise on the situations which make up the themes of the books. For instance, when the children have read about a rescue from a lighthouse, we ask them to improvise a play about it, to imagine they are lighthouse-keepers showing visitors over the lighthouse, or make up an adventure story about a lighthouse. They are also asked to make models and pictures on these topics and we find that those who have had dramatic experience usually achieve more lively and interesting results. Their feelings, impressions and observations in drama are transferred to other forms of expression.

Some suggestions for the use of creative drama with ESN children

Begin with movement and mime. The first thing we concentrate on is the art of relaxation—complete relaxation. 'Imagine you are a frozen block of ice.—That's it. You are very stiff—your head, neck, arms, fingers, legs, toes are stiff. Now the sun is coming out. As it gets hotter you begin to melt—slowly, slowly, down and down until you are a pool of water. That's right; go really loose and flabby.' Other examples such as being a football with a slow puncture, a melting candle, a dying man, can be used. We find that suitable music (we

179

always use the 'Aquarium' from the *Carnival of the Animals*) is a great help in inducing relaxation and a peaceful atmosphere. Every lesson also ends with a period of relaxation (a de-climax) so that the children leave us calm and peaceful even though the de-climax may have been immediately preceded by a noisy 'playing-up' scene.

In a group of lessons, work through the whole range of emotions. In the descriptions of situations be dramatic yourself without giving too much help. 'Imagine you are in a dark room; it's very dark. The door begins to open slowly—it creaks a little. Can you hear it? Look! Can you see something at the door?' The aim is to express a variety of emotions—love and hate, fear, pain, happiness, friendship, disgust, suspense, contentment, surprise, indifference, being accepted or rejected. The responses will vary enormously. Those of withdrawn children will at first be disappointing, being flat or inappropriate. They will certainly not show much excitement or willingness to use large movements. Practice in miming small movements is a helpful start. With encouragement, the teacher's enthusiasm and inspiration, demonstrations by children and the growing relationship between teacher and pupils, improvements take place quickly; the lessons become exciting and interesting. With restless, distractible, over-active children, the responses are often exaggerated. We use the same technique but emphasize the emotions which call for a quieter, more controlled response. With this group, we are able to move on more quickly to the next stage.

(2) At this stage, apply movement and mime to simple dance drama, similar to that used by Garrard and described in his book *Leap to Life*. We have found that 'Danse Macabre' is a useful starting point since it suggests a variety of moods and range of movements. It has several rhythms, and its quiet beginning, tremendous climax followed by de-climax, together with its story arouse children's emotions and interest. We find that some editing of music on records is often needed if expression is not to flag. We also continue to use rhythms on percussion instruments at this stage. The children derive much pleasure and stimulation from 'primitive' rhythms suggesting tribal and hunting dances, dances around the totem pole, and witch doctor scenes.

(3) The next stage is the application of these techniques to the beginnings of play-making. The subjects we have used are a variety of family situations, visits to the seaside or the country, to the circus (always very popular since children are fond of being clowns and animals), exploring in the jungle or in Polar regions, and acting the usual Wild West scenes. Sound effects either recorded or made at the time are a great help, especially with the more withdrawn children, in quickening the response and maintaining the liveliness of the

action. For instance, we find we need train and aeroplane noises, explosions, thunderstorms, street sounds and the like to make situations more realistic. Lighting effects are also useful.

By this time the children are ready to dramatize the whole or parts of well-known stories. We still emphasize movement and the expression of feelings but do not hold back spontaneous speech. Too much attention to speech has to be guarded against however lest it inhibit the expression of the whole child in movement and action. The following stories are very popular: *Snow White*, *The Pied Piper*, *Hansel and Gretel*, *Rumpelstiltskin* and pantomime themes. If the children depart from the story we do not interfere and it sometimes happens that Snow White and Hansel and Gretel get mixed up, or the lame boy is not left behind in the *Pied Piper*. We find it useful to allow the whole group to mime the various characters in a story before asking them for suggestions for role playing. In *Snow White* they mime ugliness and wickedness for the Queen, they become dwarfs, miming and dancing shyness, having temper tantrums, being sleepy, and so on.

(4) The final stage in this development of dramatic activity consists of plays composed almost entirely by the children. We have little use for the acting of scripted plays leading to a performance although reading plays within the reading ability of the pupils is enjoyed. Acting scripted plays leads to an artificial performance lacking the genuineness of real dramatic involvement. All our plays employ the arena technique and generally we use the gymnasium and its apparatus. Wall bars and window ladders become the rigging of ships or prison bars, the vaulting horse becomes a Trojan horse, sections of the box become doorways, boats or cars; Swedish benches become the edges of cliffs or the sides of houses, and high beams become aeroplanes from which paratroopers fall. We use stage blocks (3 ft by 3 ft by 1 ft) to build up sets such as rocks, upper storeys of houses, caves, etc. There is scarcely a limit to the inventiveness of ESN children if they have been nurtured in an environment which encourages it.

The new play always begins with a discussion in which a preliminary plot is developed and roles temporarily allotted. The first scene is then worked out and acted. Discussions continue, alterations and modifications are agreed upon; suitable sound effects, lighting, music and simple properties are planned and obtained. The play gradually evolves. We find that a single play can take as long as one term to complete. The following is a summary of one of these plays:

A Revenue Officer patrolling a Cornish beach finds a party of shipwrecked sailors. Their bodies suggest that they have been robbed and murdered. A second officer acting on a hunch of one of his superiors goes disguised as a traveller to a nearby inn. He talks with a man there and draws his attention to a light near some dangerous rocks. This man happens to be the leader of the wreckers. On a pretence he lures the Revenue Officer outside, where he is set upon, stabbed and left for dead. The landlord of the inn, before locking up, sends his son to look for his new guest and the boy, hearing groans, finds the wounded officer who gives him a message for the Revenue Office. The boy runs back to tell his father. Meanwhile the wreckers are at work again.

The landlord's son hastens to the Revenue Office and tells his story. The officers make a plan of campaign but the wreckers have a spy in the office who overhears the arrangements. He creeps past the guards who shoot at and wound him, but he manages to crawl to the wreckers' cave and warn its occupants.

By this time the Revenue men have reached the new wreck and get clues to the whereabouts of the wreckers' hideout, which they surround. The forward scouts make contact and hand-to-hand fighting ensues. Both sides are entrenched behind sheltering rocks. A cutlass and sabre fight follows and the hideout is captured. The wreckers' chief, making his getaway, is surprised by the Revenue Officer he wounded and left for dead. A duel follows and the wreckers' chief falls.

The background music for this play included 'Mars' from Holst's *Planets*, *Ritual Fire Dance* by De Falla, and Tchaikovsky's Overture *1812*. Some forty boys took part.

Some teachers may feel hesitant about attempting this type of drama because of lack of knowledge or experience. However, it requires no knowledge of Theatre and no previous experience of acting. The main thing is an understanding of children and a willingness to follow the children's lead in the dramatic realization of their imaginations. Teachers who have used drama in this way have been impressed with the improved teacher-child relationships which result, and have found that many disciplinary problems have been resolved.[1]

Music

It is an interesting reflection that ESN children will have more chance of hearing music after they have left school than they will have of experiencing any other of the creative activities enjoyed in school days. Most of them will be brought daily into contact with

[1] We are indebted to Mr. K. G. Tucker, formerly Assistant Teacher at St. Francis Residential School, for his contribution to our work in drama.

music by means of television, wireless or the cinema. Even though the quality of the music will often be poor and their attention to it marginal, the reflection does underline the importance of anything we can do in school to promote their ability to enjoy music. Enjoyment is certainly the first essential of music in school, but, in addition, the more children know about and understand the music, the more will their area of enjoyment be widened. Music should include not only singing but listening and moving to music and acquiring simple ideas and information which are likely to sharpen interest and increase pleasure.

What can be done at later stages of the ESN school will depend on what has been achieved earlier. The youngest classes should have ample opportunity for learning to sing a range of nursery rhymes, action songs, simple hymns and carols similar to those customary in the infant school. Children's ability to learn tunes varies and is not necessarily tied to mental level. Some quite mentally retarded children can pick up tunes surprisingly well. Listening to these same tunes on wireless programmes such as 'Listen with Mother' or on gramophone records will encourage this learning and help to train them to listen.

The ability to recognize qualities in music will be helped by their activity in music and movement. The broad differentiation of high from low sounds, of quick from slow tempos, and different rhythms (e.g. skipping, hopping, marching) will be increasingly appreciated as they respond with movement to sound and rhythm. There is also a need for including some means of experimenting with sounds and rhythms by the children themselves. Just as children go through a stage of experimenting with paint or through a scribbling stage in drawing, there is equal justification for some opportunity for personal discovery of pitch and rhythm in playing with musical instruments such as chime bells, drums and other percussion instruments. One must be wary of introducing formal percussion playing too early before children have developed the ability to listen, and to recognize the pulse of the music. An extended period of freer activity with percussion instruments is needed.

More formal activities can be developed as the children mature and become more capable of a fuller response. The repertoire of songs can be widened and should range from good popular tunes to suitable serious songs. The BBC's music pamphlets are a useful source, but teachers often find that ESN children need rather more preparation to keep up with the broadcasts. There should be humour and seriousness, jollity and sadness in the songs, for music is one way of learning to express and respond to different emotions. There should be the occasional song which is rehearsed for the school

183

Festival or Open Day; there should be others which children will want to sing at school camp or on the school journey.

The children's difficulty with reading or memorizing the words of songs is a constant problem. There is no point in working through many verses of songs unless the children can cope with the reading and can understand the words. The problem can be helped to some extent by selecting songs with a refrain or a repeating pattern which assists memorization. Preference should be given to songs which have a simple and direct story, or which express experiences and feelings which are not too difficult for the children to comprehend. At the same time, there will be songs worth inclusion for their musical quality even though the words are too difficult.

In getting children to sing well, the first requirement is enjoyment. This is achieved when children realize that they are not singing *for* teacher but *with* the teacher. On this foundation of enjoyment, it is possible to achieve some variation in the way songs are sung. For example, children can be helped to appreciate and then express the mood of the songs: sad—gay; exciting—peaceful; humorous—serious. They enjoy trying to portray these qualities for it is a way of acting. Additional inspiration can be given by the teacher's dramatic actions and tones of voice in talking about or singing the song, i.e. ESN children need more than abstract words to convey what is required. The rhythm of the song is important for a song may be sung accurately yet be lifeless. The accompanist and the conductor can help here but nothing will suffice if the children do not feel themselves into the song. This can be promoted by doing the actions referred to in a song, or by dramatizing while they sing, or watching a group acting in front of them.

While one would not want to make a fetish of correlation, of relating singing to other school experiences, the reminder is perhaps worth making that a song may often be chosen because it is related to the theme of a story the class has heard or has been reading about. For example, if children have been reading about the sea and ships, or about other countries, it is obviously worth while to introduce a few appropriate songs. In this way, music can play a part in making other learning more vivid and effective.

Unfortunately, most instruments are too difficult for ESN children to play. We find the occasional child who has an unexpected ability, and in a residential school this type of child can often be catered for. For example, in one school there has been the occasional child who could learn to play a trumpet or to play simple tunes from music on the piano or violin. Obviously such children are very much the exception, but there is much to be said for the enthusiastic teacher to experiment with other ways of letting children make music, for example, using the recorder, mouth organ, dulcimers, chime bells and home-made instruments. Having made, with the teacher's help, an instrument such as a bamboo pipe will increase the motivation for trying to play it. Older children continue to enjoy percussion but, as with younger children, there is little to be gained from stressing the use of scores. In our music-making clubs, we have used drums with wire brushes, the tea-chest bass, bones, spoons, and guitars to provide the rhythm for tunes played on combs and paper, or sung. One or two boys have shown great interest in guitars and they could quite well learn the tonic, dominant, and sub-dominant chords in the common keys, or use an instrument with a chording attachment.

Listening to music

ESN children should be given many opportunities to listen to music of various types—good popular music, light music and serious or 'classical' music. Interest and attention can be increased by using music which has a story, such as the *Sorcerer's Apprentice, Peter and the Wolf, Danse Macabre*. Short excerpts can be played which are descriptive of a topic, for example, storm scenes from Beethoven's *Pastoral Symphony*, or the *William Tell Overture*. Recorded music is often best edited, at least in the first place, rather than have children listening throughout a whole piece. Playing some of the melodies and getting them to hum or sing them is a good preparation. But programme or descriptive music should not be relied on exclusively since music with a regular pattern and clear melodies is often suitable —e.g. some tunes of Mozart, Haydn, Schubert.

Wherever possible it is a good thing to have live performances. In some areas schools are able to hear a section of an orchestra play and to have brief talks about the music and demonstrations of the instruments. Failing this, it is often possible to get someone to play an instrument to the children and demonstrate some of its possibilities. With a stringed instrument, for example, the children can see as well as hear the difference between plucking and bowing, what happens when each open string is plucked, and can appreciate the different effects the player achieves with music of different moods and types. For many backward children, seeing instruments at close quarters will be a new or rare experience yet surely a very desirable one if they are to get the most out of listening to music on gramophone records or the wireless. One need not fear that ESN children will be inattentive when they are played to like this. Perhaps it is the relative infrequency of the experience, but they are usually most attentive and enthusiastic.

Music is often the Cinderella subject of the curriculum. Sometimes this is due to a feeling that what can be done in music is limited by its obvious difficulties for ESN children. Yet within limits much can be done to widen appreciation, interest and enjoyment. It not infrequently happens that a small staff is left without someone able to play an instrument, but there is usually someone who is interested in music and can undertake some of the activities we have described. Certainly music should not be lightly neglected since it plays no small part in creating enjoyment.

FURTHER READING

UNESCO. *Education and Art.* H.M.S.O., 1953.
CROFTON, K., DENTY, P., and MILNE R. *Creative Work in the Junior School.* E.S.A., 1955.
ROBERTSON, S. *Creative Crafts in Education.* Routledge and Kegan Paul, 1952.
TOMLINSON, R. R. *Children as Artists.* King Penguin.
VIOLA, W. *Child Art.* U.L.P., 1944.
BUCHER, L. DE C. *The Teaching of Art.* Blackie.
LOWENFELD, V. *Creative and Mental Growth.* Macmillan, 1947.
ELLIS, C. and R. *Modelling for Amateurs.* Studio, 1939
ECCOTT, R. and A. *Teaching Creative Art to Children.* Evans, 1930.
ENG, H. *The Psychology of Children's Drawings.* Routledge and Kegan Paul, 1957.
ASH, B. and RAPAPORT, B. *Creative Work in the Junior School.* Methuen, 1957.
CHURCHILL, E. M. *Counting and Measuring.* Routledge & Kegan Paul, 1961.
LOVELL, K. *The Growth of Basic Mathematical and Scientific Concepts in Children.* U.L.P., 1961.
ISAACS, N. *New Light on Children's Ideas of Number.* E.S.A., 1960.
NICHOLLS, R. *Primary School Mathematics,* Vol. 1, No. 1.

Drama

SLADE, P. *Child Drama.* U.L.P. 1954.
SLADE, P. *Teacher's Handbook of Child Drama,* U. L. P., 1958.
WILES, J. and GARRARD, G. A. *Leap to Life.* Chatto and Windus, 1957.
COGGIN, P. A. *Drama and Education.* Thames and Hudson, 1956.
LANGDON, E. M. *An Introduction to Dramatic Work with Children.* Dobson.
BRUFORD, R. *Speech and Drama.* Methuen, 1948.

Music and Dance

MAINWARING. *Teaching Music in Schools.* Paxton, 1951.
DRIVER, ANN. *Music and Movement.* O.U.P., 1936.
RUSSEL, JOAN. *Modern Dance in Education.* MacDonald and Evans, 1958.
LABAN, R. *Modern Educational Dance.* MacDonald and Evans, 1948.

X

THE GROWTH OF KNOWLEDGE AND AWARENESS

ONE of the main tasks of education is to help children develop awareness and understanding of the world around them. It is a development that is taking place all the time to some extent irrespective of what is done in school. The urge to know and master the environment is the source and purpose of spontaneous play, of the manipulative exploration and verbal questioning of early childhood, of the eager interests and acquisition of knowledge in the primary school years, and of the deeper personal interests and academic studies of adolescence. The subnormal child cannot travel so far on this path nor can he understand so much or so well. Intellectual limitations, often reinforced by social and cultural ones, restrict the range of his experience as well as the depth of his understanding. His difficulties in acquiring reading and language skills mean that he is handicapped in one of the chief ways of learning about the world. The necessity of concentrating more time and effort on the acquisition of these skills means that there is less time for exploring wider fields of knowledge and experience.

Yet whatever can be done to increase subnormal children's awareness of their human and natural environment is not merely an agreeable addition to the basic curriculum but makes an essential contribution to it. The child's activity in relation to his environment nourishes his mental growth and language development. As Watts remarks, 'The enrichment and illumination of experience by observation and discussion is a surer way to the enlargement of vocabulary than can be secured by formal exercises in the use of words, the need for which is not personally felt.' It is all the more important to consider ways of enriching and illuminating experience since the simple reading materials on which ESN children spend a more prolonged period are usually rather limited in the amount of information and general knowledge they impart—in fact, more books for backward readers with a stronger informational content would be a useful addition to those already available. Even so, the knowledge assumed in reading books may not be really familiar to some ESN children. It is necessary to widen their experience in order to make more meaningful the words they are learning to recognize and to increase the comprehension of what they read. Moreover, interests and experiences can often be harnessed to the task of learning to read as well as to stimulating oral and written expression.

The fundamental reason, however, for developing as much knowledge and understanding as possible is that they contribute to feelings of confidence and security. The ESN child is often uncertain of himself not only because he is aware of his limitations but because he lacks knowledge. The truth of this can be most obvious at school-leaving, or when the residential school child leaves a relatively sheltered environment to go out into the community. If the new environment is one he understands and in which he knows how to act, the process of adjustment will be easier. We can introspect upon a similar experience in ourselves when we are in a strange country, the geography, customs and organization of which we do not fully understand. But at a deeper level than this utilitarian one, to *know* is to have a sense of mastery which is basic to the sense of confidence in oneself as a person. Hence the pleasure with which young children assert—'I know', or 'I can do this'.

There are two directions in which awareness should be developing. *First, the child needs to gain an understanding of his human environment*—the home and family, the class and school community, the services provided in the village or town, different kinds of work and the facilities for leisure. Although geography or history are not taught formally, his own locality can become known to him and will provide opportunities for him to realize how it is related to other places. He can acquire some awareness of how people live in other parts of his country or in other lands, and how they lived in former times. What is done in these respects will have to start from points of interest in the locality since such work needs to be related to things the children can visit.

Second, there should be some understanding of the natural environment, both animate and inanimate. Nature study is usually given most emphasis since children's interest is easily aroused in living things. But nature needs to be interpreted in a broad sense to include other observations of the natural world. Children will want to know something, at a simple level, about the air we breathe, the earth which gives us food and material resources, water which affects us in so many ways. At the latest ages in the ESN school, simple scientific experiments can be used to elaborate that knowledge with the more able pupils. Children also need some simple notions about physical geography—broad differences between mountains, valleys, the seas, rivers and forests, dealt with in relation to the locality or in connection with school journeys and holidays. Schools placed in the middle of industrial towns rarely have adequate means of studying the natural environment, but at least the wonders of the man-made environment offer many possibilities for observation and discussion —the buildings going up, modern methods of construction, new machines for factories or transport, the sources of fuel and power. While these are not topics that need be pursued to any depth, they are aspects of experience that children can be stimulated to notice more, so that they have some ideas about them as well as words in their vocabulary for talking about them.

The method

In thinking about the way these aspects of awareness can be developed in the ESN school, it is useful to recall the stages through which the normal child develops in his knowledge of his environment. In the first stage, the child learns about the world in the play which is so strong an urge in normal development. He learns about the qualities and properties of things in manipulating them and in his constructive and imaginative use of them. In make-believe play, he represents the happenings which he has observed in his surroundings. He may dramatize for himself, or with others, some of the things he has watched adults doing. In rehearsing these events for himself, he learns more about them; he makes himself familiar with and begins to comprehend the everyday activities of the world around him.

Because of their slower development, many of the youngest children in the ESN school are still in need of this first stage of learning through play, up to the ages of eight or nine years depending on their level of maturity and previous experience. Adequate opportunities at this stage will hasten their progress into the next stage in which their activities are increasingly channelled into more formal learning.

In the second stage, learning about the world continues to come through the child's active exploration in play but is increasingly assisted by verbal means—talking and questioning. At the same time, the interest of the normal primary school child widens out until by the end of the junior school period he is ready to be interested in almost anything in the Universe. He wants to know what things are, why and how things happen, although he is not ready for complicated explanations, scientific principles and laws. He wants to know about *things* and what they do: that diesels run on oil whereas the steam engine works by steam; that gas and coke come from coal; that electricity is made in power stations; how animals live; what people do for their work; how people live in other countries and how they lived long ago. He collects names and facts rather as he collects conkers, train numbers, stamps and Dinkies. It is rather a process of cataloguing his experience so that he knows what things are and what they do.

As Susan Isaacs has remarked, up to the age of 11 or 12 years the child is interested in activities not subjects, and it is not until the third stage leading into adolescence that the child is ready and inclined to parcel out aspects of experience and study them in more detail in the form of subjects.

It is useful to think of the older ESN child as being in many respects at the second stage—one similar to that of the normal child from 7 to 11 years. He has the same need to start from things and events in his immediate experience, the same need to learn through his natural interests and through activity. His range of experience is narrower than that of most junior children but there is plenty of scope in the average environment to provide material for observation and discussion at his level. Visits to such places as museums, castles, factories and shops are most desirable to broaden experience. In most cases, visits should be arranged to fit in with some current interest or work of the class so that children have some preliminary knowledge of what to look for. The visit should be followed by some recording of its results either in discussion, or by making models and pictures, or producing a class book which can be shown to other people or referred to later.

The ESN child has greater difficulty than the average child in thinking about things which are removed from him in space and time so that ideas of a geographical and historical nature are less easily comprehended. This does not mean that such ideas should be avoided altogether but that they should always be introduced in ways that are as concrete and personal as possible.

The ESN child may display fewer interests than the normal child but that does not imply that he cannot be interested; he may show a less active curiosity but that does not mean that he cannot be excited to curiosity and a sense of wonder. In so far as curiosity and interest have been submerged by failure and a dull school experience, it is the job of special educational treatment to try to arouse curiosity and interest. As with the junior child, the ESN child is interested in learning by doing rather than by sitting and listening; he may, however, need more prompting to remember the purpose of his activity so that what he is learning is clear to him.

He is further handicapped in comparison with the ordinary child by his lack of ability to think all round an experience. His attention may centre on some outstanding, but not necessarily the most relevant, feature of his experience and his attention needs to be drawn to features that he would otherwise overlook.

Normal children can learn about the world through the medium of reading. ESN children can use reading less effectively, some not at all. There is much knowledge, however, that can come from using pictures—from picture scrapbooks, pictorial magazines, illustrated information books, film-strips and films. Television can also be a means by which general knowledge is increased.

A final difficulty is that of written expression. Whereas the average child consolidates his learning by writing about it in diaries, topic books or class records, the ESN child can make less use of this. The poorest writer, however, can label pictures, write short captions; some can write a few sentences, and others may be capable of more extensive written accounts of what they have observed.

The teacher who has become accustomed to working through schemes in history, geography and other subjects with ordinary children may feel rather dissatisfied with the apparently casual and fragmentary approach, and may be left with a feeling that nothing has been achieved. Alternatively, the fact that there may be nothing on the timetable or in the schemes of work about these topics may lead to their being overlooked. If, however, it is recognized that one of the teacher's tasks is to make children more aware of the life around them and help them to understand it, there will be satisfaction in any small signs of growing awareness and knowledge. Those signs will often come in the children's contributions to oral work, their drawings and paintings, perhaps in drama and in written work. Although the method is mainly an incidental one using opportunities as they arise, the aims should be firmly held in mind—the two aspects of awareness as we have outlined them. The fact that the teacher has certain aims in mind will help to give cohesion to the diversity of small experiences.

The human environment

The importance of an understanding of the human environment needs no stressing since it is basic to the ability to function satisfactorily in life after leaving school. Many aspects of school experience play a part in developing this understanding. It is not something that comes only from occasional projects on home, food, shops, transport —useful though these can be. Talk in the classroom about everyday experiences is most fruitful in the younger age groups—talk about their families, events at home or in the neighbourhood, about the people they meet such as shopkeepers, postmen, policemen, doctors and nurses, and workmen they have watched. Make-believe play continuing into the creative drama we have described in Chapter X is another way. Stories familiarize children with a variety of human situations and emotions—fairy stories and folk tales with the younger age groups, stories of real events, adventures, and the doings of great people with older children. What they understand about relationships between people will also be absorbed unconsciously from the atmosphere of the school.

As children grow older, they can become more aware of the world outside school and home. It is surprising what gaps there are in the knowledge of common things that we rather take for granted. Some children may not have been on a railway station, or on a train. Some may have only the vaguest ideas of what a farm is, know few of the names of farm animals and little about the typical activities of farms. Many will not have seen the sea. The harbours, lighthouses, caves and ships which we hope will captivate their interest in the simple story of adventures at the seaside may only be hazy impressions. Wherever possible we need to enlarge their horizons and stimulate them in that process of knowing their environment which comes so much more quickly with the normal junior school child.

What can be done will depend on the possibilities of the environment and the interests of the children and the teacher. Some houses being erected near the school will suggest a visit to see how houses are built and may extend to a consideration of the homes the children live in, and perhaps to some simple treatment of homes in other countries. If there are some old houses near by, it may be suitable, depending on the age and ability of the children, to think about homes in former times. In one residential school a class made a series of visits to places of interest in the nearby town—the fire station, the railway station, the post-office, the library and the church. On these visits they also talked about other places they passed—the hospital, the parks, the police station, the employment exchange and the different shops. Later there was talk about their own home towns or villages and some of the abler ones accepted the challenge to write a little about their own towns as though to tell a visitor what to go and see.

Wherever possible, experiences which have personal significance should be looked for and used. The eagerly anticipated school journey can be prepared for; pictures of things that will be seen on the journey can be looked at and discussed. Places that children have been to for day-trips or holidays can be talked about. If a class corresponds with a similar class in another town, there is often increased personal interest. In one instance, a class in the Midlands corresponded with a class in the Isle of Wight. Picture postcards of the Isle of Wight arrived and were displayed on the wall. There was great eagerness from 11-year-old ESN children to ask the teacher about all the things that could be seen. Some chalk from the cliffs was passed round and compared with the classroom chalk. The Midland children sent back samples and packages of a familiar and favourite commodity from a Midland factory. In another case, children from a Lancashire cotton town sent samples of cotton, pictures of local mills and factories and, of course, their First Division football team to a Midland school. One can embark on such ventures knowing that in all probability they will be fairly short-lived. When the interest has served its purpose there is little point in trying to prolong it when interest has waned. However, it can later be repeated in a different way.

With the oldest age groups in the ESN school, the study should concentrate more on those aspects of the human environment which children will need to understand when they have left school: the shops, transport and leisure facilities which they will use; the offices and departments which they may have contact with. One important aspect is the discussion of life at work—the different kinds of job available, the problems they will meet in working conditions. The use of factory visits and the discussion of working conditions is considered at length in Chapter XII.

The natural environment

Nature study is one of the most suitable and enjoyable ways of getting children to be more interested in and observant of their environment. There are few children who are not fascinated by watching living things or who do not sense the magic of things that grow. Moreover, the enjoyment of natural life does not depend on the child's level of intelligence; it can be enjoyed in some measure at all levels of mental maturity. Nature study, if it is the real thing and not some remote and unreal classroom subject, appeals to many of the children's fundamental interests—the desire to know, the pleasure in being active, the satisfaction of feeding and looking after living things. Children like things that move, whether they be working models or animals; they are also attracted by colour and enjoy the sensation of touching things. These perceptual and active experiences in Nature Study provide the initial incentive through which we can develop their awareness of and simple concepts about the working of the natural world.

Some teachers feel that they do not know enough about Nature Study and are therefore diffident about taking it. Any teacher of ESN children is likely to know enough to be able to teach Nature Study adequately as long as he appreciates what he is trying to do.

Special knowledge about nature and about the methods of teaching it are obviously an advantage and can have the effect of enthusing a whole class to the benefit not only of their natural history but also of their reading and written English. The teacher's diffidence often arises from the misconception that to teach Nature Study one must know the names of plants, birds, pond creatures, and so on. It is certainly useful to be able to identify, but there are plenty of straight-forward illustrated guides that the teacher can use and which the older children will enjoy referring to. The main thing is that the teacher should feel something of the sense of wonder and be able to share the children's curiosity and pleasure in the things which can be collected. It is important to conceive of Nature Study not as identi-fication but as an activity of observing, collecting and finding out which can be used to help children acquire such basic notions as growth, the need for food and the different ways of getting it, the effect of the seasons, and the different places in which plants and animals live.

Although this study depends partly on the environment of the school, the following principles stated by Seguin, an early worker with subnormal children, are generally applicable.

Teach nothing indoors that can be learned outdoors.

Teach nothing with dead things when you can make observa-tions on living things.

Nature should be the classroom and the school book except in cases of insuperable difficulty.

In urban schools, separated from nature by miles of brick, it may seem impossible to apply these principles, but much can be done by growing things in the classroom, by having pets and aquaria, and by arranging the occasional expedition. The need to have real things to look at is all the more important for town children. Fortunately, many ESN schools arrange camps and school holidays, which pro-vide many of the simple experiences we are often tempted to take for granted.

The nature walk

ESN children (or adults for that matter) are not very good at noticing the variety of things that can be seen on a Nature walk. The ability to observe depends on previous experience—having noticed and learned about things on previous occasions makes them more likely to be noticed on the next. Observation can also be im-proved by giving the walk a definite purpose so that attention is directed to the quests for certain things. For example, 'It is Autumn —what happens in Autumn? What can we see and find that tells us

194

about Autumn?' The walk can become a game to find and bring back things which are evidence of the end of the year—fallen leaves, beech nuts, acorns, berries, dry grasses, straw from the cornfield. 'Let us see how many different colours we can find.' Older children can compare what they are seeing now with what they saw in the same place before the summer holidays. Only old, unused nests can be found, there are few birds singing, the fields and gardens look different. Extra incentive to notice can be provided by having little notebooks in which sketches, however crude, can be made of what is seen—the combine-harvester, the tractor ploughing, the stacks of straw or hay.

With older children different habitats can be observed and compared. The lane with its many flowers and plants may be compared with the middle of the beech wood; the meadow with the common. The question 'How many different trees can we find?' can lead to a variety of activities such as collecting leaves, twigs, fruits and making bark rubbings.

As with any educational visit, some previous preparation helps children to observe. This is best done with the aid of pictures or a few specimens. Verbal descriptions of things which they have not yet seen do not mean much to subnormal children. If pond dipping is the purpose of the walk they can be shown pictures of creatures and plants they may find, and they can discuss what apparatus will be required.

Much of the value of the walk comes from the activity in the classroom on return. Some children may be willing to record what has been found in lists, drawings or a nature book; leaves can be used in art for stencilling or printing; the reference books can be brought out to look at pictures of things seen or found; the nature table can be laid out.

The *nature table* is an important feature of the classroom, and every effort should be made to maintain it as an attractive one. It is easy for the table to become a repository of dying flowers and dusty specimens; it is better to clear it when exhibits have served their purpose. Attractive labelling helps—labelling not only with names but short sentences saying where the specimen was found or posing questions—'What is this?' 'Where was it found?' Colourful illustrations pinned at the back or a reference book lying open at the appropriate page may promote some further activity in relation to the display. Arranging the specimens upon some simple classification principle is to be recommended even if it is simply arrangement by colour. The arrangement can be made according to the place (wood, field) where the specimens were found; according to mode of dispersal in the case of seeds; or grouped into plants, animals and non-living things if the collection permits it. As we have noted previously, it is useful to draw children's attention to similarities and differences since ESN children are poorer at noticing them for themselves.

Children, especially ESN children, are generally not very observant of birds, partly because it is difficult to get near enough to them, and partly because they move so quickly. The bird watcher notices many more birds than the average person because he learns to look for the bird after he has heard a call-note or song. A few of the more interested children may take to the idea of tracking a bird quietly to see whether they can catch a glimpse of it, although the noises of the rest of the group often are not conducive to bird watching.

The best way of approaching the study of birds is to have a bird-table outside the classroom. Watching daily the arrival of the same few birds enables the children to become familiar with them, and provides a useful foundation for creating further interest. A knowledge of the size, colour and behaviour of half a dozen common birds (sparrow, starling, blackbird, thrush, chaffinch, blue tit and great tit) enables differences to be more distinguishable in new ones that are seen. Most town areas not enclosed by endless streets and factories can attract the above birds; every London or Birmingham park has them and often several others as well. Attempts to watch real birds is far more profitable and enjoyable than lessons on beaks and feet!

There is no doubt that children, especially boys, prefer things which are active, and the aquarium has a special appeal since it involves the activity of pond dipping and the watching of creatures once found. For younger children a tank with fish is a good start; older children will enjoy the variety of creatures that can be collected from ponds. The teacher who wants to start an aquarium cannot do better than read the advice on equipment for pond-dipping and how to set up an aquarium in Hutchinson's *Children as Naturalists*. A summary of suggestions of how to keep insects and other creatures in the classroom is given in the UNESCO *Source Book for Science Teaching*, noted at the end of this chapter.

It is, of course, almost an essential for children to have at some time the experience of looking after pets, rabbits and hamsters being the most suitable. Apart from the knowledge of living things gained from this, it is an important piece of training that they should learn desirable attitudes towards animals and what is involved in looking after them. Attention must be given to whether a particular group is ready for this experience since one does not want animals to be exposed to mishandling by children who are not sufficiently mature to realize what they may be doing to helpless creatures. Nor must one forget to grade the responsibility given to children according to their capacity to undertake it. Looking after pets must involve a great deal of adult oversight.

Growing things is another essential experience for subnormal children to have. Whether there is a school garden or not there should be the annual planting of bulbs for decorating the school and the classroom. The more of this operation they can perform for themselves, even to buying the fibre and the bulbs, the more likely they are to appreciate the aesthetic value as well as to enjoy watching them grow. Younger children should certainly have the chance to see the development of root and shoot in growing beans and other seeds in jars, and with older children the conventional experiments to show the seed's need for air, water and warmth should be arranged. Simple experiments showing the effect of different growing conditions on plants are also worth undertaking.

The school garden

The extent to which the school garden can be used to teach gardening varies with the facilities, and the previous experience of the children —whether the school draws from a rural area or an old industrial one. At the simplest level, children can appreciate the school garden as something that makes the school more beautiful, both by providing a more attractive setting outside and by supplying flowers for inside the school. Undertaking jobs in the garden provides another opportunity for development in practical competence and work habits. Its value in terms of providing physical exercise in the open air should not be overlooked, particularly for those ESN children whose physical condition is poor.

Perhaps more important than learning how to garden is the fact that gardening provides an additional means for developing knowledge and awareness. Children can learn to distinguish some of the commoner flowers and vegetables and understand something of gardening operations such as digging and sowing. A close link with Nature Study should be made to increase their understanding of the cycle of growth from seed to flower, the conditions needed by plants for growth and, with older children, the effect of insects and other garden pests. The typical gardening operations at different seasons can be linked with their observation of farming and the countryside generally. With town children, noticing what fruits and vegetables are in shops at different times of the year can be discussed in relation to what is growing in the garden. Their thinking can also be directed to making simple classifications of garden plants, e.g. according to whether the root, leaf or seed provides the food; according to the time of year they are harvested; according to the method of propagation; according to different growth conditions needed (this can again be linked to the time of sowing and harvesting). In this way, gardening can play a valuable part in the development of knowledge and thinking even though children may not become competent at gardening themselves.

Actual learning about gardening is probably proportional to the amount of personal involvement in the activity. Few of us have learned much about gardening from digging other people's potatoes or performing gardening operations under somebody else's direction. The more, therefore, that children can be brought into the actual planning of the garden work, the consulting of seed catalogues, the purchase of seeds, deciding on planting times and other operations, the more they will learn. There are many incidental opportunities for learning in the form of writing letters, working out costs, measuring and weighing. If personal involvement can reach the point where children can take on individual or group plots on their own responsibility, some real knowledge and skill can be acquired—as many residential ESN schools have found. It is perhaps worth quoting in this connection the experience reported by Duncan. For two years individual plots were a failure, in spite of practical demonstrations and explanation. It was not until the third year that gardening inexplicably became a success. The eventual success is probably not so inexplicable. Knowledge takes a long time to soak in and to be changed by trial and error into a skill. The average suburban gardener probably takes three years to absorb from books, conversation and his own failures how to do things. We cannot hope to turn many ESN children into competent gardeners but for the sake of the one or two who will continue it is worthwhile, and for the rest there are, as we have noted, many incidental benefits.

Elementary science

A proposal to include elementary science in the curriculum for ESN children may appear over-ambitious. However, the special school teacher is often surprised at the interest and knowledge of his pupils in scientific matters. Radio, television, science fiction and comics undoubtedly have an influence in this connection. Such subjects as space travel, rocket and jet propulsion, car engines, simple electrical machinery and gadgets, the working of household appliances, wireless and television are certainly of interest to ESN boys. Some girls are also keen and interested. This was illustrated in a lesson designed to develop concept formation in older ESN girls. The lesson was taken soon after an earth satellite had been launched and when the news of this historic event was fresh in the girls' minds. The word *satellite* was written on the board and the girls were asked to tell the teacher anything which 'came into their heads' about the word. More than half of the group of some thirty girls had something to offer and the blackboard was soon covered with their suggestions. These included the following words and phrases: *rocket, space travel, fireworks, moon, going round the world in the sky, wireless messages, it had a dog inside, the dog died because it could not breathe, the Russians did it, the Americans are making a satellite.*

Three ESN boys aged 12, 13 and 14 years from the school's camping club have just walked in, each carrying a primus stove. A simple science discussion has ensued and the boys have used such words as *paraffin, methylated spirits, jet, air, gas, pressure* and *pump.* As a result of questioning and experimenting they appear to have discovered how their stoves work. Such experiences provide daily opportunities for widening and deepening their knowledge and for satisfying the lively curiosity born out of good motivation.

We suggest, therefore, that the curriculum should include some science topics, modified to suit the children's interests and limitations and presented in simple non-quantitative terms. Few ESN children will ever reach the stage where they understand physical laws or have reasonable ideas of causality. Nevertheless even a little knowledge will be good for their self-esteem, useful in helping them to take an interest in the applications of science in the home, at work and in leisure activities, and in letting them experience something of the excitement, fascination and wonder associated with man's attempt to control and understand himself and his environment. The problem is to know what to include and how to teach it. The time available is too short and has too many important calls made upon it to allow the inclusion of a systematic science programme, even were this desirable. A formal syllabus would in any case be of doubtful value since it might lead to the science lesson which becomes divorced from an integrated programme for developing awareness and knowledge. Much of the science we teach will be dealt with incidentally with the emphasis on practical application, repetition and experiment. It will be included as the occasion arises in connection with reading, conversation, practical work, educational visits, music and films. The odd science lesson will have its place when the teacher will demonstrate some particular scientific principle or deal with a topical interest. For example, he may wish to show how a camera works, how oxygen is necessary for combustion, or how a simple telescope is constructed. He may also wish to demonstrate how a knowledge of simple science can prevent accidents in the home, e.g. in connection with electricity.

Wherever possible the children should do their own simple experiments using home-made apparatus. Such experiments will usually be carried out in connection with the children's questions about the way things work and why things happen, i.e. the approach should be based on verification or problem-solving. We have seen ESN children absorbed in these simple experiments. For instance, an ESN boy asked how a jet plane moved forward. A crude explanation was given and he tested it out by using a balloon. He was proud of his new knowledge and felt important as a result. The explanation and verification were completely satisfying to him at his level of understanding. Another boy asked how a rainbow formed. He tested the explanation by seeing the colours of the spectrum as the sun shone through a fine spray of water made with a garden hose.

Knowledge acquired in this incidental way may not be very certain or be retained. Year by year the information can be repeated, first simply and later at levels appropriate to the child's widening experience and learning capacity. The teacher should keep in mind a small body of factual information useful in the everyday lives of his pupils and which he wishes to impart. This basic information might be organized under the following topics:

The story of fire. Importance of friction and heat; use of flints in cigarette lighters; sandpaper on a matchbox; science of burning as applied in the home for heating the air, water, and food; domestic heating appliances; fire as a source of light—bonfire beacons, torches, the sun, candles, oil lamps, gas and electric lights; dangers of fire and heat.

The story of air. Composition of the atmosphere with particular reference to water-vapour and oxygen: the movement of air; air pressure; simple science of weather; ventilation; production of sounds; other gases.

The story of water. Rain, sea and rivers: water as source of power; domestic water supply—wells, reservoirs, water pump: purification; other liquids.

The story of power. Energy supplied by human beings, wind, water, steam; electricity supply; electricity in the home and in industry.

The use of science in communication and transport. Elementary knowledge of engines—steam, internal combustion, diesel, electric motors; radio and television—making a crystal set; telephone and telegraph.

THE GROWTH OF KNOWLEDGE AND AWARENESS

FURTHER READING

ATKINSON, M. *Junior School Community.* Longmans.

BOYCE, E. R. *Play in the Infants School.* Methuen.

CONS, C. J. and FLETCHER, C. *Actuality in School.* Methuen.

GOLDSTEIN, H. and SEIGLE, D. M. *The Illinois Curriculum Guide.* Interstate Publishers, Danville, Illinois.

HUNT, H. C. *Working with Children in Science.* Hubler.

HUTCHINSON, N. M. *Children as Naturalists.* Allen and Unwin.

ISAACS, S. *The Children We Teach.* U.L.P., 1932.

UNESCO. *UNESCO Source Book for Science Teaching.* Educational Productions, Wakefield, Yorkshire.

XI

PRACTICAL SUBJECTS; PHYSICAL EDUCATION; RELIGIOUS EDUCATION

WORK in practical subjects should not be viewed as something separate but as a continuation and extension of work done elsewhere in the school. What the child can do in the practical room depends partly on experiences he has had of practical work in various forms in younger age groups. A woodwork bench is not out of place in any classroom and the provision of simple tools can provide preparatory experience of making things in wood.

There are few children who are not eager to engage in woodwork, metal work or some other craft, and the teacher who can utilize that eagerness effectively can make an important contribution to the work of the school. This section is not concerned with techniques but with the place of crafts in the education of ESN children.

Practical work is one of several fields in which ESN children can often more easily achieve success or have it engineered for them. The work done must therefore be suited to the capacity of the individual children; it should also be something which produces evidence of success by looking good or being useful. In the early stages at least, ESN children need quick success; they cannot be expected to persist for too long without tangible results. While standards of proficiency in execution are not to be ignored, they should never be stressed to the point that children sense failure and lose the pleasure and satisfaction of achievement. It may be difficult for the specialist to tolerate poorer standards than those to which he is accustomed, but children are more likely to raise their own standards if they first feel that what they are doing is worthwhile and enjoyable. As they get more involved in the work, they will themselves want to finish jobs better. In a new school recently, the intake included boys of thirteen and fourteen from ordinary schools whose attitude to school had become most unfavourable and negative. The fact that they were sent to a special school increased their negativism. One of the chief means of transforming their attitudes

202

to school and to themselves was some quick success in making Christmas toys for brothers and sisters and a present for Mum. The models were as simple as possible; joints were reduced to a minimum and the teacher gave some help where needed to ensure a strong and satisfactory job. The results of this activity were: (1) Good relationships with the teacher which carried over to other aspects of school work. (2) Improved attitudes to themselves. (3) Enjoyment of woodwork which made possible further progress towards the acquisition of some real skills. The first essentials then are that success should be ensured, and that what is done should be valuable in the eyes of the pupil.

One of the chief values of practical work is the development of habits of work and attitudes towards work. The old debate about vocational training is largely irrelevant since the ESN school can hardly provide training in the variety of operations and for the many situations that may be met after leaving school. In any case, if there is any training to be done, employers usually prefer to train young-sters themselves in their own way for the job. But practical work can develop some of the characteristics of the good worker—persistence and the habit of sticking at a job until finished; the ability to think out how to do a task and to carry on without waiting for someone else to say what should be done next. Children who have not been encouraged to do things for themselves at home (or even in the classroom) may reveal their lack of practical sense and personal competence in the craft rooms. Although these characteristics may be related to personal handicaps and limitations, they may also be due to lack of opportunity to acquire them. The craft teacher can do much to encourage independence and competence. There can be as much satisfaction for the teacher in trying to coax such children forward as there is in having lots of coffee tables to display to visitors. No one who does not know the children intimately can possibly judge how effective the work is.

If the acquisition of skills is not the first priority, it is nevertheless important. ESN children are often poor in co-ordination and badly need opportunities for developing it, not merely for the sake of skills themselves, but because of the confidence that comes from knowing how to do things. Moreover, while they may not use these skills at work there may be many occasions at home when it is useful for them to know how to look after tools and use them in some of the simple operations involved in household jobs. They should learn to appreciate that there are right and wrong ways of using tools and of going about a job. They should also be made aware of the impor-tance of safety precautions, particularly when the abler ones are given experience of working a machine.

There is, too, a great deal of useful knowledge that comes through practical work—the names and uses of different woods, materials, tools and processes. There is the learning about how things are made; where materials come from; how much materials and tools cost; measurement and the appreciation of size and quantity. Wherever possible, opportunities should be taken to use interest in the craft as a starting point for the incidental discovery of more knowledge and understanding of the world around.

There is much to be said for children seeing an adult doing something well and helping adults on a project. There is sometimes a suggestion that helping adults make a canoe or, as was done in one school recently, a small building, is not of value to the children who should be learning from their own efforts. Apart from the fact that there are many operations in a large undertaking of this kind in which children can help, it is sufficient justification that their experience can be considerably enlarged by actively assisting in such work—especially if the work is discussed at every stage. In helping to build a small bungalow, for example, the boys gained real insight into how a building is made, the nature of the materials used and where they were obtained. They gained self-esteem, confidence and knowledge from doing a man-sized job.

The specialist teacher sometimes senses a certain isolation from the rest of the school, and is uncertain how his work can contribute to the work in the classrooms. This is most unfortunate and it is incumbent on both the specialist and the class teacher to get together and appreciate how they are both working towards the same ends. The possibility of practical subjects contributing to progress in basic subjects is often a first line of thought, but it would be a mistake to think of the specialist's contribution too narrowly in this way. It is certainly worth while utilizing any natural needs for reading and writing that occur—reading and writing the names of tools, models and materials—if doing so is within the child's range. The practical room should also have some reference books for children to refer to. However, attempts to bring in reading by requiring children to read instructions before making a model may have negative results on reading and practical work in the early stages of both. Slow-learning children do not want reading interposed between them and their favourite activities at every turn. However, practical work can contribute to verbal development when children are allowed to talk about what they are doing so that they get practice in explanations and in using the right words for tools and processes. There are also many occasions for the application of number knowledge—in measuring and estimating costs. Some schools operate a penny bank so that children can save up and buy models which they would really like to have but usually say they cannot afford. There are also many occasions when the need for a model or some other construction arises out of classroom work—making easels, puppet theatres, number apparatus, models of boats, houses, etc.

It is obviously beneficial when class and practical work can be associated in this way. The real co-operation between the class teacher and the specialist comes, however, in the interchange of observation and information about individual children. It is not just that the child may reveal himself in a different light in practical work, or that the craft teacher may be ignorant of particular handicaps and difficulties. Without such discussion, opportunities may be missed of following up interests or achievements which could be of real value.

Home management

The curriculum of all Senior ESN schools includes various aspects of homemaking. There is, however, a tendency to treat these as isolated subjects such as cookery, needlework or home crafts rather than as integral parts of the school's contribution to preparation for living. The 'domestic science' room is often isolated geographically and educationally from the rest of the school and in consequence the work in it is not co-ordinated with the overall educational approach. (This is unfortunate at any stage but with older children it is inimical to the success of the efforts being made to achieve personal and social adjustment.) Home management, broadly conceived, can become a unifying element in the curriculum since most subjects are involved and, through it, the use and purpose of learning can be easily demonstrated to the children. They will appreciate the value of reading as applied to recipes, advertisements, instructions, letter writing, making out orders; of arithmetic applied to shopping, ordering, cooking, budgeting; of art and craft in decoration and furnishing; of needlework in knitting, patching, embroidery and in the making of clothes and household requirements; of laundering, in the care of clothes and household linen; of woodwork in performing simple repairs to the house and its fittings; of gardening in keeping the home's surroundings attractive; of cooking; and of other skills and habits which make for a well-planned, happy and worthwhile home life. *If this correlation and integration is to be successful there must be the closest liaison possible between the various members of the staff concerned.* No one can or should be allowed to work in isolation. All should be willing to make a contribution to the general scheme. Such co-operation often reveals inadequacies and omissions in classroom work. For instance, one specialist in home management bravely remarked during a staff meeting that she was rather dismayed by the number of older girls who appeared to be quite unable to deal adequately and independently with shopping situations. The class teachers were surprised at this because, in class, the same girls could produce pages of addition and subtraction money sums which were correct. Further investigations revealed that the specialist's observations were substantially true. Improvements in number teaching resulted since the class teachers appreciated even more the importance of teaching the use of number concepts in real life situations.

Home-management is, therefore, a very important element in the curriculum. Teaching it calls for particularly good teaching ability. It can so easily be taught without any reference to the children's abilities and by methods which are educationally unsound. One occasionally finds that no attempt is made to adapt the organization to individual differences. Often a whole group of girls do exactly the same thing. The teacher tells them what to do and never provides the opportunity to think, to plan, to work independently or to make mistakes and profit by them. There will, of course, be some ESN children who cannot experience success without a great deal of help but the teacher should not allow the majority to be held back because of difficulties created by the few. As in other areas of the curriculum, the aim should be to organize the teaching so that each child is working to capacity as independently and purposefully as possible. The best way to achieve this is by making use of graded assignments the range of which will be bigger the older the class.

Every school which caters for senior pupils should have a flat or home in which the pupils can be taught. The aim of the house management course should be to teach as many girls (and perhaps boys) as possible how to cope with the buying, preparing, cooking and serving of food for a small family meal; the planning of a week's home cleaning and maintenance; the laundering and repair of clothes, linen and soft furnishings; and the types of household equipment they are likely to use. Few will be capable of reaching this standard but many should be capable of getting near to it.

The programme for home management studies may be discussed in two parts—one for the home management centre itself and one for the rest of the school. (a) The centre should provide facilities for cooking, using gas, electric and solid fuel cookers; for laundering with gas and electric washers, electric irons and drying equipment; for training in the efficient use of kitchen utensils.

The flat should comprise a dining-room, bathroom, bedroom and kitchen, fully-furnished and well-equipped with the type of household requisites and appliances the boys and girls are likely to use in the future. Preferably it should have its own flower and kitchen garden to be cared for by the children.

The cookery programme should aim at teaching children:

(i) The basic techniques of cooking, ranging from how to make a cup of tea and a snack to the preparation and serving of a three-course meal for four people.

(ii) The correct and hygienic way of using cooking equipment.

(iii) The study of food and diets; the purchasing and economical use of foods with particular emphasis on the use of measures, scales and estimations of quantity. The choice, preparation and serving of processed foods should not be overlooked.

The laundry programme should result in girls being capable of planning 'the wash' and using equipment efficiently. They should know how to use detergents, starches and dyes; how to iron, press and air clothes. The programme should also include the darning, patching and mending, and general care of linen and soft furnishings.

The centre should also give practice in such aspects of running a home as general cleaning, care of equipment, organization of work, tasteful decoration, laying tables, making beds, and so on. The teaching should stress, at all times, the importance of cleanliness, care and good personal appearance.

(b) The rest of the school should have a contribution to make to this programme. The reading scheme should include reading recipes, instructions and patterns, and provide help for poorer readers to acquire the specialized vocabulary. Number lessons should prepare the children for the social arithmetic of the home. This preparation with older children should be as practical as possible. It should include the use of real money in shopping, how to buy well and to budget wisely for rent, hire purchase, fuel, light and clothing.

There are many ways in which practical subjects can contribute. In pottery lessons vases and ash trays can be made; in woodwork stools, trays, coffee tables, and lamp stands. Vegetables and flowers from the school garden can be used in the home management centre. If simple greenhouse work is attempted a variety of bedding-out, pot and climbing plants can be grown. Art and craft lessons can provide things for the home and show the importance of colour and design in decoration. In some schools, for instance, boys and girls do fabric printing and the fabrics are later used for curtains and cushion covers. They make baskets and trays for the school flat and offices; they paint pictures which are framed in the woodwork centre and then hung in various rooms. In one school the senior boys and girls discussed the redecoration of the flat. They bought wall paper, paint, stains, distemper, brushes and some new rugs and fittings and completed the redecoration with a minimum of help and supervision.

The end-result was naturally very amateurish but the experience was of tremendous educational value.

Needlework

Work with needles is very important. There is often a tendency, however, to include it in the curriculum for its value as a particular skill rather than for its contribution to the educational process as a whole. It is occasionally taught without due regard to the children's abilities, to good learning procedures and to its ultimate usefulness in developing social competence. The use of a big needle and thick wool should be introduced to both boys and girls as soon as seems advisable—usually at about 7–8 years. Even at this early age, the children should be allowed to make patterns on pieces of old material and encouraged to see that a needle and cotton are generally used to join pieces of cloth together. As hand-eye co-ordination and manipulation develop the size of needle and thickness of materials should be reduced. The children should be encouraged to make articles for a definite purpose, e.g. younger boys are usually very keen on needlework when they can make costumes, however crudely, for their puppets. Boys' interest in this craft will decrease with age and they should then be allowed to dispense with it. With girls, the programme should be so graded on an assignment basis that continuing success is assured. The teacher should not expect all the girls by the end of the course to be able to make a dress from a pattern with good finish. Indeed, since mass-produced clothes of good quality and at reasonable prices are available, it is doubtful whether the making of a dress is really important. From a utilitarian point of view, it is more important that the girls should concentrate on the maintenance of clothes and household linen and spend any surplus time on knitting and embroidery which they will probably continue to use as leisure activities after leaving school. As far as clothes are concerned, it is essential to teach both boys and girls how to choose clothes which are sensible and appropriate. Many of the older boys and girls need help in choosing clothes which are suitable for different seasons and situations, and tasteful in colour and design.

Physical Education

Physical education must not be solely concerned with the development of strength and physical skills, or indeed with physical development alone. It should be viewed as an integral part of the whole programme for personality development. Nor should physical education be looked upon as something which only happens in the gymnasium or the hall at a set time. It should be occurring at all sorts of times and in all kinds of situations. For example, attention to posture and general bearing should be given whenever appropriate—while sitting at a desk or table, walking about the school, standing informally in a group, or when being spoken to by a teacher. Attention should be drawn to correct breathing when speaking, reading orally, or singing; help in learning to skip, to catch or kick a ball should be given when suitable opportunities arise in casual play situations.

Physical education should include, at all levels, training in personal hygiene and general fitness, and the development of co-operation, courage and confidence, perseverance and independence. It should provide opportunities for exploration and experiment in the use of physical activity and the use of skill and strength in work and play. Because of their poor home environment, or as a result of rejection, ESN children have often missed the opportunities for skill learning which arise naturally in play. It should be noted that the adverse effects of these missed opportunities are cumulative. Primary skills are not developed and consequently more mature ones are harder to learn. This may lead to further rejection and isolation. Play and experimenting is often all they need in order to improve in such skills as catching, bouncing, aiming, throwing, batting, climbing and skipping. They are ready to learn and, given the opportunity, learn readily.

Physical education should take into account and help to minimize those physical limitations which occur most frequently in ESN children—poor posture and muscular incoordination, lack of stamina, specific physical defects. These limitations may call for medical treatment and the attention of experts in remedial physical education. Thus in 20 boys in a residential ESN school who took part in a special programme of physical education, Oliver found 15 boys who were suffering from orthopaedic defects of one kind or another, e.g. droopy posture, kyphosis, flat feet.

Finally physical education should take advantage of the many opportunities it will have (because ESN children are physically nearer normal) to compensate for other limitations and to ensure feelings of accomplishment and success.

The physical education programme

In the section on physical characteristics we observed that in any group of ESN children there is likely to be a wide variation in physical development. Although an average for height, weight, or height-weight ratio may not be significantly different from that for a corresponding normal group, the individual variations within any group are certain to be greater. These differences create a difficult problem of organization in the physical education lessons, particularly in smaller schools. In these, any one class will have a considerable range of height, weight, physical strength, skills and over-all maturity within its pupils. It is impossible, therefore, to devise a rigid programme of physical education for the class as a whole. As in all the other areas of the curriculum, individual differences will have to be recognized and catered for. In physical education particularly, the manifestations of unevenness of personal development will be clear and the problems associated with it highlighted. On the one hand we may have the child whose physical growth is normal but who is very immature emotionally and socially. Because of his physique he may be expected to take responsibilities and perform in group activities for which he is emotionally and socially inadequate. On the other hand, although less usually, there will be the child whose physical development is very retarded but who is emotionally and socially adequate. He will probably be unable to keep up with the rest in speed, skills, rhythm and strength. The physical education lesson, therefore, calls for good organizing ability on the part of the teacher if it is adequately to play its part in educational treatment.

The following programme is suggested as being the basis of physical education lessons and activities in the ESN school.

(a) In the early stages, up to about eleven years of age, lessons should be as free and informal as possible. They should encourage children to use their natural activity, e.g. climbing, walking, running, skipping, catching, throwing, and to develop other physical skills. Apparatus should include large and small balls, bean bags, hoops, skittles, mats, skipping ropes, balance benches, climbing frames, beams for hanging and crawling activities, and targets for aiming practice. The best physical education lessons we have seen are those in which our younger children are allowed to use the gymnasium with its fixed, portable and small apparatus for a free physical activity period. It is an educational treat to observe children using the varied apparatus in a multitude of ways and often with surprising ingenuity; to see the individual children's different reactions; to notice over a period of a few lessons the increase in confidence, initiative and co-operativeness and the ways in which highly individualistic activity gradually develops into group activities.

In these early stages of physical education, much use should be made of rhythms. These should be uncomplicated and used in conjunction with many forms of locomotion, e.g. skipping, walking, tiptoeing, crawling and marching to the rhythms beaten on a drum or played as chords on a piano or sung by the children as they move. These rhythmic activities can be combined with music and movement to lead to simple free dance or dramatic activity. It is a good thing to include some form of rhythmic activity in all lessons at this stage: indeed, suitably adapted for age and ability, it is popular even with senior children, e.g. dance drama is very stimulating and provides excellent physical and mental exercise for boys and girls of fifteen years. The younger children should be encouraged to become more aware of their own bodies and what they can do. Exercises which ask the children to make themselves as tall, as fat, as thin, as stiff, as loose as they can, or which ask them to trace out shapes with their hands, feet and head and make varied configurations with their whole body, are extremely useful.

(b) All these activities will lead to a gradual increase in control and refinement of movement and stimulate the desire to participate in more formal work and team games. The children will want to copy the activities of their older friends and use their new skills in more traditional ways. The boy who has learned to jump over a cane supported by two skittles will want to jump on to and finally over, the box or buck. The boy who has learned how to hang on to a rope and swing will try to climb it: the boy who has acquired skill in kicking and controlling a ball will ask if he can play soccer. The girl who has learned to catch and throw will enjoy playing netball or corner spry. In this way, the early stages prepare for later ones when more formal and controlled activities are introduced. It is quite surprising how agile and accomplished many ESN children can become when their physical development and skills are encouraged and nurtured in this way. The standard of agility and individual prowess in older ESN children can be well within normal limits. Nevertheless the teacher must not be so keen on developing the formal aspects of physical education that informal activities are neglected.

There is need at all stages for allowing the children to experiment, within the bounds of safety, with exercises and games. Oliver records how a group of senior ESN children were encouraged to invent their own exercises with the use of logs. Great ingenuity was shown in devising these exercises and the boys demonstrated them to the others. They also made simple drawings with brief written explanations to show how they should be done. One boy wrote:

MY EXERCISE
First you lay on your stomach on the log. Then you tighten your back muscles you shape yourself like a banana and at the same time try to put your little fingers together and do not forget to keep your balance, stay there fore five seconds.

Rhythmic activities will still be valuable whether given in the form

211

of movement or dance, or even occasional free standing exercises to a musical accompaniment. Indeed, rhythm should be emphasized with ESN children because they need a great deal of practice before their movements are relaxed and rhythmic. Social dancing in its various forms—country, square, and ballroom—should be included for both boys and girls, not only for its physical value but also because it encourages the sexes to mix more readily and sensibly.

(c) Physical education, as we have noted, should not be confined to the gymnasium or hall. Games, athletics and swimming are essential components. Team games are particularly useful for encouraging co-operation, team spirit, and social relationships generally. However, ESN children need assistance and practice before they can become useful members of a team, and it is as well to start training in team work, perhaps in small groups, as early as possible. Athletics and swimming are more individual and, therefore, have the advantage of allowing the child to compete against himself. Adventure training in the form of camping, canoeing, rambling, cross-country running, and mountain climbing and fell walking where possible, is of obvious value. Camping for both boys and girls not only fosters physical fitness but introduces the children to new experiences and provides opportunities for a wide range of educational activities. We would also recommend the use of adventure or 'junk' playgrounds which can be a great asset to the special school. With such things as old immobilized cars and lorries, old sheds, rope ladders, low balancing bars, logs, large bore concrete or iron pipes, bricks, broken slabs, and a sand pit, all kinds of physical activity and individual and group play can be stimulated. In addition, an adventure playground provides unique opportunities for emotional release, language development and the growth of confidence and self-reliance.

(d) The physical education programme must include health education. There are many incidental opportunities in physical education for helping children to appreciate how their bodies work and what are the requirements for healthy living. In the gymnasium, they should always wear appropriate clothing, be made aware of the need for good lighting and ventilation, cleanliness and tidiness, and the value of co-operation. In the changing rooms attention should be paid to the care of clothing, the use of lavatories and regard for other people's property. In games and athletics the value of physical fitness should be stressed—e.g. the harmful effects of smoking, unbalanced diet, over-strain, and irregularities in sleep.

At present there is a shortage of physical education specialists who are willing to take up work with ESN children. In any case, many special schools are too small to warrant the appointment of a specialist. However, excellent work can be done by the class teacher who has had some training in physical education and who is keen and enthusiastic and aware of the aims and purposes of his teaching. If he pays due attention to the preparation of lessons, anticipates the organizational difficulties that are bound to occur with a hetero-geneous group, avoids obvious dangers and makes his lessons lively, cheerful and interesting, he will be successful. He need not be a good performer himself since getting one child to help or give a demon-stration to others is a sound educational technique.

Religious education

Religious education of ESN children is of great importance for their development as persons and as one aspect of their preparation for living. Nevertheless, it is perhaps one of the most difficult parts of the curriculum to teach because it is partly concerned with abstract ideas. We have stressed repeatedly that the ESN child, even the older one, is limited in his capacity for dealing with such ideas unless they can be related in concrete form to his experience. Only then are they likely to have significance for him. We have, therefore, to face up to the ever-present difficulties of communication. Many of the commonly used words in religious teaching are only imper-fectly understood—faith, repentance, mercy, spirit, holy. It is worth noting that this problem of communication was one met by Christ and solved by the use of parables and stories related to the life of His time. But even these for ESN children will need further simple explanation and relating to living. In practice, therefore, no matter how strong the teacher's religious beliefs are, he will have to avoid too much emphasis on doctrines in favour of a more simple approach which relates the meaning of religious experiences to practical living.

A further difficulty arises from the lack of harmony between the moral and spiritual values the school tries to introduce and those prevailing in the children's home and community. For many ESN children, the religious education received in their own homes will be meagre. Few will attend Sunday School or Church; many will not have experienced from birth the affection and security upon which moral values and judgments are based. The only religious education they will receive will be that given in school, and even this may mean little to them since they will be confused by the obvious discrepancy between what they are taught and experience in school and what happens in their own society.

213

What the special school can do

Great though the difficulties are, the ESN school can certainly do much to help the child appreciate what living a good life means. It can, by the activities and experiences it provides, by its spirit and Christian atmosphere introduce the child to truth, beauty and goodness in human experience, to the value of service and co-operation in social living, and to the importance of human personality.

To do so it must distinguish between religious *education* and religious *instruction*, i.e. the imparting of religious knowledge. Religious education is not confined to the Scripture lesson but includes the experience of worship in the school assembly; the experience of living in a school community motivated by the simple faith of doing to others as you would have them do to you; the absorbing of attitudes through relationships with adults who are kind and gentle.

The set Scripture lesson can be limited in its value if it is approached in too conventional a way. ESN children enjoy hearing the stories of the Bible and there is much that they absorb unconsciously from them. However, these can be supplemented by narratives based on the lives of famous heroes and heroines, and of children and adults known to the children themselves. Suitable references to the good actions of people in the news or in the children's own environment can be most useful.

The form which the daily act of worship takes needs careful consideration if it is to mean anything to the pupils. It is almost impossible to select prayers and hymns suitable to the whole school. For this reason it is often useful to have one general assembly each week and to make different arrangements for other days. Some of the best forms of service we have seen are the short, intimate ones taken in a classroom. These have included the unaccompanied singing of one or two verses of appropriate hymns, simple prayers (sometimes composed earlier by the children), a brief reference to the beauty and wonder of day-to-day experiences and a short time for individual prayer. This type of daily service is particularly useful for the younger children in an all-age ESN school. Even with older children the material should be carefully selected. Prayers especially should be chosen so that they can be related to the ideals and spirit of the school and to the children's lives. Allowing the children to discuss the form of worship, or ask for specific prayers or favourite hymns, makes the worship all the more personal and meaningful. At certain festival times, they should be allowed to decorate the assembly hall, e.g. by making a crib at Christmas, by pictures and models of the Easter story, by a display of flowers, fruit and vegetables at Harvest time. On occasions a class can be made responsible for the whole service or it can perform a dramatic presentation of a Bible story or part of a simple miracle or morality play.

As in other areas of the curriculum it is surprising what ESN children can do in religious education if they are given the opportunity. They should be encouraged to relate stories, invent stories, make models, devise plays, compose hymns and tunes, think up their own prayers and discuss the meaning of what they see and hear. By such means, they relate the lessons to their own lives and grow in moral and perhaps spiritual understanding. How much they learn in a factual sense is less important than how sincerely they feel. 'God bless you, sir' written spontaneously at the end of a child's letter may be prompted by a depth of sincerity we fail to appreciate.

FURTHER READING

Physical Education.
OLIVER, J. N. *Physical education for educationally subnormal children.* Ed. Review. Vol. 8, No. 2, Feb. 1956.
CHESWORTH, A. and OLIVER, J. N. *Subnormal boys are helped by logs.* Spec. Sch. J. 45, No. 3, Sept. 1956.
Ministry of Education. 1. *Moving and Growing.* 2 *Planning the programme.* H.M.S.O.
MORISON, R. *Educational gymnastics for girls.* Ling Association.
GELL, H. *Music and movement for the young child.* Australasian Publishing Co.
Religious Education.
CURR, W., LUCAS, D. R., MOSES, H. G. *The religious education of backward children.* Religion in Education. Autumn. 1959.
CURR, W. *Religious education of retarded children.* Sp. Sch. J., 1958.
DEVEREUX, H. M. *Housecraft in the education of handicapped children.* Mills & Boon, 1963.
MATHEWS, KRUSE and SHAW. *The Science of Physical Education for handicapped children.* Harper (N.Y.), 1962.

XII

EDUCATION FOR SOCIAL COMPETENCE

COLIN, a backward sixteen-year-old from a good home presented a real problem to his parents on leaving school. He had, for various reasons, not attended a special school but had attended a private school which concentrated on academic attainments. His reading was surprisingly good for one of his low ability. Over the years of schooling he had memorized a few basic number facts but had acquired no practically useful knowledge of number and could not give change for quite small amounts of money. This ruled out one job—that of helping in a shop—which his parents hoped for him. His greatest limitation, however, was his lack of practical sense and initiative. He always depended on someone else to tell him what to do. In practical matters he was extremely incompetent partly because he had always been able to rely on parents helping him and partly because his schooling had neglected practical activities which could have developed in him the confidence to tackle jobs, and to work independently. He had no real leisure interests except going to the pictures. He had no friends.

Alan, who also came from quite a good home and had a similar level of intelligence, had been fortunate in going to a special school. His reading was not as good as Colin's but he made more use of it. He was quite competent in dealing with money for ordinary purposes. In his job he was a 'sticker'. He held two jobs for long periods, long after many boys would have given up. When the hours and the conditions of the second job became too much for him he found another job through a friend who went to a club that he attended. In his leisure time he continued to do some of the craft work he had done at school. He was given considerable encouragement at home but it was encouragement that gave him freedom to increase in confidence to manage his own affairs and develop his own interests and social contacts.

The difference between these two boys illustrates the difference that can be made by training and experience at home and school which develop the qualities needed for a satisfactory adjustment to life after leaving school. When we discussed the aims of education for ESN children we stressed the importance of the social aspects and, in particular, of the development of desirable personal behaviour, the capacity for proper human relationships and social responsibility. These particular aims are, of course, applicable at all levels of education but they assume greater importance in the education of ESN children who are likely to have greater difficulty in making satisfactory adjustments at home, school and work. Their poorer endowment and achievement make it more difficult for them to obtain recognition and esteem in socially desirable ways. Their difficulties in thinking may make it harder for them to be self-critical and to anticipate the outcome of their behaviour. Their earlier unsatisfactory social experiences may have bred attitudes and ways of behaving which make their adjustment precarious. For example, the over-protected child may have difficulty in adapting to the give-and-take of group activities; the neglected child may not be able to form good relationships with others; emotional disturbance may result in irresponsible behaviour or anxieties about making social contacts.

The special school has therefore to pay special attention to ensuring the development of the qualities needed for successful adjustment to post-school life and in overcoming or minimizing some of the personal problems that can lead to failure.

The characteristics needed by the ESN school leaver may be considered under two heads—personal qualities and social relationships.

Personal qualities

The ESN school leaver should have acquired good standards of personal hygiene, in the mental as well as the physical sense. He should have developed habits of personal cleanliness, a liking for physical activity and a desire to keep fit and healthy. He should have reached a stage of maturity at which he is capable of the independent management of his affairs or failing this, of being able and willing to seek help from reliable sources. We shall expect him to organize his leisure activities and be self-sufficient so as to avoid loneliness and boredom; to realize and adapt to the difficulties of new situations; and to appreciate the importance of such qualities as punctuality, persistence, reliability, self-criticism, friendliness and cheerfulness. He should also be capable of understanding his limitations and of matching his aspirations to his abilities.

Social relationships

Our ESN leaver should appreciate the importance of getting along with other people and of acting towards them in ways which will be considered fitting. He should be ready to learn from his superiors and to meet their reasonable demands; to listen to and act upon the advice of more knowledgeable people and to reject undesirable suggestions. He should be sufficiently sensitive to the reactions of other people to avoid rejection by being too persistent in his demands for attention and friendship, and to avoid over-compensatory behaviour such as showing off, boasting and lying.

In work situations, we should expect our leaver to endeavour to keep a suitable job, to budget wisely and save cheerfully. If he changes his job it should be for good reasons, e.g. greater opportunities, more security, better health conditions, and not for such reasons as increased wages without prospects, to work with a friend, to be nearer home or his girl friend, or because of personal inadequacies and an inability to get along with other work people.

Follow-up studies

Do our ESN school leavers match up to these requirements? Follow-up studies of children leaving day and residential schools show that a large percentage are employable and provide a useful source of unskilled and semi-skilled labour. Hargrove (6) reports that out of 440 leavers 337 were fully employed. Collman (5) in a follow-up study of 98 leavers from residential schools and 125 from day schools between 1949 and 1952 states that 72 per cent were wholly or partly successful at work, 16 per cent were failures and 12 per cent were unemployable. If the unemployables were excluded 69 per cent were completely successful. Atkinson (1) followed up 45 leavers from a boys' residential school and considered that 89 per cent had settled satisfactorily in work. Twenty-nine boys were in unskilled work, 12 in semi-skilled work and 4 were unemployable. Jones (3) followed up 59 boys who left a mixed residential school between July 1952 and July 1955. Seventeen boys had been certified, 5 had left before the statutory leaving age and 37 were at work. Of the last group, 26 were followed-up in detail and Jones states that one became unemployable for health reasons, 5 had had more than two employers and more than half changed their jobs within three months of leaving school. Brown (2) in a study of the post-school adjustment of 84 boys who left a residential school for maladjusted ESN children between 1950 and 1952 found that 10 per cent were in institutions, 37 per cent had had more than five jobs before 1954.

These studies were all carried out during a period of full employment but they appear to substantiate the claim that the vast majority of ESN school leavers are capable of earning their own living. This is particularly true of day special school leavers. The studies also show that lack of intelligence is by no means the main cause of failure in the type of work that most of these children take up, i.e. semi-skilled and unskilled jobs. For example, Collman (5) gives the following figures in connection with his failure group:

IQ	40–49	50–59	60–69	70+
Percentage Employment failures	22	12	18	12
Percentage Unemployable	48	12	4	6

O'Connor (7) states that his consistent failures were found not to be boys with low IQs but boys with higher IQs who were emotionally unstable. He also asserts that the primary determinants of failure appear to be related to conditions of supervision, incentives, emotional stability and degree of home support. The above studies and our own observations suggest that the main causes of failure at work (and this is usually symptomatic of a generalized failure in social matters) are:

(1) Irresponsible behaviour arising from emotional disturbance and temperamental instability. This irresponsibility usually shows itself in lack of persistence, susceptibility to monotony, inability to put up with necessary frustrations, disinterestedness resulting in unpunctuality, poor work habits and apathy.

(2) Lack of adequate supervision and guidance at home.

(3) Lack of understanding on the part of employers and, in particular, of immediate superiors. The ESN school leaver does not readily adapt to changes and the transition from school to work can be very difficult. The leaver may have difficulty in understanding or remembering instructions; he may find the speed of work too much for him, or apparently simple processes difficult to grasp. Changes in routine, the necessary making of new social relationships with more normal people who may not appreciate the problems of the subnormal boy or girl, and the removal of the support of school make adjustment difficult. The traits which are likely to lead to success are:

(i) Attention to necessary detail, especially with reference to standards of performance.

(ii) Regard to rules and regulations. The ESN child may unwittingly disregard the rules and regulations laid down by managements —may be unable to read them or fail to grasp their significance when they are given them verbally. As we shall see later, the school can help the leaver to avoid this difficulty.

(iii) General emotional control which obviates impulsiveness and lack of perseverance.

(iv) An ability to learn from experience. The learner is bound to make mistakes at work either in a job process or in his dealings with others. Successful adjustment depends on an ability to profit from his mistakes either through his own self-criticism or through accepting the help of others.

Follow-up studies of ESN school leavers are few and not very detailed so that generalizations made from them may not be very reliable, but it would seem that, where failure at work occurs, immaturity of personality rather than lack of intelligence is the deciding factor. From the available evidence, job success and personal and social adjustment in general appear to be highly correlated. Nevertheless, the ESN leaver has other difficulties which without help and guidance can lead to tension and breakdown. Some of these difficulties arise from lack of knowledge or lack of awareness of sources of information. Interviews with many leavers, and tape recordings of conversations with boys and girls who have failed and been admitted to mental hospitals, reveal that inability to cope with personal budgeting results in personal and social difficulties. For instance, several boys and girls have been in difficulties over failure to honour hire-purchase agreements unwisely undertaken. Others have borrowed money from workmates or friends and have been unable to meet their debts. The majority are unable to understand the intricacies of their wage slips—income tax, national insurance contributions, Union dues—and few can account for their spending or anticipate future financial commitments. Some spend excessive amounts on clothes (often bought through so-called clubs), on smoking, drinking, cinema visits and girl friends.

Problems arise, particularly in the early months of post-school life, as a result of fear of new situations or inability to cope with the unexpected. These situations are often quite insignificant but can assume frightening proportions to the unprepared leaver. For instance, one girl was very worried because she did not know how to make an appointment with a hairdresser; another girl had a fear of entering the work's canteen—she did not know how to pay for her food or where she was allowed to sit. Yet another was nervous about going into shops. Difficulties over travelling are common, particularly with residential school leavers who have had too little experience of travelling to and from school.

Many ESN children come from unsatisfactory homes which are likely to cause difficulties for the school leavers. Parents may be unreasonable over money matters and lacking in understanding. We know of several boys and girls who have failed to adjust because

220

their parents encouraged them to change jobs for immediate financial gain. In a few cases, parental ambition has caused trouble. Failure of parents to insist on reasonable disciplinary standards or to offer guidance and encouragement are all too common. In a later section we shall discuss home influences in more detail when we deal with the need for hostels or other forms of residential care for ESN school leavers.

Special schools' leavers also have trouble in developing useful, interesting and absorbing leisure activities. In many areas there are no suitable further education facilities for them, although some ESN schools now organize various activities for their leavers. The ESN adolescent does not become a good club member because he lacks confidence about mixing with his brighter contemporaries, although he may well be able to hold his own in many activities, e.g. in games or crafts. Lack of reading ability often adds to his insecurity since he is very sensitive about letting others realize his deficiencies. Being afraid of joining organized clubs, the quieter, withdrawn ESN school leaver either spends too much time at home or escapes into the cinema. The more outgoing leaver joins the gang and resorts to activities which will mask his deficiencies and provide opportunities for exaggerated forms of compensatory behaviour— excessive smoking and drinking, association with good-time girls and, in some cases, delinquency.

Our criteria for successful adjustment of the ESN school leaver are naturally somewhat idealistic but the follow-up studies to which we have referred do not give too gloomy a picture. It seems reasonable to believe that at least three-quarters eventually lead independent, worth-while lives particularly when suitable care and supervision are offered them during the early post-school period. Nevertheless, there is no room for complacency. The ESN school must always make adequate and special provision for procedures designed to foster social maturity and competence. These procedures must be clearly defined, and must be psychologically sound, educationally possible and socially desirable.

Developing social competence in school

We have described on page 217 some of the qualities needed by the ESN child if he is to make a satisfactory adjustment to post-school life. It is one of the most important tasks of the ESN school to develop these qualities, but this cannot be achieved only in the last year or two at school. Social competence, in its various aspects, is something that is the result of a long process of development, the foundation of which is laid in the work done in the junior classes and consolidated and extended as children grow older. The school must adjust its environment so that the child can live and grow in it successfully. He must be able to learn from it, desire and develop acceptable attitudes and modes of behaviour from his experience in it, and eventually realize that it is helping him to prepare for independence in post-school life. In organizing the school to these ends, the following considerations should be taken into account.

(a) Children develop these qualities at different rates. While age and intelligence must be considered in setting standards of social behaviour and personal competence, any class group will vary considerably because of the pupils' previous experiences at home and school. The child's constitutional make-up and his physical development must also be taken into account. In assessing how the child is progressing in social maturity, the check list in Chapter III suggests some of the things that should be looked for.

(b) With some children, social re-education will be necessary. This is not easy because previous attitudes and forms of behaviour are often difficult to change. This is particularly true of over-demanding behaviour which has previously been successful, as in the case of Margaret, a deprived child who had learnt that she could get what she wanted (usually food or sweets) from her inexperienced foster-mother by screaming, kicking and throwing things. On admission to a residential school, she was gradually taught by the teachers and the other children that she could not get what she wanted by this type of behaviour. After two years of patient effort, decided improvement had taken place; but as so often happens, the characteristic had not completely disappeared.

(c) The above considerations indicate that there must be a certain amount of flexibility in the standards of behaviour and in the approach to children. A pattern cannot be imposed; it must develop as the majority of children in the class are becoming ready to act up to it. The school must accept that at times a child's individual activity will be contrary to what is desirable yet it is a necessary part of his attempts at adjustment. His behaviour should be regarded as his way of meeting a felt need, perhaps as an emotional release. The teacher's job is to understand the need and to try to make the necessary arrangements for meeting it, and for avoiding the reappearance of unacceptable behaviour in connection with it. For example, a child sometimes defaces his reading and exercise books and this may be his way of relieving frustrations arising from educational demands which he is incapable of meeting. The remedy, of course, lies in adjusting the difficulty of the work.

(d) Social education must be viewed as an integral part of the whole educational process—in play, in school work, at home. The school's part is so to arrange its programme that each child grows in personal awareness and develops feelings of confidence, self-esteem and self-reliance. Many children have not had experience of playing and working with others, either because mother has protected them from other children, or because they have been rejected by brighter contemporaries. Children do not learn to play and work with others in just a few days. They may need to go through the stages that normal children go through—first of playing more or less on their own, then playing *next* to another child although not in active co-operation, and only later will they make more active contact with each other. It is for this reason that ESN children need time for informal activities or play throughout the junior school, as well as continued opportunities for group activities throughout their school life. The fact that they are needing *individualized* work in basic subjects should not lead to all their work being *individual*. Group work is needed, e.g. in art, drama, the development of a centre of interest, practical subjects and, where possible, in out-of-school clubs, to give experience in working and in planning together. In the older age groups, there should be a balance between such group work and individual work so that the child learns to work by himself with the minimum of supervision. The personal relationships he makes with teachers in school may be vital since he may have had little experience of the give-and-take of good relationships in his home life.

The special school teacher must have some knowledge of the child's home and community setting and try to influence it where it seriously opposes what the school is doing. Close co-operation between parents and teachers is needed if the child is not to suffer from being exposed to conflicting codes of behaviour and morals—one for the school, another for the home, and another for the neighbourhood. The school can often do something to influence parents and, in difficult cases, can seek the help and co-operation of social workers, probation officers and others.

(*e*) The attitudes and relationships within the school are most important. ESN children will learn more about the art of living together when they are educated in an atmosphere of friendliness, consistency and respect for others than from repeated moralizing and exhortations. The head teacher should regard himself as the benevolent head of a therapeutic community in which good relationships within the staff extend throughout the school—between teaching and non-teaching staff; between teacher and class; between child and child. If this is to be done, the head teacher should not isolate himself from the staff in the fond belief that by remaining aloof he will gain in respect and esteem. He should be a leader whose tolerance and accessibility enable the collection of teachers to become a group imbued with the same aims and a common spirit.

School procedures influencing social maturity

(1) Children cannot become socially competent and mentally well if they do not have feelings of success. In school, success is often measured, rightly or wrongly, by accomplishment in basic subjects. The development of other skills as, for example, in practical pursuits or art and craft, can provide useful compensations for failure in other areas of the curriculum, but no child feels really successful in school if his failure in basic subjects is marked. Adequate competence in social situations cannot be achieved without a reasonable standard of reading and number. The school must ensure, therefore, that the basic subjects are well taught—with due regard to learning readiness, motivation, grading of work and individualization of treatment.

(2) All learning situations and procedures should be so planned as to encourage independent work habits and self-direction. These are facilitated by encouraging pupil participation in learning and planning—each child should appreciate the reasons for what he is learning and the significance of each step in the total learning situation. When difficulties arise, the teacher must encourage the child to seek help and guidance, and give assistance by careful explanation, graded examples, and remedial measures.

(3) Some aspects of social education need to be developed by step-by-step demonstration and daily practice. Many of the younger children need help and encouragement to become independent in looking after themselves in feeding, dressing, and cleanliness. There are many who come from homes where personal hygiene, table manners, courtesy, respect for other people and their property receive little attention. There are many occasions in school when these aspects can be developed, partly by example, partly by specific training and insistence.

(4) Many children come from homes where discipline is non-existent or inconsistent. Not only will they have had little teaching about what is right and wrong but may come from environments in which moral standards are extremely poor, for example, in respect of honesty, truthfulness and attitudes towards other people. In trying to remedy this there is always a danger of too much verbalizing and moralizing. Wherever possible, examples should be used so that each child can more easily understand what is expected of him. His own misdemeanours might be used not so much as a matter of punishment as an opportunity to help him develop gradually the

ability to be self-critical—to see how he has offended so that he is more likely to anticipate the result of his actions in future.

(5) The way the school and the class are run as communities can make a contribution to the development of social responsibility. Rules should be kept simple and as few as possible. They should be simple in order that children may comprehend them and so that they do not place too much disciplinary responsibility on the children. The majority of ESN children wish to conform and be helpful and co-operative. This should therefore be encouraged by positive suggestion, ample praise, and sympathetic correction. They should be allowed to participate in the making of rules and the ordering of routine. Many teachers of ESN children have made successful attempts at establishing simple forms of self-government. By timely discussion and the use of everyday experiences, they encourage the children to make their own rules and to develop a measure of group feeling and responsibility. For example, a group of children complained that the classroom always seemed untidy and that the materials they wanted to use could not always be found in the right place. A discussion ensued out of which some simple rules were formulated—each child was to be responsible for his own desk space and for replacing any books and apparatus that he had used. Failure to do this was to be punished by having to tidy up the whole room next day. (Children often tend to be severe on each other in the matter of punishment and the teacher may need to moderate their 'punishments'.)

Most teachers realize that self-generated standards of discipline should be aimed at and that discipline imposed by authority should be kept to a minimum. The balance between these two forms of discipline must be watched constantly. Some teachers fail in their attempts at instituting some degree of class self-government because they place too much responsibility on the children—e.g. by trying to develop courts and allowing children to decide unaided the forms punishments should take. Other teachers oppose any suggestion that children should be encouraged in self-government. There is, of course, a relationship between the teacher's personality and the disciplinary standards expected or imposed. The teacher who is rigid and authoritarian will insist that children must be compelled to conform and that to achieve conformity, any means, including rule by force and fear, are permissible. On the other hand, the teacher who is vacillating and inconsistent, and untidy and unorganized himself is unlikely to achieve good standards of discipline and class management. The latter teacher is never likely to be successful, while children taught by the former are unlikely to develop independence, self-reliance and an ability to adapt to changes.

We are often asked the question, 'What do you do about discipline?' There is no single answer but the following principles are important.

(i) Difficulties with discipline should not ordinarily arise when the children are interested and busy. If activities are well-prepared and well-organized, the children will respond suitably. Indeed, we have been frequently impressed by the way children will work with absorption and purpose for long periods without teacher direction and without apparent feelings of fatigue. With younger children, the attention span may be shorter and interests may not be sustained for very long. For them, lessons should be shorter and, more important, a wider choice of activities should be provided.

(ii) Rewards and punishments should be used with discretion. In general, encouragement and praise are more effective than threats, scoldings and punishments. Rewards and punishments should fit the child. To stop games or swimming may be a punishment for some and a reward for others. One child may enjoy tidying up the classroom; another may hate it. Consistency, fairness and tolerance are essential.

(iii) When children misbehave persistently there are always causes for that misbehaviour. Ideally, these should be discovered and treated, although this is, of course, not always possible. For the sake of general class discipline, the teacher often has to deal immediately with the symptom—i.e. the misbehaviour. There is not time, for instance, for investigating the cause of a tantrum; it has to be quietened. However, all special school teachers must try to understand the causes of behaviour and realize that, as in all forms of educational treatment, an individual approach is necessary.

In any ESN class there are likely to be one or two children whose behaviour is a more or less constant source of disturbance. The cause in these cases is likely to be acute emotional disturbance or organic damage, or a combination of these. Symptoms will be restlessness, distractibility, over-activity and lack of inhibition, and are particularly apparent in younger children. It is usually better in more formal lessons to seat these children at the side of the class and to provide a variety of activities for them. The more seriously disturbed children need individual help. There will remain the child who continues to be difficult despite all efforts to control and help him. In extreme cases exclusion may be necessary. Although head teachers are naturally very reluctant to take this very serious step it is occasionally necessary if the disturbing behaviour is detrimental to the welfare and education of other children.

(iv) Sarcasm should never be used.

(v) No punishment should be used which is likely to tempt the child into further misdemeanours. For instance, in residential schools it would seem inadvisable to withdraw the whole of a child's pocket money or his sweets allocation if, as is common with deprived children, he cannot manage without sweets.

(vi) 'Issues' with children should be avoided. Many disciplinary episodes are created by teachers putting themselves into positions from which they cannot withdraw gracefully and without loss of dignity, e.g. by issuing threats which cannot be carried out.

(vii) Favouritism should be avoided. Many ESN children, especially the deprived, are very sensitive to anything they believe to be unjust. They will react unfavourably if they feel they are not getting their fair share of the teacher's attention and affection or if a reward is not commensurate with effort. This does not mean that children who need extra help and affection should be denied it.

(viii) Corporal punishment is hardly ever necessary when teacher-child relationships are good. It is a last resort when other devices or sanctions have failed.

(ix) Children entering the special school at a later age may need firmer discipline at first in order to give them feelings of security in what is probably a freer and more relaxed atmosphere than the one to which they have been accustomed.

(x) The healthy child should be reasonably assertive and aggressive and outlets for such behaviour need to be provided, e.g. in drama, games, adventure training.

(6) Attention should be given to class composition and arrangement in order to ensure that the child is in an environment that will help him to make the best possible adjustment. In placing a child in a class, the following questions might be considered:

(i) Are the child's attainments adequate for him to feel successful? Failing this, does the teacher individualize his treatment sufficiently for the child to make progress at his own level.

(ii) Is the child's physical development such that he can be suitably placed there?

(iii) Is the child socially mature enough?

(iv) Is he likely to make a good relationship with the teacher and the other children in the class?

(v) Is the disciplinary atmosphere appropriate for the child?

(vi) If the child is particularly difficult, nervous or insecure, is there a child in the class who might help him settle down? It is well to remember that a child can often be helped better by another child than by the teacher. For example, Josephine is a very disturbed girl with neurological evidence of brain injury. She is usually antagonistic to persons in authority but always responds satisfactorily to the help and guidance of an older girl, Jean. Again, Peter, a persistent absconder from a residential school, greatly improved when Robert, a former absconder, was asked to help him.

Procedures for helping ESN leavers develop social competence

In our summary of follow-up studies, we indicated that failure was largely due to weaknesses in character and personality, and inability to meet the demands of new situations. The ESN school cannot be held responsible for every failure but it should ensure that every feasible step has been taken to help each leaver to avoid breakdown situations at work, at home and in the community. Every child in school should be looked on as a potential school leaver. His educational treatment should aim at developing those qualities and attitudes which will lead to successful participation in all spheres of post-school life.

Since our ESN children will be placed in a job not requiring great skill, we need not attempt any narrow vocational training. The view is sometimes held that to include in the curriculum such activities as shoe repairing or tailoring will help the ESN leaver to find work in such trades. In practice, this is rarely so since training in school does not simulate actual working conditions nor are the skills taught the same as those which will later be required. Indeed, there are some instances where such training in school has been a decided handicap in the actual work situation. In any case, employers generally prefer to train their new employees in their own way under their own working conditions. This does not mean, of course, that practical work such as gardening, looking after animals, woodwork, metal work and housecraft should be disregarded. They have an important part to play in enlarging the child's general knowledge, experience in the use of different tools and materials, and for the improvement of work habits.

It is pre-vocational training in a wider sense upon which the school should concentrate. We have seen that failure is due to weaknesses in personality and inexperience rather than to low intelligence and lack of skill. The training programme should therefore include the following:

(1) The arrangement of visits which show the leaver a variety of working conditions.

(2) Introducing the pupil to new experiences similar to those he will meet in post-school life.

(3) Training in specific aspects of working life such as interviews, form-filling, details of wage slips, changing jobs, estimation of travelling time, factory rules, and the way a factory works.

(4) Advice on leisure activities and relationships with the opposite sex.

(5) Guidance about fitting in at home. This is particularly important for the residential school leaver who, in addition to meeting the difficulties of new situations at work, will possibly have to adjust to poorer living conditions and unsatisfactory family relationships at home.

(6) Personal budgeting.

(7) Educational first-aid for some individual leavers.

The programme outlined below, though by no means finalized, will be of use to teachers of senior ESN children and backward children in secondary schools. It was designed to meet the needs of children leaving a large residential school and was based on replies to questionnaires seeking information about the leavers' progress in their immediate post-school years. It was also based on the results of personal interviews with leavers and their parents, discussions with Youth Employment Officers and After-Care workers, and on research findings.

Discussion groups

Each leaver joins a discussion group at the beginning of his penultimate term in school. The group leader is either the head teacher or one of the staff. The group meets in a room which is not a classroom, e.g. the head teacher's room or the staff room. Discussions are informal and friendly and each group member is encouraged to take an active part. The leader has to ensure that quieter withdrawn children are given a chance and that the more outgoing, talkative children do not dominate the discussion. In the early stages, it may be difficult to get the members of the group to relax and talk, or to be sufficiently serious. However, if the group leader chooses interesting topics related to the children's present or past experiences and uses films or filmstrips, tape recordings or sociodrama to stimulate discussion the difficulties are quickly overcome. *The group leader must always resist the temptation to play too dominant a role himself.* Out initial difficulties have decreased because the discussion groups have become part of the school tradition and are looked upon as a great privilege. Experience has also enabled us to improve our methods of deciding the composition of groups, e.g. by paying greater attention to the children's abilities, experiences and general maturity.

The first discussions usually deal with the children's present problems and status, and with their ideas about various aspects of school life. We encourage them to discuss school organization and methods of improving treatment or discipline. We take them into our confidence about our own problems where these will help them to realize and talk about their own. For example, in one discussion group the head master admitted to having felt rather nervous and apprehensive when he first stood in front of the assembled school to take the daily service. Other adults in the same group cited similar instances from their own experience. The children were surprised to hear these admissions, and a lengthy discussion ensued. The next meeting, which dealt with the first day at work, was a memorable one. We suggested and discussed many situations, likely to be met on this eventful first day at work, which would make the boys rather nervous. At this point, it is appropriate to stress the importance of discussing the apparently most insignificant incidents since these may be the ones to cause anxiety and tension. For example, 'What time will you get up?' 'What will you wear?' 'What will you do when you arrive at the factory gate?' are questions which must be dealt with, and answered.

Whenever possible, discussion should be followed by some first-hand experience. It is important, therefore, to integrate the programme of discussions with that for educational visits. Before a work's visit, for example, the children should be given information about the type of work they will see, the working conditions, and a simple description of the manufacturing processes they will see. Each visit should be followed by discussions during which the children can analyse their impressions. These post-visit discussions are most useful since they bring up many of the problems and new situations which the leaver may have to face. For example, the problem of noisy, dirty working conditions, the degrees of skill required in different types of process, the type of people the leaver will meet, rules and regulations, degree of personal risk, difficulties of working independently or as a member of a group, can all be discussed. We have been pleasantly impressed by the degree of insight shown by our future leavers during these sessions. They can appreciate their limitations and consequently are better able to match their aspirations to their abilities. This is made apparent when, in co-operation with Youth Employment Officers, we discuss job placement with them individually.

A comprehensive programme of works visits is of course a very useful aid to the discussion of suitable types of employment. ESN children certainly need much help in making choices of job. This is particularly true of the residential school leaver who may have no idea of what jobs are available to him. The school must find out what types of work are carried on near the child's home if worthwhile suggestions and guidance are to be offered. This information can be obtained from Youth Employment Officers, but we ask the leaver to visit his local office for interview during his last school holiday. During his last term at school, we can thus offer practical help based on the information he brings back. During recent years, leavers have had no difficulty in obtaining initial employment. The leavers' difficulties arise more from being placed in unsuitable employment. In discussion, therefore, we place particular emphasis on how to keep a job, the advisability of not changing a job without seeking advice, and the importance of those attitudes and qualities (reliability, punctuality, honesty, steadiness, courtesy, and friendliness) which are necessary for work success. We stress the importance of punctuality, and willingness to take a joke. Talking about these things is not enough. Punctuality is dependent on the ability to estimate time and distance and to relate these to the type of transport available. Our programme of individual assignments includes practice in this estimation (see page 234). An ability to take a joke can be developed in those children who are easily upset because of lack of confidence and over-sensitiveness.

In these sessions which deal with changing employment, we make great use of examples from our follow-up files or of tape recordings of conversations with leavers who have returned to visit us and have talked about their success or failure. The tape recordings have proved especially useful since our group members generally know the boys and girls concerned. Indeed, when circumstances are suitable, we sometimes mention the boy's name and ask the group whether they think he will have been successful since leaving school. We discuss the reasons for their opinions, then play the recording and discuss it in detail. If a change of job has occurred, we ask the group to say whether or not the change was a good one and whether it was made for adequate reasons. If a leaver has been successful, we talk over how this has come about. The educational and therapeutic value of such discussions is very great, both for the group as a whole and for the individual members.

Since an interview may be important in obtaining a desired job, we arrange real and mock interviews as part of the programme. Using a kind of sociodrama, we let the boys and girls interview each other, and adults in the group also play the roles of interviewer and interviewee. Each interview is discussed and then re-enacted with any improvements that have been suggested—dress, deportment, clear speech, punctuality and smartness are stressed. After these rehearsals of interviews, we invite Youth Employment Officers and Personnel Officers from firms with which we have made useful contacts, to attend one of our sessions and actually interview the children.

231

When we discuss and give training in specific aspects of working conditions, we use a very practical approach based on actual procedures. We obtain from co-operating firms actual copies of rules and regulations, wage packets and slips, time sheets and application forms, union cards and sickness regulations. During visits, we ask the person who arranges the itinerary to ensure that time is allowed for the children to be shown how the topics we have previously discussed are practised in the actual work's setting, e.g. what happens if the rules are broken, paying-out procedure, and so on.

Our discussion groups emphasize working life and conditions because economic efficiency and job-satisfaction are so important in the making of satisfactory post-school adjustments. However, social competence also includes adjustment at home and in the wider community. Our discussions therefore include such topics as relationships in the home, choice of friends, club activities, choice of pastimes and personal budgeting. Again, in these parts of the programme, our approach is an essentially practical one. Actual examples are used whenever possible. For instance, we discuss known examples of boys and girls who have not been happy at home either because of their own shortcomings, or because of parental neglect, or dissatisfaction with living conditions. We visit youth clubs and arrange football, cricket and table tennis matches and square dances with them. We talk about cinema going, amusement arcades, Teddy boys and girls, smoking and drinking, television viewing, and how to avoid boredom. Personal budgeting receives particular attention. Surprisingly few children have much idea of what they are likely to earn and how their wages will be used. We therefore give many examples of how our leavers spend their money and we include such items as board and lodging, buying clothes, savings (every leaver is shown how to open a bank or Post Office savings account), paying for such things as toilet requirements, shoe repairs, hairdressing, travelling, pleasures. Hire purchase agreements receive special attention. The arithmetic programme deals with personal budgeting in detail.

Our discussions and talks about relationships with the opposite sex are, of course, most important. We realize that there are widely differing views about the value and place of sex education in the curriculum. We also appreciate the need for individualizing the approach to it. It would seem also that the ESN school leaver is likely to get into no more serious trouble over sex experiences than the dull leaver from the secondary modern school. However, we know that many ESN adolescents are not likely to receive wise guidance in sex matters from their parents. If teacher-child relationships are good, the school acting *in loco parentis* should do something to help. A biological approach or a moralizing attitude are not likely to achieve very much. A friendly discussion on the dangers of pre-marital sex relationships can help to avoid future unhappiness. We discuss the economic effects of having an illegitimate child, the personal unhappiness and tensions which can result, and the problems of the child itself. Such discussions may not prevent sexual promiscuity in all leavers but interviews with leavers who have returned to school show that our discussions have been useful in many cases.

The success of the discussion groups depends to a large degree on the group leader. He must have insight into the leavers' problems, a sensitivity to the reactions of individual members, and a friendly approach. It will be obvious that there are some persons whose presence encourages a free flow of talk, and others, well-intentioned and kindly, who would yet have the effect of freezing-up discussion. It should be noted too that the group discussion has its dangers. It can, for example, make the sensitive child who feels inadequate more nervous and insecure as a result of the increasing awareness of problems associated with leaving school. As we have mentioned, there will be individual talks with children and individual problems can be tackled in that way. The advantages of these group discussions seem so great as to outweigh any disadvantages.

Educational visits

We have already emphasized the importance of a programme of visits in the pre-vocational scheme and of preparation and discussion in connection with it. One further point is perhaps worth making. It is not sufficient to take the leavers to works which specialize in processes which they are likely to carry out, or in which first-class working conditions obtain. It is important that they should see skilled work in progress in order to help them appreciate their own limitations. They should have some experience of all types of working conditions—noisy, quiet, dirty, clean, indoor, outdoor, and in large and small firms.

Individual assignments

It is important that the ESN leaver should be capable of independent action and of working without direct supervision. The whole educational process aims at the development of these but the leaver requires more intensive and practical training. Our leavers' programme therefore includes individual assignments designed to develop self-confidence, initiative, a willingness to ask for advice and information, and an ability to meet new situations without strain· These assignments provide experiences in shopping, travelling, using the telephone, estimation of time and distance, the carrying out of requests and the following of directions.

The first step is to teach each leaver to use the telephone. Small groups are taken to a call box and given practice in the operations of making a call. The children then go out unescorted and make a call to the head teacher or a member of the staff. Once they are proficient in using the phone, they follow a scheme of graded assignments. Each assignment involves the use of public transport and the making of a telephone call which serves as a check on movements. as a means of giving instructions, and for dealing with difficulties, When the boy (or girl) phones up school, he is asked to estimate how far he thinks he has travelled, and how long he has been away from school. He is then given a specific task to perform—such as finding an address, obtaining articles from a shop, buying stamps or postal orders, finding prices of clothes, foods, hairdressing, shoe repairing and so on, obtaining pamphlets and brochures, and details about bus or train times. He might be asked to visit places of cultural interest such as an art gallery or museum and return with information about selected exhibits. We usually insist on the child visiting a café for a cup of tea or a meal not exceeding a certain amount. Our experience shows that many ESN children are afraid of asking strangers for help and information, and we therefore arrange the assignments so that their successful completion depends upon overcoming this fear. Prior consultations with shopkeepers, local officials and interested private persons are a great help in this connection.

When the child returns to school, he has to give a full description of his experiences and account for the money he has spent. (This is provided by the LEA who have always been generous and sympathetic in this matter.) Difficulties are discussed either individually with the child concerned or with the group as a whole. Future assignments are so arranged as to give further practice in difficult situations, to extend individual children's experiences and to increase the demands made upon their initiative. By the end of the scheme, we expect the majority of the children to travel distances up to fifteen miles independently, to seek information without fear, to cope with money situations, to buy a meal and to return to school within a given time. Our expectations are generally realized. However, we would point out that the grading of assignments must be adapted to individual capacities. Some children are capable of completing the whole scheme in four or five journeys. Others take much longer and some are so fearful or so lacking in drive and self-confidence that they find the experience too much for them. Such children need extra patience, encouragement and support. Each school, whether day or residential, will have to adapt the assignments to meet the needs of its own population.

Educational first-aid

Very few leavers from special schools should be totally illiterate or unable to deal with practical money problems up to a pound. Nevertheless, the school must cater for the small minority who because of irregular attendance, late entry or special difficulties have only very slight attainments. These children will generally be emotion ally disturbed and lack the confidence to deal with the assignments we have suggested. Every effort should be made to equip them with a vocabulary of useful words—road signs, words connected with travelling, shopping, employment and leisure activities. They should be given frequent practice in handling real money in practical situations. Surprising progress is often made because motivation is very great and limited success is easily experienced and appreciated. Moreover, the ESN leaver is not incapable of further learning even if actual schooling has ceased. Many of the slowest learners make considerable progress in the basic subjects after leaving school and an apparently insignificant progress during a first-aid programme may be the basis of surprising improvements later when the importance of learning to read and cope with money has become more apparent.

Post-school management

The pre-vocational training described above will certainly do much to help the ESN school leaver to meet the problems inherent in the transition from school to work. Nevertheless, further help and supervision will be necessary in the majority of cases because the child will move from a society which has been geared to his individual needs, and in which he has been taught and guided by trained personnel, into one which probably expects standards of achievement without regard to individual capacities. His connection with adults who understood him and whom he could respect and lean upon will be broken and new associations made. He will be parted from a group composed of individuals with somewhat similar inadequacies and feelings to his own, and will now have to meet, in an extremely different setting, the demands of a more mixed group. These demands may increase his feelings of inadequacy, loneliness and frustration and make apparent to others his general immaturity. Some scheme of post-school supervision and guidance is therefore essential. This scheme should provide readily available aids to vocational, social and personal adjustment.

Job placement

Obtaining suitable employment for the ESN school leaver is, of course, the first step towards eventual adjustment. We have seen that the majority of leavers are placed in jobs. However, placement is not enough—the aim is job-satisfaction. It is not always possible to achieve this at once and changes of employment can be expected in a proportion of cases. However, these changes can be kept to a minimum if the following suggestions are acted upon:

(a) There must be close liaison between the school and the Youth Employment Service. Contact between the school and individual firms should also be made, particularly in day schools serving a limited area. Personal contact between head teacher and employers can be most useful, and it should be part of the former's duties to make such contacts and to know about the local employment situation.

(b) Placement must take into account the leaver's strengths, weaknesses, interests and wishes, and parental attitudes. It must also take into account the general assumptions that (1) the ESN child may have difficulty in working with others; (2) speedy operations may be beyond his capabilities for a long time; (3) he is more likely to succeed in jobs which involve repetitive processes which call for simple manipulation; (4) he will require at first, a well ordered routine and supervision by a sympathetic adult; (5) his chances of success under suitable conditions are good.

The following types of employment appear, from follow-up studies and experience, to be suitable:

UNSKILLED

Boys	Girls
Labourer	Domestic service
Driver's mate	Ward maid
Bottle washer	Kennel maid
Warehouse assistant	Canteen work
Messenger	Laundry work
Hotel worker	
Canteen assistant	

SEMI-SKILLED

Woodwork	Dressmaking and
Garage hand	tailoring
Gardening	More complicated packing
Semi-skilled engineering	Factory work
Farm labourer	
Tailoring (mass production)	
Painting and decorating assistant	
Boot and shoe repairing	
Coal mining (unskilled jobs)	
Foundry work	
Plumber's mate	

There are a few ESN leavers who are capable of taking up training for more skilled occupations such as carpentry, plumbing, lathe operators (boys) and shop assistants (girls).

(c) If at all possible, parents should be consulted about their child's employment since their co-operation and understanding are vital. They should be invited to the first employment interview, although in some instances it is preferable that they should be interviewed by the head teacher separately because they need help in understanding their child's limitations. Many parents also need guidance on how to help their child to adjust to work situations. This guidance should take the form of practical suggestions such as how to ensure punctuality, independence, self-criticism, cheerfulness, and a willingness to take a joke; what to do when a job seems unsuitable; how and when to offer encouragement; how to help over financial matters; where further help can be obtained. The parents should be advised that changing jobs for financial gain is not always the best thing in the long run and that they should accept the child as he is, but without undue complacency.

(d) The Youth Employment Office should, where possible, have on its staff an officer who can specialize in vocational guidance for all types of handicapped persons. This is difficult in small departments, and in the larger one an officer who specializes may be placed at a professional disadvantage. We suggest that when these difficulties exist the special school might be given more responsibility for vocational guidance and job placement. In smaller schools the head teacher, and in larger schools a careers master, working in close co-operation with the YEO, could take some of this responsibility. Indeed, there seem to be strong arguments for the special school to play a much more active part in the total guidance programme for its leavers in the early stages of their post-school life.

Social and personal adjustment in post-school life

After-Care. Some form of supervision is needed by the ESN leaver for the first three years after leaving. Up to the present, supervision has been statutory for leavers notified to the Local Health Authority under Section 57(5) of the Education Act, 1944. But the use of Section 57 has varied widely. Some Authorities have notified all their ESN leavers and others less than half. Authorities have also varied in the emphasis placed on intellectual, social and personality criteria for notification. The interpretation of the section has left much to be desired.

Leavers placed under Statutory Supervision became 'subject to be dealt with' under the Mental Deficiency Acts. It was unfortunate that the Mental Deficiency Acts could be invoked on behalf of children who were not severely subnormal nor socially very inadequate. The new Mental Health Act, when fully operative, will abolish Statutory Supervision, and Section 57 of the Education Act will be revised. In future supervision will be voluntary and parents of leavers will, presumably, be advised to seek help when it is thought necessary. The form this help will take is uncertain. Present arrangements are nowhere adequate. Hargrove (6) stated that only 22 of the 97 local authorities replying to her questionnaire, reported that an after-care service was in operation. The existing schemes are organized by local authorities, voluntary bodies or voluntary after-care committees attached to schools. It is to be hoped that the current re-planning of community care will ensure adequate arrangements, in which voluntary bodies and the schools themselves will play a large part.

In Birmingham, an After-Care sub-committee and department were established over fifty years ago. This committee is comprised of elected members from the health and education committees and of co-opted members. Among the latter are all the head teachers of the authority's senior ESN schools. Apart from leavers who have been certified under the Mental Deficiency Acts, all leavers are placed either on statutory or voluntary supervision. It is the responsibility of the After-Care committee to ensure that adequate supervision is provided. This is done by an After-Care officer and social workers who are attached to the Special Services Department. The sub-committee is also responsible for the administration of the city's occupation centres and home teaching. Through a case sub-committee, careful consideration is given to each young person under supervision and recommendations are made for any change in supervision which appears desirable. Under arrangements recently made, a final decision as far as the After-Care department's responsibility is concerned has to be made before the age of twenty-one. After this age, all cases requiring supervision are handed on to the Mental Health Committee and its officers. These arrangements were initiated because it was realized that the most difficult years for the school leaver are those immediately after leaving school. It therefore seemed very desirable, on grounds of efficiency and economy of effort, that the department's social workers should concentrate on the young person and not dissipate their energies over the whole group of mentally-handicapped persons.

This scheme of After-Care appears to work very well for the majority of cases. The fact that each school head teacher is on the committee does something to ensure that each school's views are made known and that continuity is maintained. The school's part in After-Care should be a most important one and other arrangements might be made to improve the co-operation between the schools and social workers. For instance, the social worker attends the employment interview at school and this is her first contact with the leaver. We feel that earlier contacts are desirable so that good relationships are established between the child, his home and the social worker long before he leaves school. We realize that this would require the appointment of more social workers, both male and female. But subnormality is a social as well as an educational problem. It is both inefficient and uneconomical to tackle one aspect and ignore the other.

Hostels for ESN leavers

In some instances, the after-care worker is contending with very difficult and sometimes impossible conditions. These may arise from defects in the leaver's personality, but more often can be attributed to an unsuitable home background. The researches of Hargrove, Atkinson, and Brown and our own follow-up study have revealed that the personality gains which result from special educational treatment are quickly undermined when a boy has to struggle un-aided against a home which is unsatisfactory in every way. The problem is particularly acute for the residential school leaver who was probably recommended for special education in the first place because home conditions were bad. If this child returns to a home which has not improved, his chances of making a good social adjustment are slight, and the time, thought and money spent on his education will have been wasted. Furthermore, a recrudescence of instability leading to delinquency will result in his becoming a charge on public funds yet again, either because he gets into court or the M.D. Acts have to be invoked. It is important, therefore, that the problem of the bad home should be tackled vigorously. Here again a social worker engaged on field work during the child's school life would be a great asset. She might be able to make improvements but, failing this, even the negative finding that the rehabilitation of the home is impossible would be useful to those responsible for making recommendations about the leaver's placement.

At present, because of lack of suitable accommodation, the M.D. Acts have to be used. Some ESN leavers have to be certified. This is a regrettable step and is contrary to the new and more optimistic philosophy of special educational treatment implicit in the 1944 Act. Evidence given to the Royal Commission on the Law relating to Mental Health emphasized the lack of suitable accommodation and recommended that hostels would be useful. We heartily endorse this recommendation, and are pleased to see that under the new Mental Health Act 1959, the Local Authorities are now obliged to provide residential homes and hostels. The trend is therefore towards keeping the ESN leaver out of Mental Deficiency hospitals and providing treatment within the community.

Under the old arrangements, there were many difficulties in establishing hostels, principally that of deciding which committees of the Local Authority had the necessary powers. Health committees had only permissive powers and rarely used them. Two hostels have already been set up by voluntary bodies and are administered at present by the National Association for Mental Health. This is a commendable beginning but the problem is too big for voluntary action alone. It is to be hoped that Local Health Authorities will now work with vigour to provide homes and hostels. In any further re-thinking of community care, the following suggestions might be considered, particularly with reference to the provision of hostels for ESN children leaving school:

(1) It should be the duty of Education Committees to provide hostels for ESN leavers who need them. Close co-operation between Health, Children's and Welfare services would be essential.

(2) The special schools should play an important part in placement and hostel treatment.

(3) Leavers should be admitted without specifying the length of stay, but they should not normally stay for longer than five years.

(4) The size of the hostel should be such that a sense of family loyalty may be encouraged and individual attention given. Creating a family atmosphere is not merely determined by group size. The size and quality of the staff and the nature of the group are more important. However, even with good physical conditions and adequate, well-trained staff a group of fifteen should be the maximum.

(5) The hostel should be able to call in the help of a social worker whose responsibilities would include family case work, the finding of suitable foster homes or lodgings, assistance in job placement and helping individuals in personal and social development. The hostel should also have ready access to psychiatric and psychological services.

(6) In the first instance the hostel should be for ESN school leavers only. Present experience suggests that groups made up of ESN children, nervous and deprived children, and ex-approved school children are too difficult to manage successfully.

Community Education

At present, hostels are a necessity, but the need for them might be reduced if steps were taken to educate the community in the needs and potentialities of ESN children leaving school. There is still widespread misunderstanding of the types of children who are educated in special schools. The stigma of segregation remains. Employers and likely foster-parents are unwilling to accept responsibility for people they consider to be very subnormal and difficult to handle. Even the children's parents may be apprehensive or openly antagonistic, particularly in cases where delinquent and unstable behaviour have been present. A programme for community education, carried out by schools and social workers, would be valuable in changing people's attitudes to the ESN school and its leavers. Since there are already signs that the general public is more willing to be sympathetic and tolerant, it is reasonable to suppose that such a programme would have effect.

Further Education

Many, if not all, ESN leavers are still capable of further intellectual growth and learning. They become more sensitive to the felt needs of life and become more ready to accept help. For instance, although an inability to read and perform simple numerical operations may not be a marked handicap in their employment, they do sooner or later realize that reading and arithmetic are essential for promotion at work and to feel adequate in social situations. Many leavers we have interviewed have expressed disappointment at not being able to continue their studies. Experience in Birmingham, where evening classes for backward adults have been organized, suggests that such classes are very beneficial and are well attended although they only deal with reading and writing. Teachers in charge of the groups find, however, that their lessons often become therapeutic sessions in which individuals seek and receive help in a variety of personal problems, the majority of which are connected with the social repercussions of not being able to read. Classes such as these are relatively few. More provision would seem to be urgent and when County Colleges are established the ESN school leaver should not be forgotten. In the meantime, further education in the form of evening classes could be organized by the special schools themselves. The suitable venue for such classes raises certain problems, e.g. some leavers might object to attending classes held in the special school. Taylor (4), for instance, in describing a club held on school premises, says that one of the biggest difficulties was that the club was held 'at school'. Many of the boys were not keen to come back to school once they had left, and he suggests that the club would have been more successful if other premises could have been found. Against this, however, he states that of the regular attenders, the majority lived within easy travelling distance. Taylor's conclusion was that the club could be used more. Other leaders of clubs appear to have more or less the same experiences. We also know from follow-up studies that ESN leavers are seldom successful when they join other clubs because they leave once their inadequacies become apparent either to themselves or to others.

We are therefore faced with the problem of how best to satisfy the educational needs of our school leavers. It would appear that the provision of leisure activities *per se* such as dancing, billiards, table tennis, jazz clubs, etc. for ESNs only, will not attract many leavers for very long. Such activities are obviously useful but they should form part of a more comprehensive programme which is realistically related to educational and social needs. The following suggestions, which are tentative because of lack of detailed knowledge and experience, may be useful:

(*a*) The school's pre-vocational programme should include preparation for club membership and propaganda about further education, clubs and their activities. Club nights and inter-club visits are useful in this connection. We have found, for instance, that the school's affiliation to a federation of clubs is valuable.

(*b*) Parents should be asked to encourage their children to take part in worthwhile activities after leaving school.

(*c*) A club should maintain a reasonable balance between organized classes of a strictly educational type and leisure pursuits. The ESN leaver is usually quite anxious to continue his education. He wants to improve his reading, writing and arithmetic, particularly when they are taught in a way which emphasizes their usefulness at work and in life.

(*d*) The club should offer a wide variety of activities which should

242

not be a mere extension of school work but be more related to the interests of young adults. Out-of-door activities such as cycling, hiking, camping should be encouraged.

(e) Discussion groups along the lines of those held in school would be of value.

(f) The club should cater for both sexes and make arrangements whereby the leavers' friends may participate.

(g) The leaver should be given every opportunity to co-operate actively and responsibly in the running of the club.

(h) The club leader should establish close co-operation with After-Care workers, voluntary organizations and schools.

The Mental Deficiency Acts

Although the setting up of clubs within the further education service, or as part of a comprehensive system of community care, would be most useful to many leavers, there would still be a minority for whom other provision, in many cases full-time, would be necessary. At present this minority sooner or later finds its way into mental deficiency hospitals. As stated earlier this is regrettable. Evidence submitted to the Royal Commission criticized the present arrangements which often result in the young person being labelled 'mental defective', when he had not to be so-called during childhood. The evidence also included the suggestion that 'full time training or special help in regard to employment' might be needed but there were conflicting views on how and by whom this training should be provided. The members of the commission were 'not inclined to recommend any extension of the functions of the local education authorities in relation to young persons who, because of mental backwardness, need services of a special nature after leaving school'. The reason for this view is that if the ESN school leaver needs full-time training after leaving school he is likely to need general help and supervision for several years at least, and that this training can best be provided through vocational courses run by the Ministry of Labour or by local Health and Welfare departments. It seems to us, however, that what is needed for most of the leavers in this minority group is an extension of the pre-vocational programme we have outlined. Programmes of rehabilitation now being introduced into mental deficiency practice are just this—educational and social aspects of treatment are being increasingly emphasized.

EDUCATION FOR SOCIAL COMPETENCE

REFERENCES

1. ATKINSON, E. J. *Post-school adjustment of ESN boys.* 1957.
2. BROWN, E. B. *A report on the post school settlement of Birmingham Boys.* 1954.
3. JONES, D. J. *A study of the problems and needs of boys who left a residential school for ESN children.* 1957.
4. TAYLOR, G. A. *An after-care follow up of school leavers.* 1957.

All the above were Dissertations submitted as part of the requirements for the Diploma in the Teaching of ESN Children, University of Birmingham.

5. COLLMAN, R. D. *Employment success of ESN school ex-pupils in England.* The Slow Learning Child, Vol. 3, No. 2, 1956.
6. HARGROVE, A. L. *The Social Adaptation of Educationally Subnormal School leavers.* National Association for Mental Health, 1954.
7. O'CONNOR, M. *Defectives working in a Community.* Amer. J. of Mental Deficiency, Vol. 59, No. 2, 1954.
8. Report of the Royal Commission on the Law Relating to Mental Illness and Mental Deficiency, 1954–7. H.M.S.O.

FURTHER READING

BRENNAN, W. K. *Preparation for learning.* Special Education, Vol. LII, No. 2.
BRENNAN, W. K. and TANSLEY, A. E. *The School leaver's handbook and teacher's pamphlet.* E. J. Arnold, 1963.
BRITISH COUNCIL FOR REHABILITATION. *The Handicapped School leaver.*
COLLMAN, R. D. and NEWLYN, D. *Employment success of educationally subnormal ex-pupils in England.* Amer. J. ment. Defic. Vol. 60, No. 4 April, 1956
COLLMAN, R. D. and NEWLYN, D. *Employment success of mentally dull and intellectually normal ex-pupils in England.* Amer. J. ment. Defic. Vol. 61, No. 3 Jan., 1957.
COLLMAN, R. D. *Leisure activities of educationally subnormal and other ex-pupils in England.* Amer. J. ment. Defic. Vol. 62, No. 3, Nov., 1957
FERGUSON, T. and KERR, A. W. *Handicapped Youth.* O.U.P., 1960.
GUNZBURG, H. C. *Social Rehabilitation of the Subnormal.* Bailliére, Tindall & Cox, 1961.
MAXTED, G. W. *Following-up ESN school leavers.* Special Schools J., XLV, No. 3, Sept., 1956.

Appendix A

INTELLIGENCE AND ATTAINMENT TESTS

Individual Tests of Intelligence

INDIVIDUAL tests can be placed in two groups: verbal and non-verbal tests. The most frequently used *verbal* test is the New Revised Stanford-Binet Scale, commonly called the Terman-Merrill, after its authors. It is a development of the original test devised by Binet at the beginning of this century. The items in the scale are of a variety of types: for example, vocabulary; verbal reasoning and comprehension; memory for sentences, words and digits; description and interpretation of pictures; copying shapes and patterns by drawing. Although there are some practical tests, it is mainly a verbal test. The tests are grouped into age-levels and the examiner proceeds from a year group of tests which are answered correctly (the basal age) through to a year group in which all the tests are failed. Each test passed obtains two months of mental age and the total is added to the basal age. This total is the mental age, and the IQ is then calculated by the formula:

$$IQ = \frac{\text{Mental age}}{\text{Chronological age}} \times 100$$

Example. Chronological Age (C.A.) = 11 – 6.

	No. of sub-test								year	months
	1	2	3	4	5	6				
Year VI	+	+	+	+	+	+		Basal age	6	0
Year VII	+	–	+	+	+	+		5 passes		10
Year VIII	+	–	+	–	–	–		2 passes		4
Year IX	+	–	+	–	–	–		2 passes		4
Year X	–	+	–	–	–	–		1 pass		2
Year XI	–	–	–	–	–	–		0 passes		0
									7	8

$$\frac{\text{M.A}}{\text{C.A}} \times 100 = \frac{7-8}{11-6} \times 100 = 67$$

It will be noted that this boy's passes scatter through several year groups. In this case, the passes on Years IX and X are in practical and picture tests and he fails earlier on verbal tests.

Teachers who are interested may like to consult the Terman-Merrill book to see the type of tests included in the scale. It must be pointed out,

245

however, that individual tests should only be given by people who have been trained in their use and interpretation.

Individual non-verbal tests. These avoid the use of words as much as possible. A distinction can be made between non-language tests (using pictures, designs, patterns) and performance tests (in which materials such as bricks, formboards and jig-saws have to be manipulated). The Raven's Progressive Matrices tests are examples of the former; the Drever Collins Scale, Alexander Scale, Kohs Blocks Designs are examples of the latter. These tests sample rather different aspects of intelligence from verbal tests.

A performance test is often used to supplement the information derived from a verbal test. This is especially needed if there is any reason to suspect that a test conducted with language will underestimate the child, for example, if he is extremely shy and inarticulate, has a speech or hearing defect, has had little schooling or comes from an unusual social background.

A non-language test which is sometimes used is the Porteus Maze test. This consists of a series of printed line mazes through which the child has to trace the shortest path. The results are claimed to be a measure of foresight and planning and Porteus believes the test is superior to a verbal test as a measure of those aspects of intelligence important in practical, social efficiency.

An individual test which combines both verbal and non-verbal material is the *Wechsler Scale.* In the Verbal Scale, there are tests of vocabulary, information, verbal similarities, comprehension, and a short test of simple number thinking. In the Performance Scale, there are tests of picture completion and arrangement, block designs, object assembly and coding. The treatment of the scores is such that the child's level of functioning on the verbal and performance scales and also on the sub-tests within each scale may be compared.

Another method of assessment sometimes used by doctors or psychologists in examining children with a view to special schooling is the *Drawing a Man Test.* Drawings of man a can be placed at an approximate age-level by comparing them with average drawings for different ages. (See Burt, Mental and Scholastic Tests.) A more refined method of scoring has been worked out by Goodenough (*Measurement of Intelligence by Drawing,* published by Harrap). Emphasis is placed in these assessments on the accuracy of the child's observation and the details he includes rather than his drawing skill.

Group tests. In work with backward children in the ordinary school group tests are sometimes useful as a rough measure of ability. It may happen, for example, that a child does surprisingly well on a group test and this acts as a corrective to a poor opinion of him based on his very low attainments, and his lack of response in class. However, a low score on a group test from a backward child is not conclusive evidence of low ability. Children who have been failing in school tasks are usually lacking in confidence, have not developed good habits of work, especially in pencil and paper tasks, and may be unable to do their best in the impersonal situation of a group test. Verbal tests requiring reading are, of course, inappropriate for poor readers. Non-verbal tests, using pictures and patterns, are, however, not necessarily highly predictive of school achievement, and need to be supplemented by a verbal test (e.g. the Cornwell Oral Group Test). The results of group testing with backward children certainly need to be viewed with caution.

Non-Verbal Group Tests
Moray House Picture Tests (for ages 6½–8½), U.L.P.
Deeside Picture Tests (for ages 6½–8½), Harrap.
N.F.E.R. Non-Verbal Tests 1–5 (each designed for certain ages), Newnes.

Verbal Group Tests.
Simplex Tests, Harrap.
Essential Intelligence Tests, Oliver and Boyd.
N.F.E.R. Verbal Tests, Newnes.
Cornwell Oral Group Test (8–11 years), Methuen.

Tests for Young Children
Pre-school children, or children with mental ages below 5 years, may be tested on the Terman-Merrill Scale in which there are tests down to a two-year level. The testing is done through the medium of attractive materials—toys, bricks, pictures—which can be used in a way which makes the test as informal and as much like a play situation as possible. There are other tests for pre-school children, the Merrill-Palmer Scale being fairly frequently used. It has a preponderance of performance material—bricks, formboards, picture puzzles, picture matching—but also contains language items.

The mental assessment of children depends on obtaining their interest and co-operation and this is often not easy with the young mentally handicapped child. The results should not, therefore, be accepted uncritically. Moreover, mental assessments obtained in the pre-school years do not correlate so highly with mental test results later in childhood.

Gesell's Norms of Development
Gesell has charted the sequences of normal development in the four aspects: motor, adaptive, language and personal-social behaviour. These are occasionally used for making an assessment of development in young mentally-handicapped children. The teacher of these children would find it interesting to refer to some of Gesell's books, e.g. *The First Five Years of Life* (Methuen), *The Infant and Child in the Culture of Today* (Hamish Hamilton).

Attainment Tests
Attainment tests are useful tools but, to avoid over-testing children, it is always worth asking what information is wanted and whether the test will give it. Too frequent testing, merely for the sake of testing, can have a disheartening effect on the slow learning child. After all, the teacher usually knows when a child is making progress. Attainment tests can be used:

(i) To find levels of attainment with a view to planning future work for the child or to make groups within a class.

(ii) To obtain diagnostic information about the child's difficulties or weaknesses.

(iii) To assess progress at intervals.

(iv) To make an objective assessment when this is needed.

Reading. Word recognition

Burt's Graded Vocabulary Test (in *Mental and Scholastic Tests*, Staples).

Schonell's Graded Word Reading Test (in *Diagnostic and Attainment Testing or Psychology* and *Teaching of Reading*, both published by Oliver and Boyd).

Vernon's Graded Word Reading Test (in *Standardisation of a Graded Word Reading Test*, U.L.P.).

These tests have slightly different standards. A conversion table from which corrected scores may be read off is given in the Appendix to Ministry of Education Pamphlet, No. 18 (H.M.S.O.). These tests are given individually, the child reading from a list of words graded in difficulty to give a measure of the skill in recognizing individual words. (There should, of course, be no coaching, or teaching of the words.)

Watt's Holborn Reading Scale (Harrap) can be used either as a measure of word recognition or of comprehension. It consists of thirty-three sentences of increasing difficulty, the word recognition level being indicated by the point at which the fourth error occurs.

Reading for Comprehension

The most frequently used tests of reading comprehension are Schonell's *Silent Reading Tests A and B* (Oliver and Boyd). For individual testing, the *Neale Analysis of Reading* (Macmillan) is the most satisfactory. This has three parallel forms consisting of short passages of interesting reading material graded for difficulty from R.A. 6 to 10 years. Scores for comprehension, accuracy and speed are obtained.

Diagnostic reading tests.

Daniells, J. C. and Diack, H. *The Standard Reading Tests.* Chatto and Windus. This series of tests provides material for the systematic study of reading difficulties, e.g. weaknesses in visual and auditory discrimination, gaps and confusions in the knowledge of letters and sounds. 10–20 minutes is usually sufficient to assess: 1. abilities which can be relied on in teaching reading 2. weaknesses which need planned remedial attention.

Schonell's Diagnostic Reading Tests (in Backwardness in the Basic Subjects or Diagnostic and Attainment Testing, Oliver and Boyd) serve a similar purpose.

Spelling

Burt's Spelling Test (*Mental and Scholastic Tests*, Staples).

Schonell's Spelling Tests A and B (*Diagnostic and Attainment Testing*, Oliver and Boyd).

Schonell's Regular and Irregular Words (*Essentials of Teaching and Testing Spelling*, Macmillan).

Tests of Language

There are few satisfactory tests of this important aspect. Reference might be made to *Crichton Vocabulary Scale* (H. K. Lewis) and Watt's *Language Tests* (Harrap).

Appendix B

LIST OF READING BOOKS

Books starting with reading ages below 7 years
Janet and John (ample supplementary material) (Nisbet).
Gay Way (Macmillan).
Happy Venture (with film strips and supplementaries) (Oliver and Boyd).
McKee Readers (Nelson).
Quinlan Readers (Macmillan).
Today's Work-Play Books (Macmillan).
Gates Readers (Macmillan).
Activity Reading Scheme (Macmillan).
Pilot Reading Scheme (many supplementaries) (Arnold).
John and Mary (Schofield and Sims).
The Vanguard Readers (MacDougall).
Activity Readers (Sand, Wood, Clay, Shopping, etc.) (Evans).
Reading through Interest (twelve booklets) (Collins).
Round and About Books (Oliver and Boyd).
Town Books (Oliver and Boyd).
Pinkwell Family (Arnold).
The Five Friends (E.S.A.).
Sound Sense (E. J. Arnold).

Books with older interest starting with reading ages below 7 years
Adventures in Reading (and Writing), 1–6 (O.U.P.).
Griffin Books, 1 and 2 (Arnold).
Kingsway Readers, 1–3 (Evans).
Pathfinders. Intro. Books A, B, C (Oliver and Boyd).
Active Reading Scheme (*Bonfire Night*) (Ginn).
Play-Learn Readers (and Reading Games), (Harrap).
Royal Road (Chatto and Windus).
Modern Reading (U.L.P.).

Reading books about or more than 7 years
With younger interest
Most of the books listed in first section above.
Wide Range. Books 1–6 (Oliver and Boyd).
Our Every day World, Series 1 (O.U.P.).
How? Why? Where? A reading book and work book (Arnold).
Dolphin Books (U.L.P.).

With older interest
Story Path to Reading (Blackie).
More Adventure in Reading (*and Writing*) (O.U.P.).
Griffin Readers, 1–12 (Arnold).
Explorer Readers, 1–3 (Schofield and Sims).
Discovery Readers, 1st series (boys).
    2nd series (girls), (Harrap).

Pioneer Readers, five books. Older interest and more difficult than last series (Harrap).
Pathfinder Series, 1–2 (Oliver and Boyd).
Family Affairs (for girls) (Oliver and Boyd).
Challenge Books, 1–12 (McDougall).
Interest Books: *Peter and His Football*, 1–4, *Betty and Her Friends*, 1–4 (Warne).
Picture Story Readers (Murray).
Active Reading Scheme (and work books) (Ginn).
Peter Brown Stories (U.L.P.).
New Adventures in Reading (O.U.P.).

Reading Ages about and more than 8 years
Pathfinder Books 3 and 4 (Oliver and Boyd).
Our Everyday World, Series 2 (O.U.P.).
Adventure of Bill and Betty (O.U.P.).
No. 5 Charles Street, for girls (O.U.P.).
Adventures in Work (older boys and girls) (O.U.P.).
Burgess Books (U.L.P.).
Onward Readers (Cassell).
Far and Near Readers (13 books) (Chambers).
Forward Books (Methuen).
Question time series (simple information booklets) (Macmillan).
Headway Series (book of the Town, Sea, etc.) (Evans).
New Reading (Readers Digest).
Janet's Journal, *Janet's Move*, etc. (Allen and Unwin).
Picture Tales (Collins).
Wide Horizon (Heinemann).
Active Readers (*White Hawk*, etc.) (Ginn).

Other Books
Heath Elementary Science (Heath).
Information Books (E.S.A.).
Tropical Library (Longmans).
Ready Readers (Longmans).
Animals of the World (O.U.P.).
Looking at History (Unstead) (A. and C. Black).
Adventure and Detection (O.U.P.).
Look Ahead Readers (Heinemann).
Classical stories (O.U.P.).
Crusader series (Blackie).
Pond Dwellers, Aquaria, Wasps (U.L.P.).
Using Your Reading (Arnold).
Reading to Some Purpose (Oliver and Boyd).
Systematic Crosswords (2 series) (Evans).
Let's Make Something (for younger children) (Arnold).
Read and Make (for older children) (Murray).

INDEX

Page numbers in bold type indicate where the topic is chiefly discussed.